THE
LATVIANS

STUDIES OF NATIONALITIES
Wayne S. Vucinich, General Editor

The Crimean Tatars
Alan Fisher

The Volga Tatars: A Profile in National Resilience
Azade-Ayşe Rorlich

The Making of the Georgian Nation
Ronald Grigor Suny
(copublished with Indiana University Press)

*The Modern Uzbeks: From the Fourteenth Century to the Present;
A Cultural History*
Edward A. Allworth

Estonia and the Estonians, second edition
Toivo U. Raun

The Azerbaijani Turks: Power and Identity under Russian Rule
Audrey L. Altstadt

The Kazakhs, second edition
Martha Brill Olcott

The Latvians: A Short History
Andrejs Plakans

The Moldovans: Romania, Russia, and the Politics of Culture
Charles King

THE LATVIANS

A Short History

Andrejs Plakans

HOOVER INSTITUTION PRESS
Stanford University
Stanford, California

Hoover Institution Press Publication 422

First printing, 1995
01 00 99 98 97 96 95   9 8 7 6 5 4 3 2 1

Simultaneous first paperback printing, 1995
01 00   9 8 7 6 5 4

Manufactured in the United States of America
Printed on acid-free paper

Library of Congress Cataloging-in-Publication Data
Plakans, Andrejs.
    The Latvians : a short history / Andrejs Plakans.
        p.   cm. — (Studies of nationalities)
    Includes bibliographical references and index.
    ISBN 0-8179-9301-0 (alk. paper)
    ISBN 0-8179-9302-9 (alk. paper)
    1. Latvia—History.   I. Title.   II. Series.
DK504.54.P57   1995   95-765
947'.43—dc20   CIP

Design by P. Kelley Baker

To Barbara

Contents

Maps

Tables

Foreword

With this scholarly and well-written work, Professor Andrejs Plakans of Iowa State University has substantially enriched the existing historiography on Latvia and the Latvians. The book, which critically examines a large amount of literature, contains many of the author's authoritative insights and interpretations. Plakans goes deep into history to find the signs of the first human habitation in the Baltic region and explains the complexities of ethnolinguistic questions in an area in which the peoples speaking the Indo-European and Finno-Ugrian languages coexisted and influenced one another through the centuries. He traces the evolution of the local societies from their earliest tribal stages to modern nationhood. Written records shed light on the contacts of the Baltic peoples with Romans, other ancient peoples of prominence, and, toward the end of the first millennium A.D., Christianity. In their more recent history, Latvians mingled with and suffered incursions from Vikings, Russians, Teutonic knights, Poles, and Swedes until the eighteenth century, when the Baltic region, including Latvia, came under Russian rule and remained thus subjugated until the end of the First World War. Of special interest in this connection is the land-owning class of German barons who established themselves in the Baltic region in the thirteenth century and retained their privileged status until they were dispossessed by the first Latvian state following the Bolshevik revolution of 1917. (Later, in 1939–1940, they were transplanted to Germany.)

After coming under Russian rule in the eighteenth century, the Latvians experienced no major war on their soil for more than a century. But the life of the Latvian peasant remained harsh under the serfdom of both the German barons and the Russian tsars, and periodic peasant unrest and famine continued. The oppression hindered, but did not prevent, the development of a Latvian literature, learning, media, and economic development. Baltic industry and urban centers grew, especially Riga, and Latvian towns became increasingly more Latvian and less German in character. The Baltic region became a window to Europe and was influenced culturally and socially by both Russia and Europe.

By the end of the nineteenth century, Latvia had developed an active intelligentsia, a school of literati and revolutionaries who were inspired by rising nationalism and socialism. Latvians participated in the revolution of 1905 and played an active role in the First World War as volunteers organized into so-called rifle regiments (*strēlnieki*), which split into nationalist and Bolshevik formations after the revolution of 1917. The Latvian *strēlnieki* were among the best units in the Soviet military system and contributed greatly to the Soviet cause. In 1919, after Germany collapsed, Soviet troops, including units of Latvian rifle regiments, entered Latvia. For a time, Latvian nationalist and Bolshevik riflemen fought each other until the Latvian rationalists defeated the German and Soviet forces by early 1920 with the support of the Poles.

On November 18, 1918, the Latvian Provisional National Council declared Latvia independence, an act considered then and now a momentous event in Latvian history (it should be noted that before 1918 Latvia did not appear on any map of Europe). Bolshevik groups moved into Latvia shortly after the October revolution but withdrew in early 1918 in the face of a German offensive. With German support, the Provisional Council and others joined in November 1918 to form a preparliament, the Latvian People's Council, which elected a provisional government and named Kārlis Ulmanis president. Between 1918 and 1920, Great Britain, Germany, and the Soviet Union recognized Latvia as an independent state. Of particular importance was the peace treaty between the Soviet Union and Latvia, signed in August 1920, in which the Soviet Union renounced all claims to Latvian territory.

Latvia lost no time in building a state. It adopted a democratic constitution in 1922, elected a unicameral legislature, became a member of the League of Nations, passed an all-important land reform law, and adopted measures regulating minority rights. But the instability of Western Europe, the menace of the Soviet Union, and political polarization at home were continual sources of instability. For those reasons as well as his personal ambition, in May 1934 President Ulmanis took power into his own hands, dissolved the parliament, and established an authoritarian state. Latvia's experiment with democracy ended with the fourth Parliament (*Saeima*). Although the idea of an independent and democratic Latvian state never died, Latvia disappeared as an independent state in 1939–1941, when it was occupied by the Soviet Union. From 1941 to 1946, it was occupied by Germany, and in 1944 it was reoccupied by the Soviet Union, under whose rule Latvia stayed until August 21, 1991.

Plakans discusses a number of historiographic questions, particularly noting the Soviet distortion of Latvian history, which judged people and events by the objectives and policies of the Communist Party and the Soviet state. In recent years, as the Soviet Union began to break up, the Latvians began openly honoring prominent Latvian personalities and commemorating and celebrating important moments in the nation's history.

Perhaps nothing has aroused Latvian ire as much as the liquidation of thousands of Latvians during the Soviet military occupation of 1940–41, when it is believed that thousands of Latvians died or disappeared. President Ulmanis and the commander of the Latvian forces, J. Balodis, were both deported. Ulmanis died in Soviet exile in 1942; Balodis was not allowed to return to Latvia until 1956. After the Nazis were expelled in 1944–1945, many more thousands of Latvians were deported, imprisoned, executed, or driven into exile by the Soviets. As late as 1948 the nationalists who fought against the Soviets were subjected to similar treatment. The 1948 forced collectivization was accompanied by many brutalities, the memory of which will never be eradicated from the minds of the Latvian people.

The Latvians accumulated a whole list of grievances against the Soviet Union, one of which was the systematic effort of the communist regime to weaken Latvia as a political and cultural force by various denationalizing policies that threatened to reduce the Latvian population to a minority in their own republic. The fear of extinction was a legitimate concern to Latvians; their share of the republic's population went from 75.5 percent in 1935 to 52.5 percent in 1993. (The slight increase in total population was attributable to the immigration of non-Latvians into the republic.)

Of particular concern to Latvians was the Russification of the population. The immigrant Russians have been in no hurry to learn Latvian; moreover, many Latvians born outside the republic did not speak adequate Latvian. Sensitive to the threat of national and cultural extinction, Latvians began complaining about the small number of Latvian nationals represented in party and government. Furthermore, they contended that most Latvians in the government and the party felt themselves to be more Russian than Latvian and that they barely spoke Latvian. Those who dared voice such criticisms were removed from their positions during the purges of 1959–60.

Latvians then began conducting cautious discussions of specific questions to be resolved with the Soviet leadership in order to avoid any possible violence but lost little time in demanding national sovereignty. Latvia again proclaimed independence on August 21, 1991. Plakans plows through the intricate maze of Soviet-Latvian relations and party-state entanglements to discuss the impasse of 1990, the crackdown that never came (January 1991), the Soviet coup of August 1991, economic reforms and privatization, the parliamentary elections of 1993, and the Latvian ecological movement.

In the final chapter, Plakans speculates on the continuities and discontinuities in contemporary Latvia, that is, which past experiences should be retained and which should be abandoned. After a great deal of discussion and political maneuvering, and some foreign pressure, Russia and Latvia reached agreements on several crucial questions including the definition of citizenship, the evacuation of Russian army personnel, and the dismantling of former Soviet military installations. Plakans discusses with authority the implications of these and other important questions in relations between Latvia and Russia.

In the short time since Latvia declared its independence, much has been achieved. The economy has been stabilized, privatization pushed ahead, the brakes put on inflation, and unemployment kept down. The process of political liberalization has made marked progress, as his Latvia's determination to identify with the West and build a market economy. But the Soviet Union has passed on to Latvia a costly legacy—damage to the environment from careless industrial and military development that will require much time and huge financial resources to repair. It will be necessary to rehabilitate, refocus, and reform many institutions to satisfy the needs of a national and democratic society. Agriculture and industry must be modernized, and secure sources of fuel and energy provided. A national military and security system will have to be established. Solid relations with foreign states, especially Russia, will have to be built. In the meantime, Latvia has been admitted to the United Nations and a number of other international organizations and continues to press for admission to the North Atlantic Treaty Organization, to which the country attaches great importance. In addition, Latvia has entered into close cultural and economic relations with many European countries. It can be said with some certainty in light of what Latvia has already accomplished that the country's transition to modern democracy is well advanced.

April 1995   WAYNE S. VUCINICH

Preface

The year 1996 marks the two hundredth anniversary of Garlieb Merkel's *Die Letten, vorzüglich in Liefland, am ende des philosophischen Jahrhunderts*, published in Leipzig in 1796.[1] This youthful antiserfdom polemic argued, in the Herderian spirit of the late eighteenth century, that the enserfed Latvian-speaking peasants of the Russian Baltic province of Livonia (Livland) were not simply a *Bauernstand* (peasant order) but were a *Volk* (nation) that differed from the Baltic German nobles, burghers, and clergy. Merkel developed this point at length in a work called *Die Vorzeit Livlands*, published in 1798–1799. Both these books, written in German and not read by many Latvians until they were translated in the second half of the nineteenth century, began the process of separating the southern population of the Baltic provinces' past into that of the Baltic German ruling orders and that of the subordinated Latvians. Merkel was thus calling for a history of the Baltic region "from the bottom up" (to use the shorthand of recent Western social historians), but, given the cultural layering of Baltic society, such an approach meant validating Latvian "national" history.

During 1800–1850, this differentiation process continued among the Baltic German writers, and a newly emergent Latvian intelligentsia entered the debate after 1850, when the Latvian "national awakening" called for seizing control of the past as well as the future. After World War I in the new Republic of Latvia, the professional study of history was possible at the University of Latvia (established in 1919) and at the Institute of History (established 1936). These initiatives, however, were cut short by World War II: in 1939 the Baltic German population left Latvia, in 1944 a substantial proportion of the interwar generation of Latvian historians emigrated to the West, and after 1945 the writing of Latvian history in the Latvian Soviet Socialist Republic (SSR) was carefully watched and guided by the ideologues of the Latvian Communist Party. Thus world events continued to deny Latvian history the institutional continuity that allows for reflection and reduces the need for historians to always be defending one or another new orthodoxy imposed by a "national mission" or a "proletarian struggle."

In the half century after 1945, writing about the Latvian past was done by three distinguishable groups: Baltic Germans, working in the Federal Republic of Germany and concentrating primarily, though not exclusively, on the history of the Baltic German population; émigré Latvians, working in Sweden, North America, Australia, and West Germany, with little access to primary sources in the Latvian SSR; and Soviet Latvians, working in the university system and the Institute of History of the Latvian SSR's Academy of Sciences. Occasionally, a scholar not belonging to any of these groupings would make a significant contribution, but such "in-wanderers" were rare. After the events of 1987–1990, however, there was a merging of efforts, the full effects of which are still in the offing.

The Latvian émigré and Soviet Latvian schools of Latvian history produced, besides much specialized research, two general English-language surveys of Latvian history and two multivolume Latvian-language surveys, all of which need to be mentioned as the larger context for the present work. The two English-language histories, written by the historian-diplomats Alfrēds Bīlmanis and Arnolds Spekke, appeared during the 1940s and 1950s, when émigré Latvian authors were preoccupied with the recent loss of their country's independence, and both stop with the events of World War II.[2]

In the period from 1958 to 1984, the Latvian publisher Daugava in Sweden issued a ten-volume 7,300-page series called *Latvijas vēsture* (History of Latvia) for the period 1500–1945.[3] This series, which united the work of two generations of émigré Latvian historians, demonstrated the amplitude of the Latvian past in terms of sources, problems, and descriptive possibilities and became the standard reference for all (Latvian-reading) Western specialists in the field. In 1986, under the editorial direction of the academician Arvīds Drīzulis, the two-volume 900-page third edition of *Latvijas PSR vēsture* (History of the Latvian Soviet Socialist Republic) was published in Riga; the seventeen authors surveyed where the "science of history" in Latvia stood as of that date.[4] Because of the events of 1990–1991, both these series have become documents of their times. The Daugava series, however, is likely to remain a monument of Latvian historiography for a much longer period.

Against this background, the present survey cannot be put forward as anything but a relatively short essay in English on a people who, despite their small numbers, have a complicated past that requires many thousands of pages to describe thoroughly, as the Daugava series demonstrates. Moreover, the history of the area in which the Latvians live is also complicated, involving not only the Latvians' story but also those of the Baltic Germans and the Russians (to name only two of the other nationality groups of the Latvian territories) as well as the plans and movements of the large neighboring states that had almost uninterrupted control of the Latvian lands from the thirteenth century onward.

Ideally, these interwoven stories should be told simultaneously, but that would require a multivolume approach. The present work is mostly about the Latvians themselves, with the larger historical dramas in which they were involved serving principally as contexts. Although Latvians had little impact on these larger contexts until the twentieth century, their existence and activities as a distinct Baltic subpopulation must be distinguished from those of the peoples who surrounded them and lived among them. The balance between these separate but connected histories is hard to strike and might well be struck differently by other authors.

The present work benefited from the help of numerous people. I would first like to express my gratitude to the authors of the Daugava series, who did the primary-source research that others such as myself can build on. I am also grateful to the Woodrow Wilson Center for International Scholars in Washington, D.C., for a fellowship during the fall semester of 1992, which gave me free time to work on the last chapters of the book. Iowa State University granted me leave for the spring semester 1993, which permitted me to continue writing in Riga, Latvia, and the History Department at Iowa State and its chair, George McJimsey, made the arrangements possible. I am also grateful to the International Research and Exchanges Board (IREX) for short-term travel support during 1990–1993 and to the Baltic Academic Center in Riga (sponsored jointly by IREX, the Association for the Advancement of Baltic Studies, and the Baltic Research Foundation) for allowing me to use its facilities.

Colleagues and friends who must be thanked for enlightening conversations about Latvian and Baltic history include, in the United States, Professors Toivo U. Raun of Indiana University (whose *Estonia and the Estonians* in the Hoover Studies of Nationalities series traverses some of the same ground as the present work), Andrew Ezergailis of Ithaca College, and John J. Peniķis of Indiana University at South Bend. In Latvia, Heinrihs Strods, former head of the *katēdra* of Latvian History at the University of Latvia,

Ilgvars Misāns, head of the *katēdra* of Medieval History, Indulis Ronis, director of the Institute of History, and Rita Brambe, researcher at the Institute of History graciously shared their time and expertise. At the Hoover Press, three anonymous reviewers and Patricia A. Baker, executive editor, and her staff provided many helpful suggestions for improving the book. Finally, I am grateful to my wife, Barbara S. Plakans, who as a Fulbright scholar joined me in the spring 1993 Riga adventure and whose support has always been long lasting and inadequately rewarded.

1 The Populations of the Eastern Baltic Littoral

In itself, the prehistory of the Baltic region does not offer good reasons for treating the territory that lies within the borders of present-day Latvia as a distinct region. The lines archaeologists put on their maps for these early millennia are educated guesswork and do not coincide with the boundaries modern mapmakers use to separate Estonia from Latvia, Latvia from Lithuania, and those three states from their immediate neighbors. Who lived in the territory that is now Latvia is important because this land is now occupied by a people—the Latvians—to whom origins are of great significance. Credibly demonstrating continuous residence over the millennia in the territory of present-day Latvia is important for Latvian self-definition, buttressing the idea of Latvians as the basic nation (in Latvian, *pamattauta*): a people neighbors have frequently conquered and overrun but failed to dislodge.[1]

To talk about a specifically *Latvian* territory and its residents first requires a discussion of an inclusive Baltic region. Although the earliest mention of inhabitants in the eastern Baltic littoral appears in Roman writings in the first century A.D., archaeological evidence suggests that the first permanent human settlements in the region, dating from around 9000 B.C., were made by in-migrants from the south and southwest. We must infer more-precise information about the next nine millennia (some 360 human generations) from the sparse physical remains. In light of this, it seems presumptuous to assume continuity of settlement because we know so little about the discontinuities that must have occurred over so long a period. Indeed, during these millennia even the physical features of the area were changing, with the riverbeds and the coastline of the Baltic Sea not assuming their present shapes until around 4000 B.C.

Most archaeologists refer to these earliest in-wanderers as *proto-Balts* and describe their numbers as increasing over time mostly because of new arrivals. Such a population expansion must have meant conflict and displacement, about which we know nothing. Still, enough of an archaeological record exists for a rough periodization, and researchers describe the people of the region as living through a Mesolithic period (5000–4500 B.C.), an early Neolithic period (4500 B.C.–3500 B.C.), a middle Neolithic period (3500–2000 B.C.), a late Neolithic period (2000–1000 B.C.), and a Bronze Age (1000–500 B.C.) followed by an Iron Age. In this scheme, the Iron Age extends into the Christian era, but the residents of the eastern Baltic littoral came in contact with Christianity much later, at the end of the first millennium A.D. Continuing archaeological research has increased the amount of evidence that characterizes these long stretches of time. Thus, in the 1920s Latvian researchers were able to use artifacts from only four settlements of the Neolithic period; today's researchers can employ the remains from several dozens. Earlier, only eighteen artifacts were available from the Bronze Age; archaeologists now can base their generalizations on hundreds of such findings.[2]

ETHNOLINGUISTIC AND CULTURAL DIFFERENTIATIONS

The late Neolithic period (2000–1000 B.C.) in the eastern Baltic littoral appears to have included at least one important break in prevailing patterns. Around 2000 B.C. there was a major change in population composition (again, because of new arrivals), and archaeologists begin to employ with some confidence the term *early Baltic peoples* from about 1000 B.C. on (as contrasted with *proto-Balts*) and to describe these early Balts as a branch of Indo-Europeans who were also arriving in Central European territories. These relative latecomers to the Baltic coastal area merged with some Finnic peoples (as designated by archaeologists) already there, while displacing other Finnic peoples who moved northward.

These dynamics are said to account for the later coresidence, in a small corner of the European continent, of Baltic-language speakers (Latvians and Lithuanians) and Finno-Ugric speakers (Livs, Estonians, Finns), but the displacement processes that produced such a configuration cannot be dated with any degree of precision. Moreover, these early Balts established themselves permanently in a territory much larger than the eastern Baltic littoral, and researchers describing this period usually distinguish between a central and a peripheral Baltic region. The central Balts lived in the area around the Baltic Sea and were in cultural contact with the surrounding Germanic, Slavic, and Finnic peoples. The peripheral Balts, living far from these central territories but still forming a continuum with them, appear to have had cultural contacts with Persians, Illyrians, Thracians, and perhaps even Scythians.

With the emergence of identifiable Baltic peoples, some degree of ethnolinguistic differentiation probably occurred as well. The historical-linguistic literature speaks of Western Balts in territories around the Vistula River in what is now Poland, Eastern Balts in what are now Latvia, Lithuania, and Belorus, and Dnieper Balts in territories around the source of the Dnieper River in Russia and to the east. The peoples designated as the Eastern Balts—at least those segments that remained permanently settled in the eastern Baltic littoral—were probably the ancestors of the "Latvians," an ethnolinguistic term that does not become relevant until the nineteenth century.

Why the Baltic peoples were internally differentiated is not certain. Some archaeologists argue that the differentiations reflected alternative ways of using metals in the various parts of the Balt-settled area; a more purely linguistic interpretation stresses the development of dialects that in turn promoted other group differences. There is agreement, however, that the Eastern Balts became increasingly distinguishable from the other Baltic groupings and that that internal differentiation continued in the centuries leading to the Christian era.[3]

MOVEMENT AND PERSISTENCE

The archaeological literature agrees that by A.D. 100–300 sub-populations in the eastern Baltic littoral can be distinguished fairly clearly using certain kinds of burial practices to judge where boundaries fell among them. To discuss the peoples of this and subsequent centuries, archaeologists use collective terms, some of which are surely drawn from much later periods when written evidence became available. Thus, for example, there is general consensus that in the western parts of the territory of present-day Latvia and extending into what is now northwestern Lithuania there lived the *kurši* (in English, Couronians), whose language apparently developed from dialects of the Western Balts. Reflecting this, the westernmost administrative region of the Latvian territory bore the name *Kurzeme* (land of the Cours; in German, *Kurland*; in English, Courland) into the present era. The south-central part of present-day Latvia and the

Map 1. Distribution of peoples throughout the Baltic littoral, ca. 1210

north-central part of modern Lithuania was the territory of the *zemgaļi* (in English, Semigallians), whose language evidently contained elements of both western and eastern Baltic dialects.

Correspondingly, the term *Zemgale* appears in both the full name of the old Duchy of Courland and Semigallia and the name of the southern administrative region of the independent Latvian state after 1918. In what is now the eastern part of Latvia there lived the *sēļi* (in English, Selians or Selonians) and the *latgaļi* (in English, Lettgallians), whose languages and cultural attributes absorbed more eastern than western Baltic influences. Although the Selians did not have their name enshrined in any major administrative divisions of the Latvian state, their former residence is still frequently referred to in popular Latvian parlance as *Sēlija*. By contrast, the Lettgallians bequeathed to later generations not only the name of an important state-administrative division—*Latgale*—but also a distinctive cultural history (after the Protestant Reformation) in which Roman Catholic and Slavic, particularly Polish, influences remained strong until the present day. (The Lettgallians also may have been the source of the term *Latvians*.)

The Selians, the Couronians, the Lettgallians, and the Semigallians all spoke Baltic languages. Thus the *līvi* or *lībji* (in English, Livs or Livonians), who lived in the territories adjoining what would become the Gulf of Riga and spoke a Finnic language, were linguistically unique in this otherwise Baltic region. Their name is perhaps best known in subsequent history because it entered the formal designation of the medieval state—Livonia—which included all the other territories.[4]

Those peoples and their territories remained relatively unstable for a long time, and, in fact, from the fourth century A.D. onward the entire eastern Baltic littoral was affected by the same great "wandering of peoples" that brought the so-called barbarians into the Roman Empire and changed the population composition of Central Europe. A migration of Slavic peoples westward not only absorbed many Far Eastern Balts (into what became Russia) but forced the Lettgallians to move further west into present-day Latvia. The Selians too had to move in a west-northwest direction, which in turn affected the Livs on the eastern shore of what was to become the Gulf of Riga. In addition, a determined northward migration by the Couronians pressed against the Western Livs on the western shore of the gulf.

The most powerful migration was that of the Lettgallians, doubtless because they appear to have been the numerically largest eastern littoral people, estimated at about half the population of those Baltic societies, which explains the growing influence of their language. Although population movements changed the external boundaries of those societies, boundary shifts appear to have slowed down sometime in the tenth century A.D., resulting in a handful of more-or-less permanent territorial societies for which the earlier designations continue to be used by researchers.[5]

Some scholars describe the period between the second and fifth centuries A.D. as the first golden age of the Baltic peoples. Population growth, refinements in agricultural practices, improvements in metals production, expansion of trade, and accumulation of wealth led to social and political stratification within the distinguishable populations. Village communities ceased being sited only on hilltops and spread downward over hillsides. Across the region, the scythe joined the sickle as an important agricultural implement. Storage pits for grain proliferated, suggesting better harvests and an expansion of arable land. The smelting of iron and other metals became widespread, and blacksmithing apparently became an independent activity. Trade in amber and furs grew in volume, and personal ornamentation (especially for women) became more elaborate. Although it is impossible to distinguish variations of these practices and characteristics among the different peoples, archaeologists seem comfortable extending generalizations, based on artifacts uncovered in specific locations, to entire peoples and regions. Thus, improvements in the level of material culture appear to have continued, although at a slower pace, even as peoples began to move and boundaries to shift in the sixth century A.D.[6]

TERRITORIAL SOCIETIES AND POLITICAL ORGANIZATION

The frequency of boundary changes among the Couronians, Semigallians, Livs, Lettgallians, and Selians had evidently diminished by the end of the tenth century, when archaeologists detect another period of increasing prosperity as "lands remained intact, economy and trade progressed, arts and crafts flourished."[7] Also, for the centuries just before A.D. 1000, we can make reliable statements about political and social organization, though we still need to extend generalizations from place-specific archaeological finds in the territory of a given people to the territory of the others. In this era there was never a single political system that united all five, nor did any of the five at any point have a single leader. Later documents, in Latin, refer to the leaders of these peoples as *rex* (king) and the territories they led as *civitates* (states), but the suggested parallels with Western institutions are probably misleading. It is safest to think of these five territorial societies as having been multicentric because numerous castle sites have been discovered in each territory, suggesting a multiplicity of leaders, each with a collection of reliable supporters.

The use of the term *feudalism* to describe the political ties between those leaders and their supporters is questionable, if the term is meant to suggest analogies with Western Europe. Among the Baltic peoples, political organization was hierarchical up to a point, but the hierarchy had no apex, meaning that there was no monarch for the entire area who could disburse fiefs to secure the loyalty of vassals and probably no subinfeudation (vassals of vassals). There appear to have been, however, regional chieftains who could recruit followers for occasional military actions against one another, but we do not know about reciprocal obligations for leaders and followers before and after such periodic conflicts.

What concepts we should use to think about social organization below the political elites remains a problem. The English term *tribe* does not have the same connotation as the Latvian term *cilts,* which suggests a strong, kin-based organization. Both terms have been used interchangeably to suggest that some kind of social organization did exist—that the followers of chieftains were not simple undifferentiated bands—but the information is less reliable than Latvian historians would like to think.[8] Latvian historians, when writing for a popular audience, use the term *tautas* (in German, *Völker*) for these territorial societies, which seems unwarranted because convincing evidence is lacking for any consciousness of common membership. Even the term *confederation,* when employed to describe temporary coalitions among the chieftains (kings) of any one people, is, among archaeologists, admittedly a "deduction."[9]

The leaders of Couronia, Livonia, Selonia, Semigallia, and Lettgallia lived in some four hundred or so fortified places in the centuries just before A.D. 1000. The task of allocating them among the different territorial societies remains difficult, however. Ninth-century chronicles mention five (sometimes eight) political subdivisions among the Couronians, but evidence about such subdivisions among the other peoples is uneven. Later written sources identify some leaders by name—Lamekins among the Couronians, Ako among the Livs, Nameisis and Viestarts among the Semigallians, Tālivaldis among the Lettgallians—but provide little with which to evaluate their relative importance or the extent of their authority. We must assume that, in the centuries leading up to A.D. 1000, there were many such leaders (one archaeologist calls them *dukes*),[10] but none of them emerged as unifiers of the people they ruled over or of the five peoples with whom we are concerned.

Evidence about stratification based on wealth is somewhat better, especially among the Couronians. Couronian grave sites and Scandinavian sagas describing Couronian practices suggest that persons were buried with materials symbolic of their status in life, which has permitted archaeologists to distinguish among the graves of elders (referred to in later documents as *seniores*), military leaders (*meliores*), and common people. The same evidence also suggests a stratum of the poor—possibly slaves or captives—who were buried with virtually no possessions. Burial sites, however, are not evenly spread throughout the territories of the five peoples under discussion; thus any general statements about social stratification must be made carefully. We also do not know whether Couronian, Semigallian, Selonian, Liv, or Lettgallian societies rewarded talent and energy by permitting upward social mobility or whether the identifiable rich, middling, and poor strata were castelike.[11]

THE ECONOMICS OF
EVERYDAY LIFE

Most people in the five societies tilled the soil and supplemented their diets through hunting, fishing, and beekeeping. Because the eastern Baltic littoral was heavily forested, land had to be cleared and branches and stumps burned, adding ash to the soil. The horse, more than the ox, pulled the plow. Researchers agree that both the two-field and the three-field systems were in use, leaving a large part of the arable land fallow during each growing season.

Archaeological evidence suggests that by the ninth and tenth centuries all littoral societies were using a full complement of tools for their various activities: the plow for breaking the soil, sickles and scythes for harvesting, narrow- and broadheaded axes for cutting down and shaping trees. Many tools from this period exhibit fine workmanship, and specialized metalworking skills are also apparent in their armaments—arrowheads, spears, axes, and later various kinds of partial body armor. Wooden houses dominated the communities of those peoples, though they used clay for their house ovens. Cookware of this period also suggests specialized occupations because of the care with which it was created. Not only persons but also horses, weapons, and houses were elaborately and extensively decorated.[12]

CULTURAL AND ECONOMIC
CONTACTS

Because of their location, the Couronians, Semigallians, Livs, Selonians, and Lettgallians must have been involved with one another and the outside world. Their territories were well situated for the development of regular economic interaction of various kinds, given the proximity of the

Baltic Sea and the navigable Daugava (Dvina) River flowing out of Russia into the Gulf of Riga. Byzantine coins found in the seacoast areas indicate visits by Scandinavian traders; other finds suggest that the Daugava was also used by traders from the south and southeast. Coinage from Western European cities has also been found in substantial quantities, and graves have yielded counterweights suggesting that precious metals were weighed and measured.

Thus trading relations existed among the five peoples and both eastern and western lands, but the evidence does not reveal which direction was dominant. The argument proposed by Latvian historians of the Soviet period—that goods arriving from the east were especially attractive to the lower classes, while those from the west appealed mostly to the upper social orders—has no basis, for there is insufficient information about the use of imported goods. Scattered information does exist about continuous foreign influences on the fringes of the area inhabited by those five peoples, but it is questionable how lasting such influences were. Vikings from Gotland, for example, appear to have established a colony in Grobiņa (in the southwestern part of the Couronian territory) and later to have abandoned it. The Baltic area was traversed by long-distance traders, but the extent to which the Baltic-area peoples themselves traded over long distances is an open question. Some of them certainly had the capacity to do so; the Couronians, for example, developed a reputation as raiders of the Scandinavian seacoast across the Baltic Sea.[13]

Contact with other peoples also meant mild political subordination. For various periods of time, chieftains of the eastern districts in the Lettgallian, Liv, and Selonian lands made tribute payments to the Russian principalities of Novgorod, Pskov, and Polotsk, which is also why Christianity in its eastern form first made an appearance in these Baltic societies. Many Latvian words associated with church organization were borrowed from Russian, possibly in this early period. The claim that these easternmost territories were ruled by local vassals of the Russian principalities bears reexamination, however, though there were certainly tribute payments. The Couronians and the Semigallians, by contrast, appear to have escaped subordination of this kind, possibly by virtue of their distance from more powerful non-Baltic centers.[14]

Thus there is evidence that the Couronian, Semigallian, Selonian, Lettgallian, and Liv societies were open to the outside world and that outsiders moved among them. Yet we do not know how deeply such international contacts penetrated, how long they endured, or what long-term consequences they might have had, other than the few traces in what was to become the Latvian language.

BELIEF SYSTEMS

Because we must infer virtually all aspects of the lives of the Couronians, Livs, Semigallians, Selonians, and Lettgallians from archaeological evidence, we cannot expect a firm evidentiary base for a phenomenon as evanescent as belief systems. Decorations and ornaments yield some information about aesthetic choices: there is a preference for geometric designs, and even the most practical implements are decorated. The paucity of information about spiritual culture led earlier generations of Latvian scholars (and even some contemporary ones) into an uncontrolled concatenation of evidence across space and time. Although the chroniclers of the thirteenth century found non-Christian (i.e., pagan) religious beliefs and practices in place among the peoples then coming under Christian control, it is not clear that these beliefs and practices had remained sufficiently unchanged for three or four centuries so as to be ascribed to the A.D. pre-1000 populations.

Nor is there much warrant for reading into the pre-Christian past information from the oral tradition (particularly folk songs [in Latvian, *dainas*] transcribed hundreds of years later) or for attaching to the five pre-Christian "Latvian" peoples the beliefs of Lithuanians or Old Prussians because linguists have placed them all in a single language family. If we demand that evidence about the belief systems of a people at a particular point in time be contemporaneous with and derive directly from the people being described, then we know almost nothing about the spiritual component of these A.D. pre-1000 societies. The observation by a leading archaeologist that "the [post-1100] Christian stratum is recent and can be easily detached"[15] also assumes an unchanging stratum of pagan beliefs that came into being before A.D. 1000 and remained unchanged until much later. If we do not accept this assumption, then the pagan thought world remains closed to us and later evidence must be analyzed as the product not of earlier minds but of contemporaries who espoused them.[16]

The beliefs the early Christian missionaries found and mentioned casually throughout the texts of the medieval period (after 1200) appear to have included a heavenly father called *Dievs* as well as a host of other semi- or quasi-divine figures whose relationship to *Dievs* remains uncertain.[17] There was, for example, *Pērkons* (thunder), *Dieva dēli* (the sons of God), *Saules meitas* (daughters of the sun), *Laima* (fate or fortune), and *Māra* (Mary). All these figures and others survived by name in the *daina* texts and could be used—depending on the interpretative thrust—as evidence for the existence of a pre-Christian faith or for a merger of pre-Christian and Christian beliefs (e.g., for *Māra* read Mary). *Dainas* and legends also suggest beliefs in benign and evil spirits (in Latvian, *labie un ļaunie gari*), in a nature suffused with the workings of the divine, and in ancestors who periodically returned in spirit form (in Latvian, *veļi*). Mediation between the human and the spiritual worlds was apparently performed not by an organized priesthood but by individuals (in Latvian, *burtnieki* or *zīlnieki*) in the community; such mediation evidently involved places of worship (e.g., sacred oaks) and perhaps sacrifices. There is a strong likelihood that, even in pre-Christian times, the summer solstice (June 23–24) was marked by special celebrations that, in due course, became John's Day (in Latvian, *Jāņi*).

Cleanly separating pagan and Christian beliefs into strata remains problematic in those Baltic tribal societies, but there is evidence that various kinds of non-Christian beliefs retained an influence after the thirteenth century. The early Christian clergy mentioned them repeatedly, and as late as the eighteenth century, Lutheran pastors working to develop a written Latvian language complained about the prominence of the oral tradition (especially the *dainas*) in the thinking of their parishioners. By that time, of course, the institutions of the Christian church were as traditional as any non-Christian beliefs because the oral and the Christian traditions had coexisted for some six hundred years.

CHANGE AND DEVELOPMENT

Historians and archaeologists writing about eastern Baltic societies in the first millennium A.D. have been caught in an evidentiary bind. They have had to make sense of a great deal of physical evidence without reliable nomenclatural information about peoples and territories, which does not appear until the post-1000 written chronicles. Hence artifacts from the earlier period tend to be sorted and arranged not only by the logic of the activities that create them but also by territorial designations, political arrangements, and collective names that were not observed and described until many generations later and then only by newcomers to the Baltic area rather than by the Balts themselves. This results in a portrait of the region before A.D. 1000 that is most certainly too seamless both chronologically and spatially. We use such terms as Couronians, Lettgallians, Semigallians, Selonians, and Livs for the earlier period, knowing full well that we are engaged in retrospective reconstruction and that these names do not distinguish these peoples from one another as well as we would wish them to.

Several generations of Latvian historians, first in the independence period (1981–40) and then in the Soviet period (1945–91), have exploited the relative pliability of evidence about the early medieval Baltic peoples to propose that the cultural orientation of the Latvian-area Balts was western or eastern.[19] There is no unambiguous evidence, however, that the cultural and economic contacts we know about led to any special geographic tilt. The controversy is in fact unnecessary because those territorial societies were self-sustaining and inventive enough to develop attributes of their own, which are visible in the jewelry and weapons decorations obtained from the grave sites of the period. Because no scholar has argued that these peoples depended on external trade, it follows that they were capable of dealing with commercial contacts with outsiders without risking absorption into neighboring societies and cultures.

There is evidence from the fifth century onward that the societies of the Couronians, Semigallians, Lettgallians, Livs, and Selonians were changing. Increased commercial activity, adopting or inventing agricultural and military tools, elaborate handicrafts and weaving techniques, understanding the function of fortifications and how to build them, the appearance of Christianity among peripheral subpopulations, security purchased with tribute payments to principalities in the east, and raiding trips across the Baltic Sea suggest the ability to generate new ways of doing things as well as the ability to borrow such ways from near neighbors.

Change, however, is not development in the sense of continuous improvement, and none of the archaeological or historical evidence persuades one that these tribal societies were "developing" in that sense. They were changing—that is, not stagnating—but the periods about which we know little are too long to conclude that the change had an identifiable trajectory.

There have been various reasons for scholars to discover developmental change in this period. On the one hand, Latvian historians of the first independence period needed to demonstrate that change among the pre-Christian peoples in what later became Latvian territory was dynamic and purposeful *before* the arrival of the German crusading orders in the thirteenth century, so that German claims to have brought civilization to the Baltic could be shown to be empty. Soviet Latvian historians, on the other hand, were obligated to cite all historical change as developmental and to claim that there was an important transition from a primitive "prefeudalism" to "feudalism" during that early period. Those researchers also had to promote the notion that it was proximity to Russian principalities and their inhabitants that had "progressive" consequences for the Baltic societies. A persuasive argument that change in this period was developmental, however, will need much more convincing evidence than that which is currently available. At the same time, the absence of demonstrable developmental change in those centuries is not in itself an argument that such indigenous changes would *not* eventually have assumed an identifiable direction. Such a possibility, however, was denied forever at the end of the twelfth century and the beginning of the thirteenth, when merchants, crusaders, and churchmen from the Holy Roman Empire decided that the eastern Baltic littoral was a promising arena for their expansionary activities. With their arrival, the nature of change in the eastern Baltic littoral took on an entirely new dynamic.

2 Invasion, Conquest, and the Creation of Livonia

In the new millennium the peoples of the eastern Baltic littoral remained receptive to outsiders and, in a limited fashion, ventured beyond their own territories. Vikings and Russians as well as merchants of assorted backgrounds made their way in and out of these lands, and the Couronians periodically sailed across the Baltic to raid the coastal settlements of the Scandinavian peninsula. Christianity in its Eastern Orthodox variant had arrived on the peripheries of the littoral, and people of the eastern littoral lands paid tribute to the principalities of Polotsk, Pskov, and Novgorod. As far as we can judge, however, none of these contacts resulted in important permanent settlements, either by foreigners settling in the littoral or by littoral inhabitants settling elsewhere. Thus the Couronians, Semigallians, Livs, Selians, and Lettgallians generally remained in the territories they had marked out for themselves by the end of the ninth century.

Starting with the second half of the twelfth century, however, western in-wanderers began to think of the Baltic littoral as a permanent source of income and its peoples as pagans in need of Christianization. For the papacy, which was concerned primarily with consolidating its influence on the monarchical states of Western Europe, the Baltic area was peripheral but promising.

CHURCHMEN, MERCHANTS, AND CRUSADERS

Merchants from the German territories of the Holy Roman Empire had been making regular stops in the territory of the Livs around the mouth of the Daugava River. In the mid-1160s they were accompanied by Father Meinhard (ca. 1125–96), an Augustinian monk from Holstein intent on Christianizing the Baltic pagans. He constructed a church in Ikšķile (in German, Uexküll) on the Daugava River, and from there missionaries sought converts among the surrounding Livs. In 1188, to formalize those efforts, Pope Clement III confirmed Meinhard as the first bishop of Ikšķile. Those early missions, however, did not yield much for the church because the Livs, though not antagonistic to the presence of foreigners, proved resistant to Christianity. Meinhard was evidently prepared to bribe the Livs by building them a castle, but, when this did not work, he began thinking about a crusade. In 1196 Meinhard died without converting many of the people he had lived among.[1]

Western appetites had been whetted by this experience nonetheless, and the next phase of the incursion coincided with the ascension in 1198 of Innocent III to the throne of Saint Peter. Perhaps the most ambitious of the medieval popes, Innocent entertained notions of ruling over both the religious and the secular world but was ambivalent on the subject of crusades within Europe. Although he felt that the greatest threat to the church in Europe was heresy, he did not think it proper for Christians to war against other Christians. Despite his doubts, Innocent did proclaim a crusade against the "pagan Balts"; it is in this context that another churchman, Berthold, a Cistercian abbot from Loccum, was named the second bishop of Ikšķile and arrived in 1198 at the mouth of the Daugava, this time with a contingent of soldiers. He, however, was killed in a skirmish with the Livs in the year of his arrival.

A year passed, and in 1199 Albert of Buxhovden, a nephew of the archbishop of Bremen, was named as third bishop. Albert was far more ambitious—an empire-builder, in fact—and a much better strategist than his predecessors; before coming to the Baltic, he convinced Innocent III to proclaim a second Baltic crusade. Thus Albert arrived at the mouth of the Daugava in the spring of 1200 with twenty-three ships and five hundred Saxon soldiers, having decided that a serious Christianizing effort required a permanent and intimidating presence and territorial control. To accomplish his goals, Albert first co-opted the Liv elders in the immediate area by taking them hostage and forcing them to agree to his terms. Recognizing that the earlier fortification in Ikšķile (far inland from the mouth of the Daugava) was militarily unjustifiable, in 1201 he began building the city of Riga close to the mouth of the Daugava near a cluster of Liv villages on the Ridzene River. In 1202 Albert transformed his military contingent into an order of knights called the Swordbrothers (in German, Schwertbrüder, sometimes also called the Brothers of the Militia of Christ or the Livonian Brothers of the Sword). Finally, like a feudal lord, he began making land grants (fiefs) to his soldiers, who thereby became his vassals.

The chronicles of the period do not fully explain these transactions or tell how Albert came into possession of the fiefs in the first place. We must assume that possession of the lands occupied by the Livs was simply asserted, just as designating the entire littoral as *Livonia* was asserted before the territory was fully conquered. We can further assume that those fiefs included their Liv inhabitants; later chronicles describe Albert's vassals as having fiefs populated by farmers.[2] In any event, Albert was the first Westerner to superimpose onto the territorial arrangements of the eastern littoral not only his control but also his geographic nomenclature. With his arrival began the construction of the medieval state known as Livonia.

MILITARY ACTION

The Swordbrothers wasted no time in moving against the pagans closest at hand, namely, most of the unconverted Liv population. In 1205 Salaspils, the center of Liv resistance, was taken by an armed force consisting of the Brothers, merchants, and already-converted Livs. In his battle against the Livs, Albert was able to strengthen the crusaders' cause by taking advantage of internal antagonisms and rivalries of the native populations; he thus called on the Semigallians, as well as the Christianized Livs, to do battle against their pagan brethren. By 1207, military action against the Livs had been concluded; the bishop of Livonia (Albert) received two-thirds of the captured territory and the Swordbrothers, one-third.

The Selonians were next in line. Their important centers were taken in 1207–1208 (Koknese) and in 1209 (Jersika). In Jersika the Swordbrothers took captive the wife of Visvaldis, the Jersika chieftain; Visvaldis then assented to become Albert's vassal and received part of his former lands as a fief. Simultaneous with the military actions in the southeast, Albert and the Swordbrothers moved northeast and in 1206 built a castle in Cēsis (in German, Wenden), which became the center for military action against the surrounding Lettgallian and Estonian territories.

In 1208 the Swordbrothers formed a military alliance with the Lettgallians of the Tālava region in order to move against the pagan Estonians to the north. The struggle with the Estonians weakened the Tālava Lettgallians, and in 1214 Albert added the Tālava region to his territories. Despite a brief Lettgallian-Estonian uprising in 1212 near Cēsis, Albert remained the master of this region. By 1216 the Swordbrothers had overrun nearly all of southern Estonia, and in the winter of 1216 they invaded the island of Ösel, off the Estonian coast in the Baltic Sea.

The successes of Bishop Albert and the Swordbrothers threatened the Russian principalities to the east, and in 1217 there were a series of

Estonian-Russian moves against the crusaders. In doing battle with the Estonians, Albert had to depend on both Livs and Lettgallians, especially in the battle at Viljandi in 1217, as well as assistance from the Danish king, Waldemar II. For the next ten years warfare continued between the crusader-Danish forces and the Estonian-Russian forces, but by 1227 this conflict had been concluded in favor of Albert and the Swordbrothers. The northern lands of the eastern littoral were finally under the firm control of the church, the crusaders, and the merchants who followed in their wake.[3]

As the conquest of the north proceeded, the Couronians in the western territories of the littoral were trying to head off a similar fate by launching raids against the military outposts the Swordbrothers had established on the edges of the Couronian territories. In 1210, when the Livs requested their assistance, the seagoing Couronians had sent a fleet of vessels to the mouth of the Riga. This venture, as well as the raids, came to naught, however, and in 1230–1231 the Couronians together with their Semigallian allies faced a major thrust by the crusaders to the west and southwest. The thrust was successful, and much of the Couronian territory was overrun and its inhabitants Christianized in 1230 through an agreement with Lamekin, the northern Couronian chieftain, and in 1231 with the other Couronian chiefs.

At this point, the crusaders joined in an ambitious scheme, approved by the papacy, to gain control over the entire Baltic seacoast from the Prussian lands to the northeast. The plan involved the German Order (in German, Deutsche Orden), which was founded in Jerusalem in 1189 and had moved to Prussia by the early thirteenth century. The plan called for the German Order to move north and east and the Swordbrothers south and west, thus subjugating not only the Semigallians and Couronians but also the Prussian pagans and the Lithuanians, that is, those Baltic peoples who had not yet been conquered and Christianized. In those campaigns, the battle at Saule in September 1236 gave a combined force of Lithuanians and Semigallians a decisive victory. Virtually all the leaders of the Swordbrothers were killed, including the master, the knights of the German Order having proven insufficiently strong to make a difference. That battle had three important consequences: the remnants of the Swordbrothers were incorporated into the German Order in 1237, henceforth known as the Livonian Order; the Lithuanians gained time in their battle against the crusading orders; and in the north the Couronians and Semigallians took the opportunity to revolt. In 1242 the energies of the Semigallians were also fed by the defeat of the Livonian Order on Lake Peipus by the army of Alexander Nevsky.[4]

During the next two decades the Couronians and Semigallians remained restless and unpredictable, but by the early 1250s their opposition to the Livonian Order had waned. There were some victories against the order, particularly at Durbe in July 1260, but in 1267 the defeated and exhausted Couronians signed a peace agreement. The only old territorial society that remained unsubjugated was that of the Semigallians, but a sequence of events that began with clashes in 1264 ended in their defeat. In 1265 the Livonian Order built a castle in Jelgava (in German, Mitau) that became the headquarters for the Semigallian wars. Not until twenty-five years later, however, did the Livonian Order subjugate the Semigallians and then only with the help of the main German Order, which by 1283 had defeated the Prussians and could thus send military assistance to its Baltic branch. In 1286 a particularly effective Semigallian chieftain called Nameisis even managed for a time to surround the city of Riga. In 1290, however, the last Semigallian stronghold at Sidrabene fell, and with that battle the military conquest of the eastern Baltic littoral by German churchmen, crusaders, and merchants was completed.[5]

THE FEUDAL CONFEDERATION OF LIVONIA

The Livonian Confederation, which emerged on the territories formerly controlled by the Couronians, Semigallians, Livs, Selians, Lettgallians, and Estonians, remained an important factor in the politics of northern Europe until the second half of the sixteenth century. The use of the term *Livonia* in the singular, however, belies the nature of this state because its several political elites—the ecclesiastics, the order, the Riga burghers—seldom acted in unison. The history of Livonia is one of continuous and bitter rivalry between the church and the Livonian Order, between the vassals and lords of these corporate entities and among the vassals themselves, and between the cities, especially Riga, and all the other claimants to power and influence. Although technically a confederation, Livonia was an extreme example of medieval decentralization in which cooperation and collaboration emerged only when there was an external threat and sometimes not even then.[6]

The reasons for the disputes were many, but the principal one was territorial control. In the thirteenth century the original formula for dividing newly acquired territories called for one-third of them to be placed under the jurisdiction of the order and two-thirds under the church, but this principle broke down when, after the conquest of each indigenous people, exceptions were made to the rule. This resulted in the order controlling far more territory than the church.

The number of influential ecclesiastics in Livonia, however, expanded, as in the course of the thirteenth century bishoprics were created at Tartu, Ösel, and Tallinn (all in Estonian territory). Late in the thirteenth century, a Courland bishopric was formed as well, but because it was not capable of defeating the Couronians, it had to rely on the order, which then received most of the conquered Couronian land. When the bishopric of Riga was elevated to an archbishopric in 1251, the archbishop became the spiritual leader of all the Baltic bishops except the bishop of Tallinn. By the mid–fourteenth century, the Livonian Order had become the largest land-holder in the confederation, controlling about 67,000 square kilometers of land; the ecclesiastical lands contained only about 41,000 square kilometers. The largest church state was the Riga archbishopric, which controlled about 18,000 square kilometers. The Courland bishopric was next, with control over about 4,500 square kilometers. The lands of the order were in turn divided into some forty smaller districts, each governed by an official called a *Vogt*. The distribution of the ecclesiastical and order lands in Livonia, as shown in map 2, virtually guaranteed continuous friction.[7]

Given the feudal principle (by which powerful persons voluntarily subordinate themselves to overlords), as well as the fact that both the church and the order embodied the principle of hierarchy, one might have expected a high degree of political cohesion. The problem in Livonia, however, was that feudal superiors were not powerful enough to enforce continued loyalty, especially from their most ambitious vassals. Thus, for example, although in the order the lines of authority were clear—the master was elected for life, had his seat in Livonia (in Riga and later in Cēsis rather than far away, and was therefore well positioned to be an effective feudal lord—he had trouble guaranteeing the loyalty of his vassals. Such vassals lived in fortified castles and expanded their personal power, secure in the knowledge that only through them could the master effectively govern the order's territories. The vassals, in turn, depended on low-level district (in German, *Amt*) administrators. The higher officials of the order constituted a kind of parliament (*kapituls*), which functioned as an advisory council to the master. The master was subordinate to the master of the German Order, the headquarters of which were in Marienburg in Prussia. (From the early fourteenth century onward the Livonian Order enlarged its sphere of action and became less accountable to Prussian headquarters.) There was a feudal hierarchy, but by the early fourteenth century self-interest was doing battle with pledged personal loyalty.[8]

At the apex of the Livonian ecclesiastical hierarchy stood the arch-bishop of Riga, who was also the nominal head of the Livonian Confedera-tion as well as the city of Riga. As a landholder presiding over the properties of the archbishopric, the archbishop alternated residences among the castles at Rauna, Limbāži, and Koknese. Needing an armed force, the archbishop,

Map 2. Medieval Livonia, ca. 1400

■ City of Riga
▨ Ecclesiastical lands
☐ Lands of the Livonian Order

in a practice typical of the period, granted out the lands under his jurisdiction as fiefs to secular vassals, who then constituted his military. Given the above, the Riga archbishop appeared to be a powerful personage but in fact wore too many hats, each of which brought him into conflict not only with his own ecclesiastical subordinates and secular vassals but also with the nominally religious but increasingly secularly motivated order. Thus during the fourteenth and fifteenth centuries, power flowed increasingly away from the position of archbishop in the direction of the advisory councils and the secular power centers. The bishops, the other powerful churchmen in Livonia, were not much better off; the bishop of Courland, for example, depended almost entirely on the goodwill of the Livonian Order because he had little land to grant to create his own military force.[9]

Despite the order's territorial strength, the church, by means of the Christianization process, was developing an infrastructure in the nonelite population in its own and the order's territories. The new faith was not only a matter of beliefs but also of institutions, such as parishes, congregations (in Latvian, *draudzes*), clergy, places of worship and housing for the clergy, and formalized contributions from the congregations. There were also new forms of control: rules on admitting converts to the church, regulations about impermissible marriages with close kin, required attendance at worship, the manner and frequency with which sacraments were taken, and rules about burials. It is estimated that, by the end of the fifteenth century outside the city of Riga, there were some seventy congregations in the Latvian territories, each with its own church.[10] The evidence suggests that acquiring territorial control and creating parish-level institutions were but the first steps in the long-term Christianization process. Yet how far the process reached into the rural populations is difficult to estimate because there was evidently a shortage of clergy willing to serve outside the urban centers such as Riga.

THE CHURCH, THE LIVONIAN ORDER, AND THE CITY OF RIGA

When Bishop Albert founded Riga in 1201, the eastern Baltic littoral did not have any population concentrations large enough to be called cities. The number of people in and around the fortified places of the precrusader period may sometimes have reached town size, but these concentrations appear to have been fortuitous and impermanent. The founding of Riga, therefore, was the beginning of urban history in the area; the city was immensely significant during the active crusading and

Christianizing efforts of the first century and remained so even as other cities were founded in Livonia during the course of the thirteenth and fourteenth centuries. Accurate population statistics do not exist for the medieval period, but the city is estimated to have had about ten thousand residents by the beginning of the fourteenth century.[11]

When its founder and lord, Bishop Albert, was alive, affairs in Riga were dominated by his agenda, except for a brief period before 1120, when Albert gave the city to the Danish king in gratitude for his assistance in the colonization effort. Even before this, however, the city had developed its own administrative institutions (a council of *seniores* [elders] is first mentioned in 1210) and political will. In 1221 the Rigans successfully challenged Danish rule and achieved a quasi independence, even though Albert tried to reclaim some of his prerogatives.

When Albert died in 1229, power in the city was concentrated in a council that originally had twelve members but grew as time went on. Judging by the fragmentary evidence in written sources, the social structure of the city consisted of a patriciate of wealthy merchants and tradesmen; a large middle group of artisans, craftsmen, and lesser merchants; and a fairly large number of persons who worked in various support occupations but did not have political rights. These political-economic structures became more rigid with time, particularly in the mid–fourteenth century when guilds began to control entry into urban occupations. As Riga became a typical medieval city, it also grew independent in spirit, reserving the right to choose its own patron, which was especially important after Albert died. The city adopted its charter of rights first from Visby (on the island of Gotland) and then from Hamburg when Riga became a member of the Hanseatic League in 1282.[12] In various revised forms, the charter remained in force until the seventeenth century, and all other cities in the Livonian territories copied their charters from Riga's.

Because trade had been a principal motive for the "discovery" of the Baltic littoral by central Europeans, Riga grew and thrived as a commercial center. But this also meant that the concerns and values of its permanent residents came to differ from those of the church (which was a landholder) as well as from those of the landed members of the Livonian Order. Because the Riga bishop (archbishop after 1282) remained an important figure in the area, and because the order remained a strong military force, a conflict over a host of issues was inevitable.

The main themes of these internal struggles concerned overlordship of the city, overlordship of the whole of Livonia, and, within Riga (where both the order and the archbishop had domiciles), influence over the city's political institutions. Overlordship and influence ultimately meant income, which, because of Riga's growing prosperity, made the city a particularly attractive target to both the church and the order. Normally, but not always, Riga sided with the archbishop against the Livonian Order and periodically—especially during a thirty-three-year stretch from 1297 to 1330—was at war with the order. Riga's struggles with the order became so severe that it asked for military assistance from the Lithuanians, who in 1305, 1307, 1309, and later attacked the order's lands from the south. During the Avignonese papacy (1309–77), Riga archbishops made frequent visits to southern France to argue for their rights against what they felt were the order's usurpations. Later, especially after the defeat by the Lithuanians of the German Order in 1410 at Tannenberg, the weakened Livonian Order began negotiating with the Riga archbishop to obtain his help in subjugating the independent-minded city.[13]

The conflicts among the order, the church, and Riga also involved the peasantry. Riga remained a thorn in the side of all landowners, including the church, because, in the manner of all medieval cities, it attracted peasants fleeing from the increasingly harsh obligations of life in the countryside. More generally, no landowner was spared the danger of losing some of his rural labor force because peasants sought better conditions and readily left the areas of their birth to settle on the properties of other owners. Mutually satisfactory regulations among all the landowners, and between them and the city, were never devised during the entire medieval period.[14] Some of the fleeing serfs who ended up in Riga working in support occupations became the core of a non-German subpopulation of the city and thus introduced another source of antagonism.

The conflicts among the church, the order, and Riga reflected the inevitable fault lines in Livonian society that resulted from the ambitions and powerful personalities in these corporate groupings. Even the creation in 1419 of a Livonian diet (in German, *Landtag*) did not help. This institution, called at the initiative of the Riga archbishop and meeting for the first time in 1422, consisted of four sociopolitical orders (or *curiae*). The first was the Riga archbishop and the other Livonian bishops; the second, the higher officeholders of the Livonian Order; the third, all of the persons of vassal status in Livonia; and the fourth, the representatives of the Livonian cities. Although the *Landtag* met regularly during the fifteenth century and beyond, its presence did not substantially affect the rivalries among the elites. Whereas in Western European societies one monarch after another successfully challenged the forces of feudal decentralization, Livonia remained decentralized and therefore entered the sixteenth century as an exceptionally weak state, a tempting target to ambitious neighbors because of its strategic location.

THE LIVONIAN PEASANTRY AND THE
EMERGENCE OF LATVIANS

The consolidation of power by the new elites of the eastern Baltic littoral expressed itself in the imposition of new borders and subdivisions on Baltic territory, in the appearance of chroniclers and other record keepers and through them of the first written historical sources, and in the transformation of the indigenous populations into peasants. These developments combined to make it virtually impossible to answer the question of what happened in the period 1200–1400 to those peoples who, before the arrival of the crusaders, bore the designations Couronians, Livs, Semigallians, Selonians, and Lettgallians? The written sources for the period—such as the *Chronicle* of Henry of Livonia (1225–26)—described principally the activities of the upper social orders and, in the Baltic as elsewhere in medieval European society, provided information about peasants only to the extent that they were of importance to the functioning of administrators and churchmen and to the occasional curious observer. Of even greater importance for a history of the Latvians was that the record keepers had limited interest in the processes of change affecting the non-Germans (in German, *undeutsche*) of the area, that is, those populations that did not use German (or Latin). In these medieval chronicles and accounts the Couronians, Semigallians, Livs, Selonians, and Lettgallians begin to show up as "non-Germans" or as "peasants" just at that point in Baltic history when it is important for us to know how they were changing as peoples. The problem continued beyond the medieval period, of course, because the indigenous populations did not directly create historical records in their own language until the nineteenth century.[15]

The question concerning the indigenous peoples is twofold: how did they become a peasantry, and how (and possibly whether) did they become Latvians? Although we know nothing precise about the relative sizes of the different population groups in the Livonian state, there is no doubt that the nonecclesiastical, nonmilitary, and nonmercantile groups—that is, the cultivators of the soil, the agriculturists, the peasants—made up the vast majority of the population, as they did elsewhere on the European continent. At the start of the thirteenth century, then, it is estimated that there were four to five persons per square kilometer in the "Latvian" territories of the Livonian Confederation, yielding an estimated total population of 250,000 to 350,000.[16] The upper orders constituted about 5–10 percent of this number, as elsewhere.

It would be a mistake, however, to conceive of the upper and lower orders in terms of an urban/rural division. The countryside in fact dominated: the German- and Latin-using churchmen, knights, and administrators and their entourages were, in effect, swimming in a sea of non-German rural folk and having to find ways of dealing with them on a daily basis. Only in Riga and a few other towns would this image need to be reversed, and even in Riga there appears to have been a sizable complement of non-German residents. Below the well-organized merchant and artisan guilds, there were a host of support occupations and shopkeeping enterprises in which, sources suggest, non-Germans were important numerically and perhaps even dominant.[17] Even so, the vast majority of the total population of 300,000 or so did not live in cities, and the vast majority of the rural dwellers were not recent in-wanderers.

Whereas in Western Europe by the fourteenth century, serfdom and manorialism were already rural institutions, in the Baltic littoral they were the products of the last centuries of the medieval period. Dating the appearance of Baltic serfdom (in Latvian, *dzimtbūšana*) as a formal institution is particularly tricky because a convincing case can be made that it did not begin in the littoral until the late fifteenth and the early sixteenth centuries. In this interpretation Baltic serfdom was not a medieval institution at all and did not play a formal role in transforming Balts into peasants in the fourteenth and fifteenth centuries. Those centuries involved various relationships of dependency and obligation between landholders and peasants but not, evidently, hereditary servility (in German, *Erbuntertänigkeit*) and the corvée labor associated with developed serfdom.[18]

At issue here are transformatory processes lasting some eight to ten human generations (one generation = twenty-five years), none of which there is adequate documentation for; descriptive statements must be inferred from a few words in the written sources. Personal subordination was normal in all social strata. Vassals were subordinate to lords who in turn were vassals of other lords, and, as mentioned, the highest power holders in the Baltic littoral had superiors outside the area: the pope and the master of the German Order. Some sources mention a category of slaves, who were evidently captives taken in battle, criminals sentenced to slavery, or people unable to pay their debts.

In this context, serfdom (hereditary subordination to a particular landholder) would not have been judged a remarkable invention when it did appear in individual instances and became widespread. On fiefs, peasants were already subordinated in the economic sense because most paid rent of some kind and performed some obligatory labor. Twice a year representatives of landholders traversed the countryside and gathered rents from peasant communities. In fifteenth-century sources there are a number of complaints about "fleeing" peasants, a phenomenon that originally seems to have been connected to the inability to repay accumulated debt. But later complaints appear to have been based on landholders' assumptions that peasants should stay in place regardless of whether or not they had debts. From here it was only one step to the emergence of a heritable status that carried with it perpetual labor services and dues of other kinds. Certainly by the end of the medieval period, there were more frequent appearances in the sources of such terms as *Erbbauer, Erbleute,* and *Erbherr* (hereditary peasant, hereditary persons, hereditary lord), all of which suggest that relationships of dependency had become fixed. We do not know, however, the pace at which these new relational forms spread, whether their spread was geographically differentiated, and how their intensity varied from place to place.

When manorialism emerged is a somewhat easier question to answer because it involves real estate rather than hard-to-interpret personal obligations.[19] Although we think of manorialism and serfdom in medieval Europe as two sides of the same coin, they do not have to be and, in fact, were not in the Baltic littoral. Manors (in Latvian, *muiža,* from the Liv *moiz;* in German, *Gut*) made their first appearance simultaneously with the granting of Baltic lands as fiefs to vassals in the thirteenth century, but their internal arrangements took a long time to standardize. During the centuries in question, *muižas* and peasant holdings coexisted, and free (not enserfed) peasants lived on manorial properties alongside peasants whose ties to the manorial lord were more formalized. Both peasants and manorial lords held their land from someone else, of course, but not all land being worked by peasants was manorial land. Manor holders who could not command peasant labor had to pay for it. By the end of the fifteenth century (traditionally the end of the medieval period), it is probable that a large proportion of the agricultural land in the Baltic littoral had not yet been absorbed into manorial properties, and it is certain that the vast majority of *muižas* founded by that time did not rely entirely on corvée labor.[20] The spread of the classic serf estate in the Baltic, then, did not begin until the sixteenth century.

The question of how the indigenous peoples of the Baltic littoral became peasants is answerable by reference to the new institutions that absorbed them: the Livonian statelets, the Livonian state as a whole, and the manor. A multilevel social hierarchy in which location depended on birth and upward mobility was almost impossible in part because of the German/non-German cleavage. How the indigenous peoples became Latvians is a more difficult question, not only because we do not know whether, in the precrusader period, there really existed a group identity for, say, the Semigallians that they would have sought to retain but also because we do not know what *being Latvian* would have meant in the late medieval era, beyond having a childhood language different from those of the upper orders. However useful it is to employ the term *Livonia* for the eastern Baltic littoral during the late medieval centuries, beneath this territorial designation group identities were in the process of changing. Some of these changes manifested themselves in immigrants from Central Europe beginning to feel more Livonian and less German, and others probably entailed Couronians, Semigallians, Livs, Selians, and Lettgallians coming to feel more Latvian.

There are, of course, no sources that directly describe these processes of ethnolinguistic transformation. From the thirteenth century onward, when the chronicles describing the conquest were written, historical evidence about the area continued to describe and reflect the doings of the new upper orders, with evidence about the peoples that had become the peasant stratum appearing only incidentally. The processes through which the indigenous peoples lost their group identities therefore must be inferred from various kinds of descriptions of surface events. It is clear, however, that whereas in the thirteenth century the chroniclers were liberal in their use of the old group designations, by the sixteenth century the sources tended to use the German term *Letten* (in Latvian, *latvieši*) when they did not use the designation *undeutsch* (non-Germans).[21]

What happened in the last two centuries of the medieval period is not clear. One possibility is that during the thirteenth century—the period of the most intense warfare—there was a great deal of internal migration, some of it fleeing from warfare itself and some of it, during the war century and after, searching for better places to farm because many previously populated places had lost their residents. In this supposition, the populations of the old tribal societies simply dissolved as identifiable entities, fragments of each merging with fragments of others as a result of demographic shifts. The result was a new large population, the territorial base of which was now the southern part of the Livonian Confederation. The Lettagallians, having been the most numerous, became the dominant element.

Another possibility is that, by the end of the thirteenth century, the consolidation of power by the new elites resulted, over the next eight generations, in the disappearance of the old local elites in a process of assimilation, for which the German term *Enthauptung* (decapitation) could be used. Having lost their leadership class and the possibility of restoring it, the five indigenous peoples also lost a major source of group distinctiveness and therefore the incentive to maintain group identity. The process through which the old political elite disappeared is not well known or described. Some historians maintain that the indigenous political leaders became minor vassals of the new feudal lords, adapting in the process to the ways and language of the latter; others, that the old leaders left the eastern littoral and migrated to Lithuania, where the new German elites had not been implanted. Having migrated into Lithuanian territory, they assimilated to Lithuanians in due course.[22]

Another possibility is that a confrontational situation between, on the one hand, a new set of powerful elites that had the same cultural background (German language, central European) and, on the other, the heterogeneous subordinated population evoked in the latter a unifying reaction, so that in due time the old distinctions no longer mattered. Thus by establishing themselves as the new elite, the German churchmen, merchants, and crusaders ironically became the reason the indigenous populations merged into a Latvian population—a process that had not been in evidence before the German speakers came.

There is, of course, another possibility, which is that the old group identities, never having been firmly or evenly fixed in the minds of the five indigenous peoples, gradually faded and were replaced by a more general—Latvian—identity. As a result of internal population movements, the spoken languages of the five societies ceased to be distinctive, with all the speakers of the earlier tongues adopting a more widespread language, likely some transformed version of Lettgallian. This process, however, did not need to be accompanied by the emergence of a common national or political consciousness vis-à-vis the new elites or neighboring peoples. The residents of Livonia could have remained highly conscious of linguistic differences even though they did not manifest themselves as national group boundaries. Clearly, how this question is answered for the period 1300–1500 plays a large role in how the history of the Latvians as a people is interpreted in the succeeding centuries.[23]

The meager evidence about these processes suggests that change was taking place but not enough to make unambiguous statements about it. By the end of the fifteenth century, a Livonian society had come into being that, when stabilized in terms of social structure, differed substantially from its pre-thirteenth-century predecessors. Among the Couronians, Livs, Lettgallians, Selonians, and Semigallians in those eight to ten generations, the memory of earlier social and political structures and arrangements must have dimmed and eventually disappeared. They must have lost the sense that they as individuals somehow belonged to peoples designated by such group names. How deep a new Latvian consciousness had become is an open question. That legitimate political power could be exercised by socioeconomic elites who were not Latvians gradually became an accepted aspect of life for most people, as the imperatives of daily survival took over and thoughts of revenge receded. Most Latvians at the end of the period were peasants, and most peasants in the southern regions of Livonia were Latvians. Those urban people who were non-German sought to assimilate to the German elites and probably perceived themselves as having far more in common with their fellow urbanites than with the peasantry.

3 Politics, Economics, and Religion in the Sixteenth Century

By the beginning of the sixteenth century, the new monarchies of Western Europe were on their way to becoming relatively centralized national states, but Livonia retained an increasingly archaic confederational character. It had several centers of power, with none strong enough to impose its will on the others or to give Livonia a strong definition and direction. If not a major power in the international politics of northern Europe, Livonia was nonetheless a factor. The total population of the "Latvian" (southern) districts of Livonia had grown to an estimated 404,000 (see table 1, p. 88).[1] The German-speaking subpopulations, newcomers to the Baltic littoral in 1300, made up some 4–5 percent of the total population and were now in some sense natives, with some families having lived there for four generations or more. Riga and the other Livonian cities had reached a respectable age and stature, having become centers of commerce, manufacture, and culture for the upper social orders. The institutions of the Christian church in the littoral seemed permanently established, and the Livonian Order, though with a smaller membership than in previous centuries, continued as a powerful force in Livonian society.

Persons belonging to ecclesiastical, knightly, and urban corporations constituted the governing classes, and most written sources of the period concern those classes, their cultural activities, and their struggles with one another and external enemies. Less likely to enter the written record was information about the lives of the other 95 percent of Livonian society, which consisted mostly of Latvian peasants but included also Poles, Lithuanians, Russians, Livs, and Estonians. Livonia was on the eastern edge of Western Europe, and there was a brisk movement of people, ideas, and goods between it and the larger European population centers, especially those of the German-speaking lands of the Holy Roman Empire. The currents of change that in the sixteenth century began to redesign Western European society were felt in Livonia as well.

THE ARRIVAL OF LUTHERANISM

The first Livonian institution to experience the currents of change was the Christian church. As in the German lands of the Holy Roman Empire, Martin Luther's challenge to papal authority appealed to many in Livonia. After Luther posted his Ninety-five Theses in 1517, Lutheran ideas began emerging in Livonia.[2] In the early 1520s, through the sympathetic efforts of Johann Lohmiller (d. 1560), Sylvester Tegetmeyer (d. 1552), and Andreas Knopken (d. 1539)—all men of high standing in Riga—the city became an important center of Reformation impulses. From 1520 to 1540 the questions of how and to what extent the Livonian church should be reformed were debated in various local arenas, with opinions dividing every corporation and social group. There was no dearth of fanaticism among the reformers, manifested in mob attacks on monasteries and churches and the Riga authorities being unable (or unwilling) to stop such destruction.

The reasons for the attractiveness of Lutheran reform are not difficult to list, though ranking them in terms of importance is another matter. The Riga archbishop and the bishops of Livonia, as fief-granting landowners, had been involved in Livonian politics for three centuries, most recently in the Livonian Diet. The church therefore had strong interests that went far beyond spiritual leadership, and, consequently, it had enemies. Vassals of the archbishop wanted greater say over their own holdings, as did vassals everywhere; and the Livonian Order was of course an ancient rival. Perhaps most readily antagonized by the shortcomings of the church were the homeowners, merchants, and artisans of Riga, who had serious reservations about the flow of their wealth into church coffers and possibly away from Livonia.

The effects of reform on the vast majority of the Livonian population— the peasantry—are difficult to describe because the sources are silent on the pace and the extent to which congregations in the countryside "became Lutheran."[3] The peasants of Livonia certainly did not initiate their own conversion; this step, when it happened, was taken by local landholders who "led" their peasants into the new faith. What role conviction played among peasants is therefore difficult to say. Some historians have suggested—with unwarranted certainty—that the peasants simply shifted their worship from one variant of Christian belief (the medieval church) to another (Lutheranism). For the peasantry, this argument goes, the church was an imported, outsiders' institution throughout the medieval centuries and remained so in the sixteenth century.[4] The peasantry, though fulfilling obligatory attendance rules and taking sacraments to avoid punishment, remained pagan at heart, performing non-Christian acts of worship and celebration surreptitiously whenever the opportunity arose.

There was, however, one positive effect of Lutheranism on the lower social orders, including the peasantry, flowing from Luther's insistence that the Word of God be made available to churchgoers in their native language. During the 1520s this resulted in the founding in Riga of congregations in which Latvian was the language of worship. There and in the countryside, Luther's mandate created a strong incentive for clergymen not only to learn the language of their parishioners but also to translate sacred texts into that language.[5] The reformed church in Livonia also began recruiting and promoting clerics from the non-German ranks. Such changes, of course, were slow in coming, and during the sixteenth century only isolated instances of each have been documented. But in the collective attitudes of the reformed church there appears to have been from this point onward a greater receptivity to at least the linguistic aspects of the culture of the lower orders. At the same time, those changes highlighted the linguistic differences between the clergy and worshipers; clerics who had not learned to communicate with their parishioners in their language were disdained.

In any event, by the mid-1550s Lutheranism had become dominant among the ruling elites, even though what was henceforth referred to as the *Roman Catholic* variant of Christianity remained part of the Livonian religious landscape. The majority of landholders, however renounced allegiance to Rome and "led" their dependent rural peoples into the new faith. The influential circles in Riga all adhered to the reform faith, and in 1533 the Livonian *Landtag* agreed that no obstacles should be placed in the way of such reform. In the short run at least a potentially grave conflict had been resolved in favor of something like religious toleration, with Lutheranism having the upper hand.

In the Livonian lands, however, because of the continuing presence of and struggles between Lutheranism and Catholicism, the Lutherans were unable to develop a general regional church organization, except in the city of Riga. Elsewhere in Livonia, reformed districts were on their own. After the Livonian wars and the creation of the Duchy of Courland, the first Baltic provincewide Lutheran Church was established there in 1570, with a thirteen-person Consistory, presided over by the duchy's chancellor and a superintendent, as the highest organ of church governance. In 1636 the Courland church was divided into seven districts governed by deans (in Latvian, *prāvesti*), with the Mitau (in Latvian, *Jelgava*) dean as the superintendent. The Consistory supervised the activities of about seventy congregations.[6] In the sixteenth century, before this greater level of organization was achieved, however, the presence of Lutheranism had added another fault line to the internal affairs of Livonia, weakening regional power holders further at a time when territorially ambitious neighbors—especially Muscovy—were becoming more belligerent than ever before.

LORDS, PEASANTS, AND ESTATES

Political weakness produced by internal division was one reason Livonia was becoming attractive to land-hungry neighbors. Another was economic performance. Although Livonia was not hugely wealthy, it had good seaports and a brisk import and export trade, as well as a productive peasantry whose labor sustained an expanding system of manors and estates.[7] In the southern half of Livonia, in the cities, towns, and countryside, the relatively small, though politically dominant, proportion of German-speaking inhabitants made it inevitable that non-Germans—whom we shall begin to designate as *Latvians* at this juncture—would play important support roles in the urban and rural economies.

For the history of Latvians in the sixteenth century, both the urban and the rural dimensions are important, for the changes that were affecting rural Latvians in that century were associated with the changing conditions of rural life throughout the European continent. In Western Europe, a new dynamism was evident in the growth of overseas exploration and in the economic development that expanded the market for Eastern European raw materials and foodstuffs, especially grain. There was also a long-term increase in prices that began to be appreciated in the Baltic by those who were in position to benefit by increased productivity, namely, the landholding ecclesiastical vassals, the vassals of the Livonian Order, and the urban merchants and tradesmen.

The vassals' growing interest in benefiting from the rise in agricultural incomes was reflected in their systematic effort to expand the number and size of manors (landed estates; in Latvian, *muižas*) and their attempts to control a greater proportion of their lords' lands.[8] There were also efforts to render the vassals' rights to fiefs permanent through the expansion of heritability.

Such actions were bound to affect the peasantry and to change the conditions of their lives, creating restrictions and obligations that came to look increasingly like serfdom. If, before the sixteenth century, peasants' obligations to their lords still left most of the working week free for labor on their own land, then after 1500 those obligations became more onerous, with the pace becoming especially rapid in the second half of the century. If earlier peasant families were always able to find arable land and expand it through hard work, then those who now resided on land that was being absorbed by the estate system frequently found themselves restricted, as landholders consolidated the demesne and blocked the expansion of peasant land. If earlier peasants hoped to better their lot by changing their place of residence (with or without permission), then such migration across internal boundaries became increasingly difficult, as estate holders sought to establish a permanent rural labor force.

In describing these general tendencies in the Livonian countryside— that, taken all in all, amounted to a system of serf estates coming into being—we should not overestimate the smoothness of such changes. Indeed, the process was so uneven in the sixteenth century, so ragged and patternless, that some historians date the arrival of serfdom as the early seventeenth century.[9] Nonetheless, in the sixteenth, for some four generations, the old coexisted with the new. From the peasantry's point of view none of the expanded obligations affecting its daily life was surprising or entirely new because it had already learned to live with the concept of obligatory services of various kinds rendered to immediate or regional lords. The lord's portion (in Latvian, *kunga tiesa*), agreements to return peasants to their place of origin if they moved without permission, and dispossession if a lord wanted to expand his demesne had been aspects of peasant life for a long time, setting limits to freedom of action. But in the course of the sixteenth century, in different places and at different times, rules governing daily life were made more onerous on landed estates wherein the landholder and his staff were fast becoming the alpha and omega of local power.

The seemingly random nature of this process meant, in the sixteenth century, that not all peasants were equally affected by it and that some were not affected at all. Much depended on the specific agreements among communities, individual peasants, and local landholders because the confederation principle on which the Livonian state was based did not engender statewide laws. There were entire peasant communities in the Couronian areas of Livonia, for example, that retained a charter of rights exempting them from all control by local landholders, and not all landholders had an equal interest in creating estates based on obligatory peasant labor.[10] A large proportion of peasants lived on estates that were not controlled by vassals (i.e., had not been granted as fiefs), and the holders of these did not need to increase their incomes to pay for the more costly life of the titled nobility.

Another aspect of rural life mitigated even the harshest new regulations and requirements, namely, that landholders did not have sufficient personnel to enforce total control over all aspects of peasant life. For example, tenure could become less secure, but peasant inheritance customs continued to produce predictable transfers of headships in the male line, according, as far as we can tell, to the principle of patrilineality. Also, though estate owners exercised some control over peasant marriages by refusing permission and making strong suggestions, they could not openly compel marriages or break up families through residential reassignments. Generally, peasant social customs operated on their own unless they came into sharp conflicts with the economic needs of landholders.[11] Landholders had the power to mete out various kinds of corporal punishment, but egregious cruelty was frowned on. Finally, a landed estate working with serf or free peasant labor always contained a linguistic polarity: estate holders and most of their subordinates spoke one language, whereas the peasants spoke another. In most areas of southern Livonia the language of the rural upper orders was German; in the eastern parts of the Livonian territories it tended to be Polish. But in the same territories, on the receiving end of orders and regulations, were peasants who spoke variants of Latvian. Sixteenth-century peasants could easily have taken advantage of this linguistic diversity by ignoring or deliberately misunderstanding orders and regulations, risking punishment, of course, but also delaying tasks or leaving them undone.

THE LIVONIAN WAR AND POLISH-LITHUANIAN ASCENDANCY

Although the arrival of Lutheranism and the proliferation of landed estates changed the history of the Livonian Confederation, they did not fundamentally alter its political structure. That transformation was accomplished by the confederation's external enemies, who took advantage of the fact that from the thirteenth century on Livonia's squabbling elites' sense of loyalty to the papacy and to the Holy Roman Empire had gradually diminished and thus turned the confederation into a weakened fragment. For the lower orders of Livonian society, the regional temporal and spiritual lords—not Rome or the emperor—were the most significant power wielders, but those regional rulers had shown themselves incapable of creating a state powerful enough to join the competitive fray that was the state of affairs in sixteenth-century northern Europe.

South of Livonia, Lithuanian monarchs, beginning with Mindaugas in the 1230s, had made headway in uniting the Lithuanian tribal societies and thus successfully resisted the efforts of the German Order to expand eastward. The Lithuanian kingdom then began expanding and attracting allies, and in 1385 the Lithuanians and Poles signed a treaty creating the Union of Kreva. In 1410 the united armies of Lithuanians, Poles, and Czechs decisively defeated the German Order in the Battle of Tannenberg. Thus, by the sixteenth century, the Poles and the Lithuanians had a history of several centuries of cooperation against the Germans from the west.

East of Livonia, the Russian principalities had for some time lived under the control of the Mongols; relations with their western neighbors had consisted largely of reciprocal raids by the Livonian Order and the adjacent Russian states on one another's territories. Russian weakness was evident in the relative ease with which the Lithuanian kingdom spread its boundaries eastward. This distribution of power had changed by the first three-quarters of the sixteenth century—the time of Ivan IV (Ivan the Terrible: 1530–84)—when a newly unified and expansionistic Muscovy began to look westward toward a weak Livonia. West of Livonia, of course, lay the Baltic Sea, but on its western shore was Sweden, the rulers of which were beginning to think in terms of mercantile colonies on the eastern Baltic littoral.

By the second half of the sixteenth century Livonia was more a political vacuum than a territorial state. In 1558, the Russians began the so-called Livonian war by capturing two cities in the north—Narva and Tartu (Dorpat)—and by starting a march toward Tallinn and Riga.[12] This penetration, although successful in the short term, intensified the political bewilderment of Livonia's political elites and invited the intervention of the other great powers interested in the area. Russian successes revealed that the military strength of the Livonian Order and the assorted ecclesiastical states—even when operating jointly—was ineffective, especially after the battle of Ērgeme in August 1560 in which the best forces of the order were utterly defeated.

Moreover, in the Estonian territories of Livonia, the Estonian peasantry used the military struggle to stage uprisings against their immediate overlords and to befriend the Russian invader. All this produced a flurry of desperate measures among the power holders in Livonia. The bishopric of Courland and Ösel had become a possession of the Danish kingdom in 1559, and the main Livonian territories now began searching for new masters. The elites of northern Livonia (the Estonian territories) asked for and received Swedish protection; the territories of Livonia that had not been occupied by the Russian forces asked for protection from the ruler of Poland and Lithuania, Sigismund II Augustus (1548–72). The master of the Livonian Order, the archbishop of Riga, and the representatives of the

Livonian nobility all swore loyalty to Sigismund in November 1561.[13] The only important member of the Livonian power configuration that did not seek protection was the city of Riga, which remained independent but threatened by both the Russians and the Polish-Lithuanian forces.

After this headlong flight by the Livonian elites into the arms of adjoining great powers, warfare became more intense. From the Russian viewpoint, the chief enemy now was Poland-Lithuania, which in 1569 had become a single state through the Union of Lublin. The military pressure of the Russian forces on Livonian territory increased even more after the sudden friendliness exhibited toward Sweden by Poland-Lithuania, which asked Swedish troops to join it in the struggle against the Russian presence. These allied armies engaged Russian forces throughout the 1570s and early 1580s, when the belligerents decided to settle at the table what they could not settle on the battlefield. In 1582, Poland-Lithuania and Muscovy agreed to peace, with Poland-Lithuania gaining the lion's share of the former Livonian territory. In the next year, 1583, Russia and Sweden agreed to peace as well, as a result of which Sweden gained control over the northern section of Livonia as well as the territory of Ingermanland. Denmark retained control over some islands off the Estonian coast and over the Courland bishopric (which it soon surrendered to Poland-Lithuania). Territorially, Muscovy was the loser.

With these transactions, the Livonian Confederation ceased to exist. Perhaps the clearest gainers of this reconfiguration of the eastern Baltic littoral—at the substate level, of course—were the members of the Livonian Order. The order was secularized in 1561, and its last master, Gotthard Kettler, became the duke (from 1562 to 1587) of a new province called "Courland and Semigallia" and a vassal of the Polish-Lithuanian monarch.[14] The former knights of the order were transformed into the new province's landed nobility. For the peasantry of all these territories, the Livonian war brought destruction, misery, and new nonresident sovereigns. The power of their immediate overlords, however, did not change much, except for titles, because the landholding nobilities of these territories were able to negotiate favorable arrangements with their new sovereigns in exchange for their loyalty.

The most important long-term consequence of the Livonian war for the Latvian residents of Livonia was that for the next seventy years (from 1561 to 1629) their ultimate sovereign was the monarch of the Polish-Lithuanian Commonwealth.[15] The territory acquired by Poland-Lithuania included more than just the Latvians, of course, but all Latvians now lived under the new dispensation. During this period of Polish-Lithuanian rule a rump Livonia was referred to as *Inflanty* (in Latvian, *Pārdaugavas hercogiste*: "the duchy across the Daugava River").

The Duchy of Courland and Semigallia was now a separate political entity, being the territory of the vassals of the former Livonian Order and having its own duke (who administered Inflanty for a time as well). Although the proximate masters of the Latvians were not as heterogeneous as those of the Livonian period, the territory still had no internal unity and substantial differences remained within the former Livonian regions. Although it had retained its status as an independent city for some time, Riga accepted the Polish-Lithuanian monarch as its sovereign in 1581. In terms of the pre-1200 territorial divisions, the old Couronian, Semigallian, and western Liv lands were included in the Duchy of Courland and Semigallia, whereas the territories of the eastern Livs, Selians, and Lettgallians became part of Inflanty.

Because the Counterreformation was at its height in Poland-Lithuania during this period, its (to Baltic Lutherans) reactionary religious policies were applied to Inflanty as well. The influence of the Jesuit Order grew throughout the former Livonian territories, and by the last decades of the sixteenth century the number of Catholic congregations in Inflanty probably exceeded the number of Lutheran ones.[16]

The Polish-Lithuanian crown also granted large tracts of land in Inflanty to Polish nobles, especially in the southeastern districts, where their presence remained strong for the next three hundred years. But, generally speaking, the Polish-Lithuanian monarchs, especially Stephan Batory (1533–86), were concerned primarily with the economic development of the newly acquired territories. They could not act unilaterally, however, because the landholders of Inflanty, though having transferred their loyalty, had not by any means given up wanting to retain maximum control over their lands and the peasants on them. In this, they were disadvantaged because the destructive Livonian war had raised the value of agricultural labor, and as a consequence corvée obligations had to be relaxed. It is difficult to speak of general improvements in rural areas, however, because, during the whole period of the war and for a considerable time after it, rural districts had to cope not only with the destructive actions of soldiers but also with seemingly uncontrollable banditry, perpetrated by a considerable number of adventurers from Eastern and Central Europe.

Polish-Lithuanian rule over Inflanty did not go unchallenged. In 1600, the Swedes, erstwhile allies of Poland-Lithuania during the Livonian war and counting on local support, decided to vie once again for control of the region; the ensuing so-called Polish-Swedish war lasted intermittently for almost thirty years, from 1600 until the Peace of Altmark in 1629.

The forty-year Polish-Lithuanian rule (from 1561 to 1600) convinced the political elites of Inflanty that they preferred another sovereign, at least in part because of the determined Counterreformation policies of the Polish-

Lithuanian crown.[17] Thus a generation of relative peace (1561–1600) was followed by another generation of war, which in some respects was far more severe for rural inhabitants than earlier wars because more-frequent pitched battles ravaged the countryside. Although the Polish-Lithuanian armies were initially victorious, in the early 1620s their defenses began to fail, and in 1621, the Swedes captured Riga and in 1625 Tartu. With the Peace of Altmark, Polish-Lithuanian control over most of Inflanty ended. The Polish king remained suzerain over Courland-Semigallia and kept the southeastern section of Inflanty (the southern part of the old Lettgallian territories), subsequently referred to by written sources as Polish Livonia (and sometimes, confusingly, as Inflanty) and by Latvians as Latgale.

THE EMERGENCE OF WRITTEN LATVIAN

Amid the turmoil of war in the second half of the sixteenth century, a new feature was added to the cultural life of the Livonian lands, namely, printed material in the Latvian language. In the later medieval centuries there is no doubt that a Latvianlike language—or possibly variants of an indigenous language—had coexisted with the Latin and the German used by churchmen, chroniclers, and administrators. Fragments of that language—place names, proper names, short phrases, various nouns—had appeared in the chronicles of Livonian life for a long time, suggesting the existence of a medium that the upper orders were using to communicate with the various non-Germanic peoples who tilled the soil in the countryside and performed a host of support tasks in the cities and that the lower orders were using to communicate with one another. To the historian, those nonwritten languages are a ghostly presence in the 1300–1500 period; their existence is palpable, but a deeper understanding of them, impossible.

But in the sixteenth century, this configuration changed in connection with the Lutheran Reformation. Sources as early as 1525 mention several books "in the ordinary Livonian, Latvian, and Estonian" languages that had been seized by the authorities from a suspicious-looking merchant on his way to Riga, but those books evidently did not survive.[18] In subsequent decades, mention proliferated in the sources of the existence of other such books—some probably printed, others handwritten—but none have been found. In light of the kinds of works that appeared later and did survive, we can assume that the earlier works were catechisms and other short religious writings that had been translated into the Latvian vernacular following Luther's injunction (and example) that the Word of God should be accessible to the faithful in their own language.

In view of the role of the Lutheran Reformation in the history of written Latvian, it is ironic that the first sixteenth-century book that can be examined in its entirety is a Catholic catechism—*Catechismus Catholicorum*—prepared and published by Peter Canisius (1521–97) in 1585 in Vilnius, Lithuania.[19] The work consists of fragments translated into Latvian from Canisius's Latin and German writings; specialists suggest that the translation was done by someone else—probably another churchman. That book probably represented the Counterreformation reaction to Lutheran writings in Latvian and elicited reactions among the Protestant clerics working in the Baltic area.

In 1586–87 there appeared in Königsberg a Latvian-language Lutheran handbook—an *Enchiridion*—in three parts: a catechism, fragments of the New Testament, and a hymnal. That work was produced by a commission of churchmen in Courland who had been assigned to compete with the written Counterreformation materials.

This "battle of the books" continued into the first decades of the seventeenth century, though perhaps not in as overtly a challenge-response form as in the earlier decades. Thus although the motives for publishing early printed works in Latvian were complicated, we can infer from these books' existence that individual clergymen had made an effort to probe and learn the language(s) of the peasantry. The more intellectually curious among them no doubt enjoyed translation for its own sake. Both the Renaissance and the Reformation gave rise to an interest in vernacular languages, and the principal vernaculars of Livonia—Latvian and Estonian—stood ready to be translated.

LATVIANS IN THE SIXTEENTH CENTURY

Although some 90–95 percent of the 404,000 residents of the southern regions of Livonia in the sixteenth century were not Central European in origin—as were the upper orders—the precise identity of those "indigenous peoples" remains elusive. Written sources do not help because, on the levels of either small or large deeds, no "non-German" emerges as a distinct personality in the Baltic sources of this period. Consequently, we must move into the sixteenth century with the same question we asked about the final centuries of the medieval era: who were these non-Germans and what collective noun shall we employ to refer to them?[20] Is it possible to refer to them as *Latvians*—as we have been doing—for any other reason than having to call them something?

The scribes of the fifteenth and sixteenth centuries scattered the term *undeutsch* throughout their writings; that negative definition, however, did not point to a common consciousness among the "non-Germans." We are far from being able to say whether there existed a "national" consciousness among the non-Germans, but, lacking direct evidence, we can ask whether there was among them *any* kind of group consciousness that might justify the use of the term *Latvian*. That question did not trouble people in the fifteenth and sixteenth centuries, of course, including those in Livonia. One defined oneself, if at all, through membership and participation in recognized corporate entities by virtue of a status one had inherited or had been awarded. Groups defined by nationality and language were normally not entities that yielded status.

In Livonia, however, the question was somewhat more complicated because the borders of language communities correlated with a high/low social dichotomy. But the correlation was a rough one: Latvians were never people of high social or political standing, but not all high-status persons were Germans (some were Poles, for example) nor were all persons of low standing Latvians. Most peasants in the southern regions of Livonia were Latvians, but not all Latvians were rural because in Riga and other cities and towns important minorities of non-Germans played a significant role in urban commerce and trade. Also, immigration to Livonia by persons of modest means continued throughout the late medieval centuries and into the sixteenth century. Latvians derived status (rights, privileges, obligations) from belonging to a particular congregation, a particular artisan urban brotherhood, or a particular religious order, but it is not clear that they derived or lost anything from belonging to a particular language community. Indeed, sixteenth-century sources differ on how many indigenous language communities existed in Livonia: some list as few as two (Latvian and Estonian); others list as many as four (Liv, Estonian, Latvian, and Couronian).[21]

These language listings again raise the question of how long into the postmedieval period we can detect survivals of the precrusade designations of Livs, Lettgallians, Selonians, Semigallians, and Couronians. As suggested earlier, during the late medieval centuries, these terms ceased to be used (by record keepers) as descriptions of groups and instead were used primarily as geographic designations. By the end of the sixteenth century, those place names continued to occupy a prominent niche in Baltic-area usage. There was now an entire province called Courland-Semigallia (in German, Kurland-Semgaln, usually abbreviated Kurland), roughly coextensive with the earlier territories of the Couronians and Semigallians. The term *Livonia* (in

German, Livland), having been replaced for a time by the designation *Inflanty*, returned after Polish-Lithuanian dominance ended. The terms *Lettgallia* and *Selonia* evidently continued to appear in folk speech, though contemporary documents sometimes used the term *latygoly* interchangeably with *letten* or *latyši* to refer to all speakers of Latvian. Thus in both official and folk usage the pre-Christian terms persisted, giving rise to associations with a time when the area was inhabited by distinct peoples. Those usages, however, were not standardized, nor can specific words be understood to point to specific subpopulations of permanent residents.

In fact, the events of the sixteenth century suggest that impermanence of place may have been as important as its opposite. As noted above, though serf estates (manors) were proliferating, they did not yet predominate, meaning that a considerable body of peasants still did not have the status of *Erbbauer* (hereditary peasant) and thus could move from place to place in search of a better way of life. The problem of peasants fleeing because of indebtedness and serfs fleeing onerous duties loomed large in contemporary documents, suggesting movement by peasants across political boundaries.[22] Moreover, the armies of the Baltic governing classes—especially those assembled by the Livonian Order to defend against the recurring forays of the Russians—contained non-Germans (presumably Latvians) as foot soldiers and support forces (e.g., carters), estimates of which run into the thousands. Because those armies moved across the entirety of Livonia and because those who were not the core fighting force were engaged for short periods of time and then released, we can infer that warfare played a dispersing role, picking up peasants in one place and leaving them in another. Thus, though the retention of regional names harks back to a more heterogeneous past, there are also, among non-Germans, indications of homogenization through continuous movement of various kinds.

What in the sixteenth century the non-Germans (Latvians) understood themselves to be—as many remained in place and received in-migrants while others became out-migrants—is not clear from any direct testimony in the sources. The question of the vernacular Latvian—the language(s) used by the peasantry—is intriguing. Linguistic evidence suggests that, by the late sixteenth century, when the printed word in Latvian was no longer a rarity, translators had settled on variants (dialects?) that are recognizable to speakers of modern Latvian.[23] Whether the choice was made because by that time the vast majority of non-Germans used similar variants or whether the choices were entirely idiosyncratic is not clear. Certainly excluded was the subpopulation of the Livs, whose language resembled Estonian and Finnish. By that time, however, the Livs could have been bilingual, as they were later. It is possible that, by giving certain variants of Latvian greater permanence and a new status, the translators and writers of the sixteenth century were helping Latvians begin to achieve an identity that was more than non-German. But it is equally possible that the writers and translators had learned the vernaculars imperfectly, thus producing evidence that misrepresented the linguistic uniformity among the peasantry.

On the basis of currently available evidence, then, it is impossible to make unambiguous statements about a group consciousness among the non-Germans, let alone their consciousness of being a nation. One other kind of evidence that should be mentioned is the non-Germans' folk beliefs as described in the few sixteenth-century accounts. Such accounts were mostly produced by clerical persons—some of them Jesuits—who had every reason to describe these beliefs as leftovers from a cruder, pagan age. In them we learn about a host of superstitions, local customs, and habits, as well as about the four-line folk songs (*dainas*) that were not described accurately and with regard for their intrinsic value until late in the seventeenth century. Another thing missing from these particularistic descriptions is how such elements of popular culture were distributed spatially. The describers wrote about what they saw, but none traveled throughout all of the southern Livonian territories or produced a regional description. The only way to conceptualize these scattered descriptions as evidence that the non-Germans had a consciousness of being a nation (in Latvian, *tauta*) is to assume that folk beliefs having roughly the same forms and expressed in variants of the same language among peoples inhabiting adjacent geographic space manifest a commonality. That nineteenth-century assumption is difficult to make about the Latvians in the sixteenth century.

4 The Trifurcated Littoral in the Seventeenth Century

In 1629 the Treaty of Altmark, which ended the conflict between Sweden and Poland-Lithuania, reconfigured the internal boundaries of old Livonia. For the rest of the century three separate political units would be ruled and, in part governed, from the outside. Two of them were connected to the Polish-Lithuanian sovereign, and the third, to the Swedish. The central and northern sections (henceforth referred to by the German term *Livland*) became Swedish-ruled territory and part of an empire being constructed by the Vasa dynasty. The southern and western territories, which had become the Duchy of Courland and Semigallia in the sixteenth century, were governed directly by the Kettler dynasty as an independent entity, though the dukes of Courland remained nominally vassals of the Polish-Lithuanian king. The eastern and southeastern regions (Polish Inflanty or, alternately, Lettgallia) were governed directly by the Polish-Lithuanian kings. A fourth, relatively small territory—the Pilten bishopric in the southwestern corner of Courland—passed into Polish-Lithuanian hands soon after Altmark but was subsequently added to the Duchy of Courland. Latvians made up the vast majority of the populations of Courland-Semigallia and Polish Inflanty; in Livland, they were the majority in the southern half, the peasantry of the northern half being Estonian speaking. In the last three-quarters of the seventeenth century, each of these political entities had a substantially different history and thus deserves to be reviewed separately.

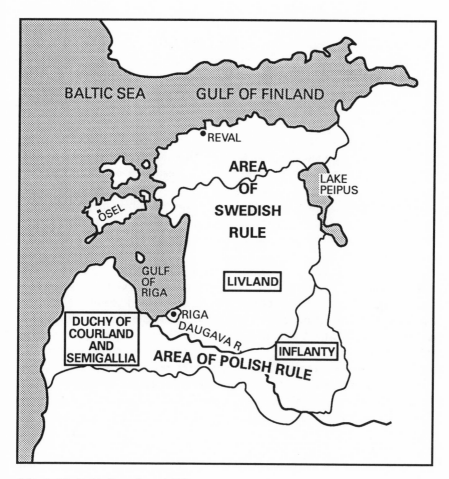

Map 3. The Baltic littoral, ca. 1680

POLISH INFLANTY (LETTGALLIA)

Although in other sections of the eastern littoral outright warfare between Poland-Lithuania and Sweden had ceased in 1629, Polish Inflanty (Lettgallia) became a kind of testing ground for the rivalries of three antagonistic powers: Poland, of which Lettgallia was a part; Sweden, which now controlled Livland and exploited the common border with Lettgallia; and Russia, which continued to try to penetrate the littoral without opening another chapter of major warfare.[1] Although conflicts were by no means continuous, there was a period of fourteen years (from 1654 to 1667) when Russian forces controlled large parts of Lettgallian territory.

We have no sources with which to estimate the total population of Polish Inflanty (Lettgallia) at the time of Altmark. Fiscal censuses toward the end of the seventeenth century yield an estimate of about 103,000 persons by 1700, suggesting that seventy years earlier the number might have been around 60,000 to 70,000.[2] Even those numbers may be too high because we do not know how Lettgallia was affected by the plague that ravaged the population of adjoining Livland in the middle of the seventeenth century.

The agrarian regime in Lettgallia had not taken as decisive a turn toward estate agriculture as had other parts of the littoral, but the structure of rural society resembled that of Livland and Courland-Semigallia in being based on enserfed peasants. Some sixty or so noble families dominated rural society, but estates were also owned and operated by churches and, in a few instances, by the Jesuit Order. Judging by names, some two-fifths of the nobles were of German extraction and the rest Polish-Lithuanian. The estimated eight hundred or so Lettgallian estates tended to be relatively small, and fewer than half the families (mostly Germans) controlled more than half the existing estates.[3] Size notwithstanding, the landed estates all contained an enserfed labor force, though it is impossible to say that all peasants who resided and worked on estates were serfs.

Throughout the seventeenth century the labor required from each peasant farmstead in Lettgallia rose steadily but evidently did not reach the levels of those in the western Latvian territories. Although Lettgallian peasant holdings tended to be smaller (both in area and population) than those in areas to the west, the tasks the peasants had to perform were just as onerous. Given Lettgallia's location and the isolation of many of its estates, carting products to market became a favored form of labor service. Predictably, many peasant-serfs responded to these conditions by fleeing, which was relatively easier in this region because all it involved was crossing a border into Belorus, Russia, or Lithuania.

Although it appears that Lettgallian agricultural productivity remained steady during the seventeenth century, there is evidence that the few urban areas in the territory—Rēzekne, Ludza, Daugavpils—experienced an economic upswing during the second part of the century by using adjacent waterways for commercial purposes. The commerce of these towns was oriented both toward the west (Livland and Courland) as well as toward the east (Russia and Belorus). The importance of these commercial centers should not be exaggerated, however, because only Daugavpils (in German, Dünaburg) was a chartered city, whereas the other centers—Rēzekne and Ludza—were towns (in Latvian, *miesti*) without the right of self-government.[4] In the estates, the peasantry lived either on isolated farmsteads or in hamlets (in Latvian, *sādžas*), though the precise distribution of these settlement types is unknown. The influence of Roman Catholicism and the Jesuit Order in Lettgallia was far stronger than in any other of the Latvian regions, but there were also a considerable number of Protestant (Lutheran) churches in the districts bordering on Swedish-held Livland.[5]

From the early seventeenth century onward, descriptions of Lettgallia, whether written by contemporaries or later historians, have tended to depict the area as Catholic- and Jesuit-dominated culturally and Polish-dominated politically, a stagnant backwater compared with the more dynamic and economically more "progressive" Protestant territories. In post–World War II histories of the Latvians, however, those depictions have been reduced, in large part because of the recognition that the seeming absence of development may stem from the absence of source-based historical research.[6]

SWEDISH LIVLAND

The 1629 Swedish acquisition of Livland (with its Latvian and Estonian populations) was part of the empire-building efforts of the Vasa dynasty. The new Baltic territories were placed under a governor-general, who administered them with the help of two governors, one for each district, Estonian and Latvian. The Latvian part of Livland was home to an estimated 50,000 persons in the first half of the century and some 142,000 in the second half, suggesting substantial growth in the interim. Although the 142,000 figure may be too high, Swedish Livland, in terms of population, was probably the largest of the three Latvian-inhabited areas.[7]

To obtain the continuing support of the Swedish nobility for the Baltic venture, the monarch distributed about 40 percent of the newly acquired land to them, with the rest remaining in the hands of the German-speaking nobles. The rights of the new and the old landowners were secured through the granting of privileges that were accorded a place in the redesigned administrative and judicial systems. In the second half of the century, there were some 198 noble families in Livland that the Swedish crown had to please, and, though initially most of them were satisfied with the new arrangements, that attitude began to wear thin. Moreover, the system found itself struggling against never-ending efforts by the landholding nobles to expand their spheres of operation, especially with respect to their freedom of action toward the peasantry. Thus the centrifugal tendencies that had surfaced with the breakup of old Livonia remained strong and were periodically expressed in the meetings of the diets (*Landtage*) of the Livland nobility.

Specifically, the conflicts arose from the widespread system of serfdom on the landed estates and the rights of landholders to expand obligatory labor.[8] On the one hand, the Swedish government wanted to curtail such rights; in 1681 Swedish king Karl XI suggested that serfdom be abolished entirely. The landholders, on the other hand, wanted to expand their rights and transform all peasants into a servile labor force. Thus, like many state-building monarchs of the seventeenth century, the Vasa kings found themselves in a bind. They needed the support and loyalty of both the Swedish and the Baltic nobilities for military ventures and administration, but a too-liberal policy toward noble rights would reduce the local authority of the monarchy. The Vasa kings of Sweden, like other monarchs, could not discover a permanent solution to this problem. Moreover, the Swedish *Riksdag* contained representatives from the Swedish peasant order who worried that expanding noble rights over peasants in Livonia might cross the Baltic to Sweden and result in practices resembling serfdom, which the Swedish peasantry had never experienced.

The high point of Swedish efforts in these matters came in the so-called estate reduction policy that began in 1681.[9] The basis on which individual landholders (and their families) held land had not been reviewed since the late sixteenth century, and the Swedish Crown claimed that the great political changes of the period—Polish rule and then Swedish rule—had created uncertainties in nobles' legal claims to the estates they controlled. The secularization of the Livonian Order, land grants and reclamations made by the Polish monarchs, and grants made by the Swedish monarchs after 1629 had left in their wake, it was said, confusion over what was Crown and what was private land and over the nature and length of particular tenures. Even more frustrating was the Crown's perception that this ill-justified system was reducing tax revenues. To establish whether or not this was true and how the Crown might reclaim "its" estates became the assignment of two reduction commissions, one of which started its labors in 1681 and the other in 1683. As a result of their work, by 1687 some five-sixths of the estates of Swedish Livland had been reclaimed by the Crown.

Whether or not these reversions were justified in each and every case is difficult to say, but as a result, Crown revenues from the Baltic estates increased substantially. As far as landholding rights were concerned, however, the reductions did not weaken the control of the Baltic nobilities over their estates. Although titles were clarified and properties "belonging" to the Crown identified, the Crown allowed the current occupants to retain their estates even when they were judged to be Crown property. The base of the landed nobilities' power was thus not reduced to any substantial degree, even though they had to pay greater taxes for the estates they held.

Moreover, the reduction policy did not penetrate into all corners of Livland, and thus numerous estate holders escaped the attention of the Crown. Although the policy engendered deep suspicions among the Baltic nobles about what the Swedish Crown would do next, the impact of the policy on the daily lives of the peasants was probably small.[10]

On Crown estates administered by trustworthy managers, the government was able to curtail some of the mistreatment to which peasants on private estates were subjected. At the same time, however, the government did not dare to abolish serfdom and, in places, introduced a host of new taxes on the nobility, most of which were passed on to the peasantry. However, given that in Livland the Crown had to rely on the local nobilities to help administer a substantial territory in a strategically crucial location, even the reduction policy was something of a surprise. The Swedish government also perhaps remembered how easily the Baltic nobilities had changed their loyalty from Poland-Lithuania to Sweden and thus could not risk such a shift by extending a too-protective policy toward the peasantry.

THE DUCHY OF COURLAND AND SEMIGALLIA

When in 1561 the Livonian Order ceased to exist, its members—the knights—did not emigrate but transformed themselves with the stroke of the pen into a new landholding order, the Courland nobility. They received, together with enlarged rights of heritability, the estates they had hitherto held as fiefs, with about a third of Courland's landed property (the order's former lands) going to the family of the master of the order, Gotthard Kettler. Gotthard was named duke of Courland and Semigallia in 1562, and the Kettlers continued to supply the duchy with its rulers until the eighteenth century. During most of the seventeenth century, the duchy was the least troubled of the three main divisions of the littoral.[11]

The dukes of Courland were nominally the vassals of the Polish king, and although this lord-vassal relationship was rocky at times, after 1629 the Polish-Lithuanian monarchs were too busy elsewhere to pay much attention to what was becoming a well-governed and economically healthy part of the realm. Historians refer to the distribution of power in the duchy as a "republic of the nobility," which in 1620 organized itself into a corporation with 121 member families, and had an extraordinary amount of influence, which was diminished only under a particularly strong duke.

By the early decades of the seventeenth century, the rights of the Courland nobility over their estates had been secured by agreements signed when the duchy was established. During the course of the century large portions of the ducal domain continued to slip out of the Kettler family's grasp both because further fiefs were granted and because the dukes used their properties to secure loans from their wealthy subjects. The strong dukes made good use of the land that remained, but the long-term pattern was one of diminishing ducal influence over the land and the people on it.

The first duke of Courland, Gotthard Kettler (1517–87), had been a member of the Livonian Order since 1537 and its master since 1559. Like many other order members, he came to the Baltic from Westphalia. After the order ended, he married a Mecklenburg princess with whom he had seven children; two sons survived to become his heirs. Kettler was a devout Lutheran and thus established Lutheranism in the duchy, following the Augsburg formula of *cujus regio, ejus religio.*

Because the order and the church had been antagonistic in old Livonia, church organization in the order's domains had been neglected; in the 1560s, the new duchy also had to repair the ravages of the Livonian war, which had been particularly destructive in the Courtland countryside. To accomplish these goals, Kettler had to persuade his unwilling nobility to pay for the founding and reconstruction of churches—some seventy in all (twenty-seven in Semigallia and forty-three in Courland). To obtain the goodwill of the landholding nobles, he had to reassure them of their privileges; thus in 1570 he issued the *Privilegium Gotthardinum,* which gave landholders virtually unlimited control over their properties and the peasantry on them.[12]

Although generally an able leader of the new duchy, Kettler mistakenly tried to be fair to his two grown sons by bequeathing the ducal title to the oldest, Friedrich, but dividing economic control of the duchy between Friedrich and his younger brother, Wilhelm. The duchy would thus have one duke and one court, but Friedrich would control the economy of Semigallia and Wilhelm, the economy of Courland. This arrangement, predictably, did not last, and in 1596 the two brothers agreed to divide power into two ducal courts, two governments, two court systems, and two economies (specifically, economic chambers). Unfortunately, that arrangement made it possible for the landholding nobility to promote its interests against those of the ducal house.

The period between 1587 and 1641—during which Friedrich was duke but Wilhelm continued to play an important role in the duchy's economy and politics—was one of considerable confusion early on but became more peaceful at the end. In 1617, with the help of Polish mediators, the ducal house and the nobility settled their relations (at least temporarily) by agreeing to a constitution (the so-called *Statuta Curlandiae*), which was something of a defeat for the duke because it enlarged the nobility's privileges.[13]

In foreign policy, the brothers had to struggle not to involve the duchy in the continuing war between Poland and Sweden (as a result of which Poland lost its Livonian territories), even while segments of the Courland nobility were complaining to the Polish monarch (whose vassal the Courtland duke was) that they were being mistreated and deserved further protection. At the same time, Wilhelm wanted Sweden to support his claims to the ducal office. The Polish king sent several royal commissions to the duchy to mediate the conflicts between the duke, his brother, and the duchy's nobles. When Wilhelm's plans were not realized, he moved to Pomerania, where he lived until the end of his life in 1640. In the meantime, the Kettler dynasty in the duchy was threatened because Friedrich had no heir; the only logical candidate to be his successor was Wilhelm's son Jacob. The last ten years of Friedrich's reign (1632–42) were peaceful, however, after the Polish *sejm* (parliament) recognized Jacob as Friedrich's heir and thus assured the Kettlers' future in the duchy. During those last years, Friedrich showed himself an able administrator, especially in the economic and urban spheres. From the point of view of the peasantry, however, this respite from ducal-noble struggles had been purchased with the strengthening of noble control over land and the intensification of serfdom on the duchy's estates.

Without doubt the most successful ruler in the Kettler line was Duke Jacob, who held that title for forty years, from 1642 to 1682.[14] To maintain good relations with the Courland nobles, Jacob could not have been a reformer in any absolute sense, especially with respect to noble control of peasants; his activities on behalf of the peasantry were restricted to the ducal domains and in no sense questioned the basic propositions embodied in serfdom. His leadership style was mercantilist, although some historians argue that his intentions were *not* to strengthen the duchy as a state but to enrich himself and his family. In any case, during the period of his rule,

Courland became a regional power to be reckoned with, for he was intent on economic development and sought to establish manufactures. Jacob was also interested in enhancing Courland's status as a sea power and thus sought to expand long-distance trade by creating a merchant navy and establishing two small overseas colonies—Gambia in West Africa and Tobago in the Caribbean. Both were successful ventures until the end of his reign, when the navy fell apart and the two colonies were lost to the English and the Dutch.

At the end of Jacob's reign the ducal house was also having trouble with its external relations. The Polish monarchy, jealous of the duke's strength in his vassal state, supported recalcitrant Courlandic nobles; the Swedes sent raiding parties into the duchy from the north with increasing frequency; and the Russians sought, through diplomatic as well as more direct means, to establish their influence on the duchy at the expense of the Poles. By the end of the century, then, the ducal government had weakened considerably, and its power would continue to decline during the first half of the eighteenth century.

RIGA: A CITY APART

The city of Riga had surrendered to the Swedes in 1621 and throughout the rest of the seventeenth century was loyal to the Vasa dynasty. The Swedish governor-general of the Livland territories had his seat in Riga, as did the commander of the Swedish armed forces in the province. Yet despite these externally imposed symbols of power, Riga's population size (some ten thousand inhabitants in the 1680s), its breadth of commercial activity, and its three hundred to four hundred merchant families' independent-mindedness set it apart, not only from the rest of the southern littoral but also from the other towns.[15] Although the other towns were also increasing in number and in size, their aggregated population was only about two thousand, and Riga thus remained the metropolitan center of the region. The city council reveled in Riga's prominence and throughout the seventeenth century repeatedly reminded the Swedes of their latecomer status by sending a stream of objections—to the Swedish king no less—about the presence of the Swedish army in the city. On many other issues as well, the Rigans tended to deal with the Swedish monarch as if his government and theirs were equal regional powers.

Riga's economy in the seventeenth century, as it had been in the sixteenth, was a complex organism dominated by some seventy different occupations organized in some forty-three guilds or brotherhoods.[16] The members of most of these organizations were German, that is, used the

German language in their internal dealings, but about ten of the brother-hoods were Latvian while some twenty others evidently accepted persons of both German and Latvian ancestry. The Latvian brotherhoods were concentrated in the mercantile and small artisan sectors and involved such activities as loading ships, sorting and weighing merchandise, as well as such trades as tailoring, blacksmithing, weaving, and butchering. Latvians, however, remained outside the large merchant and craft organizations that spawned the political leaders of the city.

Economic activity in Riga picked up on many fronts during the seventeenth century. Although the Swedish government discouraged private manufactures, preferring state-initiated enterprises, a small number of private enterprises—ironworks, sawmills, shipyards, leatherworks, brick-works—appeared on the outlying areas of Riga.[17] Most of those undertakings involved five to ten employees and were founded either by urban merchants looking for additional profits or by craftsmen seeking to escape the controls of the city.

The brisk trade through Riga's port at the end of the seventeenth century was conducted in naval supplies, grains, and wood products, with goods such as furs lacking the importance they had had in earlier centuries. Those goods came to Riga not only from the Baltic littoral but also from the eastern reaches of Byelorussia and Lithuania. Riga's merchants serviced a substantial territory, which they also supplied with finished products from abroad. Understandably, there was an uneasy relationship between the Swedish government, with its mercantilist regulatory tendencies, and the powerful merchants of the city, who wanted to impose trade regulations. Still, one result of the Swedish government's prohibitions on certain imports meant a favorable trade balance for Riga, with exports exceeding imports by a wide margin.

To the Swedish Crown, Riga was the commercial center of its new Livland colony; to the merchant elite, it was a Hanseatic German town. Thus, to the outside world, Riga was economically and culturally part of a growing urban network linking the major states and cultures of Europe. But during the seventeenth century the city was also becoming the urban center of the still largely rural Latvian population. Precise numbers do not exist, but one estimate places the proportion of Latvians in Riga in the second half of the seventeenth century at a minimum of 50 percent. Thus to many Latvians, not only in Livland but also in the Courland duchy and in Lettgallia, the cosmopolitan center of the Baltic also appeared to be "their" city.[18] Although it may also have had this meaning in the sixteenth century, in the seventeenth—when the dating of oral tradition sources is more certain—Riga was being celebrated in folk songs and stories as a

Latvian city. Outsiders may have monopolized Riga's power and commerce, but its population mix belied the notion that all Latvians were peasants.

SERFDOM IN THE SEVENTEENTH CENTURY

Although a substantial portion of Riga's population consisted of Latvians, the vast majority of the Latvian population were rural tillers of the soil in Livland, Lettgallia, and the duchy. Most of them were also, by the second half of the seventeenth century, serfs. By this time, estates (*muižas*) were proliferating with the spread of serfdom; unlike the sixteenth century, there were now few estates that did not use serf labor and fewer still in which any free peasants remained. Accepting these generalizations and the use of the term *Latvians* for *non-Germans*, however, should not lead to the notion that peasant-serf life was uniform in all three areas of the southern Baltic littoral. Judging by the main statutes regulating the status of peasant-serfs in each area, there were many similarities; judging by practices, there were also considerable differences.

In Courland-Semigallia, the main peasant statutes, which became fixed in the 1611–17 period, considered serf status both hereditary and ultimately defined by the serf's lord.[19] As a consequence, serf status in each and every locality in the duchy was defined by those nobles and wealthy commoners who held estates. Thus there was considerable variety in how much obligatory labor and dues peasants had to deliver to the estate, how free an estate holder felt to dispossess peasants for various infractions, how much and what kind of corporal punishment was meted out, and the extent to which an estate holder sought to regulate such matters as peasant marriage. Peasant custom, as well as the lord's calculations about the counterproductivity of excessive obligations and regulations, played a role in how general laws were implemented, resulting in extreme variety. In Courland-Semigallia, on the extensive ducal domains, we surmise that conditions tended to be less harsh. As mentioned earlier, however, over the century the ducal domains diminished in size and whatever protection the ducal serfs had had thereby disappeared.

In Livland, unlike Courland-Semigallia, serfdom was under challenge beginning with the Swedish ascendancy (1629) and, correspondingly, estate holders were on the defensive.[20] The general conditions of peasants in Livland were comparable to those in the duchy, but there were noticeable differences. In Livland peasant-serfs were able to complain about mistreatment and injustices to sympathetic Crown respresentatives, and peasant regulations were less categorical about how serf status was acquired and transmitted between generations. During the last three-quarters of the century the Swedish government sought to expand the number of peasants under its jurisdiction (i.e., on Crown estates), as, for example, in the reduction policy described earlier, and tried to introduce the radical—for the Baltic area—idea of abolishing serfdom, as proposed by Charles XI of Sweden. Those stances by the Baltic representatives of the Crown led peasant-serfs to believe that serfdom was a less permanent and more flexible institution than estate holders like to think. By the end of the century, however, serfdom remained in place, and the modifications that the Swedish period witnessed did not prove to be irreversible.

Unlike Courland with its locally produced peasant statutes and Livland with its protective efforts by the Crown, the enserfed peasantry of Lettgallia in the seventeenth century lived under regulations, created in 1588 in Lithuania, in which serfdom was described as hereditary and opportunities for change were minimal.[21] Juridically speaking, the lot of the Lettgallian peasant-serf was worse than in either Courland or Livland, but, as mentioned before, the demesne (lord's land) in Lettgallian estates tended to be smaller and therefore not as dependent on obligatory peasant labor. (Because little is known about population movements in or out of Lettgallia in the seventeenth century, we do not know whether peasant-serfs fled southward or eastward to settle in territories where serfdom practices were less harsh.)

Even though hereditary serf status was the lot of most peasants in the Baltic littoral, it is misleading to interpret the concept too statically. Although we should not expect that a more dynamic understanding of the term will reveal large subpopulations of heretofore unnoticed free peasants, there were pockets of free peasant populations, especially in Courland, whose rights as such continued to be observed. As a proportion of the whole, however, their numbers were minimal. Yet serf status was not hereditary for many or permanent for the entire course of all peasants' lives or lacking gradations in the restrictions it placed on peasants in it. Because there has been insufficient research on the contrasts between serf status in statute and in practice, the general situation is likely to have been far more varied than has been described.

WRITING THE WORD
OF GOD IN LATVIAN

As mentioned earlier, Courland had developed an organized Lutheran Church in the second half of the sixteenth century; the Livland church, by contrast, was not realized until Swedish rule. By the middle of the seventeenth century, however, Livland had a General Consistory with six subconsistories, three of which had authority in the Latvian regions of the province. The Swedish government, in initiating those reform measures, sought uniformity in organization, ritual, and parish affairs generally, but such uniformity was easier to command than to put into practice. The landed nobility was reluctant to surrender to a state-created church government the many privileges they had accrued over the congregations on their properties. Nonetheless, by the second half of the seventeenth century the approximately fifty parishes of the Lutheran Church in Livland were functioning as competently as their counterparts in Courland. In Polish Livland (Lettgallia), where the Counterreformation had been successful, the Catholic Church by the mid–seventeenth century was controlled entirely by Polish officials, and most parish clergy spoke Polish. The Jesuit Order founded a school in Daugavpils (in German, Dünaburg), and its college in Vilnius, Lithuania, was an important source of religious books for the Lettgallian Catholic parishes.

The imperative to use the worshipers' vernacular in religious writings yielded fruit throughout the seventeenth century among both the Lutheran clergy in Courland and Livland as well as the Catholic clergy in Lettgallia. In Courland and Livland the clerical translators and authors' first language was usually German; in Lettgallia, that of the Jesuits, frequently Polish. By the time the Jesuits began writing in Latvian, many were polyglots who had learned the other languages to further their careers in the church. Some were recent arrivals to the Baltic area; others had been born there. Numerically speaking, only about ten works in Latvian appeared during the first half of the seventeenth century. Among those authors, however, were a few whose works remained long after the authors themselves had died.

Georg Mancelius (1593–1654), for example, in 1638 published a work called *Lettus,* which contained a German-Latvian dictionary that remained a standard reference work for the next 150 years.[22] Similarly, Mancelius's *Vademecum* (1631) and *Lang-gewünschte Lettische Postill* (The long-awaited Latvian sermon collection, 1654) were extraordinarily popular, with the sermons being reprinted repeatedly in four editions until the year 1823. Despite their non-Latvian titles, all Mancelius's works were in Latvian and were not restricted to purely religious themes. Mancelius was born in Livland in a German-speaking clerical family, became a Lutheran clergyman and then a professor of theology at Tartu University in the Estonian section of the province. He preached an ethic of social responsibility that involved the peasantry recognizing its station in society and acting accordingly. Whatever the Latvian peasantry thought of this message, many generations enjoyed reading and listening to his sermons. He was one of the first of many Lutheran clergymen who learned Latvian well enough to virtually eliminate the barrier that usually exists between two language worlds.

Another of these pioneers was Christoph Fürecker (ca. 1615–84/85).[23] He was probably born in Semigallia in the Nereta region but, unlike many other authors, was not a clergyman. He started but did not finish theological studies at Livland's Dorpat University and subsequently worked as a private tutor, married a woman of Latvian birth, and became one of the most skilled non-Latvian authors writing in that language in the seventeenth century. His strength lay in translating German Lutheran hymns and adapting their language and mood to Latvian peasant audiences; his hymnal—published posthumously in 1685 and containing all his 180 hymns— continued to be a source for hymnal compilers up to the twentieth century. Fürecker's translations used Latvian idioms, proverbs, and metaphors to reduce the distance between the German-dominated Lutheran Church and its Latvian parishioners. Fürecker was more than a translator in that many of his hymns departed so far from the originals that they can be thought of as original poetry in Latvian.

The total number of new titles in Latvian during the second half of the seventeenth century was between fifty-seven and sixty, the most notable of which was the Latvian translation by Ernst Glück (1651–1705) of the Old and New Testaments (published during 1688–94, with a print run of 1,500).[24] Glück was born in Germany and studied theology and languages at the Universities of Wittenberg and Leipzig. He moved to the Baltic area in 1673 and served there in various clerical positions until, during the Great Northern War, the invading Russian army forced him to accompany it to Moscow. During his stay in Livland, Glück preached Lutheran doctrine in the language of his parishioners. His Bible translation, which was the crowning touch of his efforts, created a framework within which literary Latvian would continue to develop for the next two hundred years, until the Latvians themselves began to write.

Mancelius, Fürecker, and Glück are examples of responsible clergymen responding to the Lutheran imperative to use vernacular languages. The extent to which their dedication to written Latvian diminished the social and economic distance between themselves and their parishioners—a distance reinforced in hundreds of ways in daily life—is another question. The clergy lived for the most part in a different linguistic (and cultural) world; they wrote, spoke, published, and did most of their professional work in languages other than Latvian and for the most part were faithful servants not only of God but also of the landowners, who frequently controlled their appointments to rural parishes.

How to interpret this situation—and especially the distance created by the clergy speaking German and Latin and their parishioners speaking varieties of Latvian and in some places Liv—remains an open question, particularly because the clergymen and their parishioners had to constantly interact. Given the different languages and given that the spoken Latvian of the clergy was frequently seriously flawed, there must have been many misunderstandings if not, at times, the absence of effective communication. Yet church records indicate that many clergymen served long tenures, officiating at hundreds of peasant christenings, burials, and marriages; examining hundreds of peasant children for confirmation; and delivering hundreds of sermons. Peasant parishioners accepted this situation far more frequently than rejecting it, even though much tends to be made of the continuing presence among peasants of "pagan" (non-Christian) traditions of belief.

The language cleavage is also obvious when even the best seventeenth-century Latvian works are reviewed with attention to grammar.[25] There was likely a substantial difference between the written and the spoken versions of Latvian beyond those that normally exist between two forms of a language because those writing in Latvian in this period tended to confuse Latvian and German grammatical forms (the latter of which were not standardized either). The Latvian peasant congregations who used the prepared texts were in no position to supply alternatives because the few Latvians who became Lutheran clergymen did not write in Latvian, assimilated to the German cultural world, or left the Baltic area (e.g., Jānis Reiters [1632–ca. 1695]). The only Latvian clergyman who could be said to occupy the lower rungs of early Latvian writers was Juris Elģers (1585–1672), a Catholic priest who worked in Riga and Lettgallia and who is said to have written some books using the Liv language.

The increasing availability of books in Latvian raises the question of the relationship between that body of material and the Latvian oral tradition. Judging by descriptions in the work of the writers already mentioned as well as others writing in German, the oral tradition among Latvians remained in force throughout the seventeenth century.[26] Folk songs (dainas), stories, legends, riddles, sayings, and a host of other expressions saturated peasant celebrations, giving us enough evidence to infer those concepts and ideas that structured the peasants' view of human relations, the divine, and the natural world.

During the second half of the seventeenth century, however, and particularly in the last decades, when the Glück Bible became available, those Latvians whose thinking was disciplined by both oral and written ideas may have found some incompatibilities between the two. Direct contemporary sources do not tell us how the two traditions were combined when, as a Latvian historian put it, the Latvians became a "nation of readers";[27] nor do we know how many times such a conflict may have arisen because there are no statistics about peasant literacy (or the literacy of any other subpopulation) for this period. Observers suggest that in the countryside the number of books and the number of farmsteads in which books were to be found increased substantially. If so, then it may well have been at this juncture in the Latvian countryside that, though the book retained its character as an aid in ceremonial occasions, it also provoked the desire for literacy. Readers moreover learned the communications specifics a book entailed: the mechanisms of reproducing and transforming reality, the logical structure of information, a conceptual apparatus, and a literary language.[28]

Thus the writers and translators of the seventeenth century, in making the Word of God available to the peasantry in their language, may have begun to wean Latvians away not only from their oral tradition, which many clergymen disliked, but also, because reading need not be limited to religious writings, from the Lutheranism that the new Latvian books sought to perpetuate. The landholding nobles, in fact, for a long time suspected that teaching peasants to read was preparing them for seditious thought.

5 The Baltic Littoral in the Russian Empire

During the course of the eighteenth century, Latvian life changed dramatically as the Russian Empire, expanding southward, eastward, and westward, obtained control of the entire Baltic littoral. Ivan IV (Ivan the Terrible, 1530–84) had begun attacking Livonia in the late medieval era but without success. Peter I (Peter the Great, 1689–1725) gained a victory over Sweden in the Great Northern War (1700–1721) and control of Swedish Livland, with its estimated early-eighteenth-century population of 330,000.[1]

Polish Inflanty (Lettgallia; estimated population 103,000) and the Duchy of Courland-Semigallia (estimated population 209,000) were taken over during the second half of the 1700s as a result of the "partitions" of Poland by Austria, Prussia, and Russia. These ambitious states each received parts of an erstwhile great power, with Polish Inflanty going to Russia in the first partition in 1772. The Courland Duchy, the ruling dynasty of which was already under strong Russian influence from the late seventeenth century onward, was added to the empire in 1795 in the third partition.

This change of sovereigns did not have a profound impact on the everyday lives of the Baltic peasantry, however, because the Russian government, needing local administrators, kept in place the Baltic nobles, which meant continuing serfdom and the traditional lord-peasant relations.

In addition to changes in high politics, the eighteenth century in the littoral was marked by the secularization of Latvian writing, pietism among the peasants, and, toward the end of the century, a growing dissatisfaction with rural conditions, manifested in peasant unrest. Two phenomena of lesser magnitude were, in the first half of the century, the challenge by wealthy Latvians in Riga to the exclusionary politics of the dominant German burghers[2] and, in the second, attacks by "enlightened" writers of the Baltic German intelligentsia on the institution of serfdom. Although for the upper orders the eighteenth century may have ended in 1795 with the final act of inclusion of Courland-Semigallia, for the peasantry the century's final event was the Livland Peasant Law of 1804, the first serious effort to regulate serfdom.

THE GREAT NORTHERN WAR

By the end of the seventeenth century, Sweden's presence in the Baltic littoral had become intolerable to both Poland-Lithuania and Russia, in part because the Swedes used Livland as a base for periodic incursions into neighboring territories and in part because both the Polish and the Russian governments continued to harbor expansionist desires. Given the territories at stake, the most destructive consequences of imperial competition between these great powers was likely to be visited not on their own peoples but on the subordinated Latvian and Estonian peasantry of the Baltic littoral.

This drama was begun by Peter I (Peter the Great) of Russia, for whom acquiring access to the Baltic Sea ("window to the West") had become one of many obsessions.[3] In 1700, when Augustus II, the Polish ruler of Saxony, attacked Riga (the center of Swedish power in the littoral), the Russians (independent of the Polish action) captured the northern city of Narva in the Estonian part of Swedish territory. The young Swedish monarch, Charles XII (1682–1718, king from 1697), who was something of a visionary and an impulsive military leader, personally entered the defense of Sweden's Baltic dominions; from that point onward Livland, Inflanty (Lettgallia), and Courland-Semigallia became battlefields and remained so for the next decade. Individual battles in the Baltic littoral proved inconclusive in the short run, and the war took on an attritional character. Military ventures were accompanied by diplomatic and political machinations, as Poland became first an ally of Russia against the Swedes and then withdrew from the war to allow Sweden to concentrate on the Russian threat. Military action in the Latvian area of the southern littoral in fact ended in 1710, after the decisive defeat by Russia of the Swedish army at Poltava in Ukraine (July 1709) and the taking of Riga by General Boris Sheremetev (July 1710).

But the end of military conflict in the Latvian territories did not bring

Map 4. The Russian Baltic provinces, ca. 1850

an end to widespread mortality, for, beginning in 1710 and continuing into 1711, the Baltic populations were devastated by the bubonic and pneumonic plagues, which are estimated to have killed approximately sixty thousand rural and urban dwellers. The combined deaths from the decade-long warfare and the plague reduced the territory's inhabitants by some 40 percent, leaving the Latvian-speaking population at about 220,000.[4] By the time the Great Northern War ended (with the Treaty of Nystadt in 1721), the Latvian population numbered approximately the same as it had at the beginning of the sixteenth century. Thus the century that elsewhere in Europe was coming to be celebrated as the Era of Enlightenment began in the Baltic littoral with a demographic catastrophe of immense proportions. As a result of its victories, the Russian Empire received a province— Livland—that had been damaged economically and that in many rural areas was virtually depopulated.

CONSOLIDATING SERF ESTATES

In the decades following the end of the Great Northern War, the landholding nobility was able to convince its new sovereigns that the estate organization of agriculture and the enserfment of the peasantry should not only continue but be perfected. The high mortality rates of the first part of the century faced all estates with labor shortages, which meant that peasants were attracted by the idea of flight in the hope (however wrong-headed) of finding better conditions elsewhere. This required intensive prohibitions on peasant movements and explicit agreements regarding returning them to their original residences. The shortages and the resulting fall of productivity signaled the need to increase obligatory labor and other dues, which required a freer hand for the landholders.

To satisfy the Livland nobility, the Russian authorities permitted the legal protections created during the Swedish period to be reduced; in Courland and Lettgallia, landholders were similarly able to expand their authority because the Polish sovereign was growing weak. By midcentury the landholding nobles in all three littoral areas were in a much stronger position vis-à-vis the peasantry than they had been before. The *Landrat* of Livland, Otto von Rosen, declared that peasants were their lords' movable property, which the lord was free to buy and sell and which, by definition, could not in turn possess property of their own.[5] This attitude was extreme, but it illustrates the temper of the times. The continued absorption of peasants into the social order of hereditary serfs (in Latvian, *dzimtscilvēku kārta;* in German, *Erbbauerstand*) by the end of the century resulted in a social structure (defined by *orders* or *estates*) in which an estimated 78.9

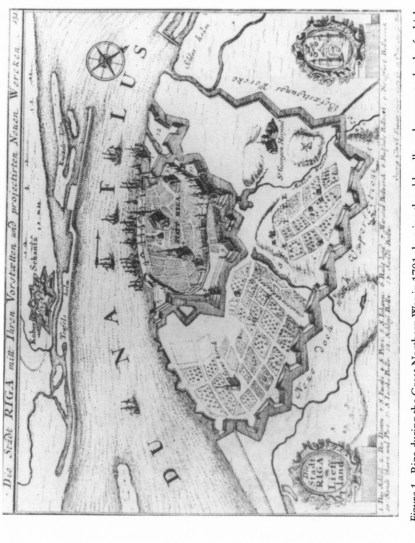

Figure 1. Riga during the Great Northern War in 1701 showing the old walls and ramparts, both of which were torn down in the 1860s, and the new ramparts that were never built.

percent of the Livland population, 87.7 percent of the Courland population, and 93.8 percent of the Letgallian population were enserfed.[6]

With no effective royal opposition to the nobility's desire to expand estates based on serf labor, the number of estates continued to grow throughout the century. In Livland in 1688 there were an estimated 537 estates; in 1816 that number had almost doubled, to 1,075.[7] In Courland-Semigallia, the number rose from 789 at the start of the century to 1,409 in 1816; in Lettgallia, where statistics for the early century are lacking, in 1784 the number of estates stood at 254. The undifferentiated numbers hide structural changes, the most of important of which was the rapid creation of half estates (in Latvian, *pusmuižas*). Still, the trend was for the proportion of persons living on smaller estates to decrease and increase on the larger estates. In Livland, the proportion of persons living on estates with fewer than one hundred persons was 7.7 percent at the start of the century and 1.6 percent at the end; the proportion on estates with more than eight hundred persons was 29.8 percent and 50.1 percent, respectively. In Courland-Semigallia, the proportions for estates with fewer than one hundred persons was 11.3 percent and 2.8 percent; for those with more than eight hundred persons, 23.5 percent and 40.0 percent. The trend toward larger estates was made possible by a constantly growing population, which in Livland's Latvian districts rose from an estimated 153,000 before 1710/11 to 293,000 at the end of the century; in Courland-Semigallia, from 209,000 to 290,000 in the same period; and in Lettgallia, from 103,000 to 190,000.

THE LUTHERAN CHURCH AND THE MORAVIAN BRETHREN *(HERRNHUT)*

The organization of the Lutheran Church in Courland and Livland remained relatively unchanged throughout the eighteenth century, with consistories heading the church government in both provinces. At the same time, the organized nobilities (in German, *Ritterschaften*) of both provinces were gradually acquiring more influence over church affairs, in part because the Russian government entrusted religious matters to them and in part because neither provincial church was able to establish a material base that would allow it to be autonomous. Estate owners had patronage rights (in German, *Patronat*) over local clerical appointments, which meant that candidates with unacceptable backgrounds (i.e., from the enserfed Baltic peasantry) had no chance of becoming pastors. Such persons had been rare earlier, but in the eighteenth century they were an impossibility.

Paralleling the absorption of the Baltic peasants into the serf-estate system were phenomena that suggest that peasants were estranged from certain aspects of established Baltic institutions, including the Lutheran Church. The easiest of these phenomena to follow in Livland is the rapid spread of pietistic ideas among the peasantry during the late 1720s and 1730s. Pietism, which stressed the importance of personal religious experience and an individualistic interpretation of the Scriptures, came to the Baltic littoral via missionaries from the Herrnhut (Moravian Brethren) movement in Germany, who began to preach their gospel of spiritual egalitarianism in the Wolmar (Valmiera) district of Livland at the invitation of Magdalene Elisabeth Hallart, the widow of General Ludwig Hallart.[8] That branch of pietism was founded by Count Nicolaus Ludwig von Zinzendorf in 1727 in Bohemia. The Herrnhut missionaries went about their business of conversion quietly but effectively and in 1738 established a seminary in Wolmar to train local lay leaders. By 1742 the Herrnhut congregations in the central part of Livonia were estimated to have had some four thousand members.

The higher officials of the Lutheran Church in Livland, as well as the parish clergy, were of two minds about this development. On the one hand, the Moravians were supported by the Livonian nobility, who initially insisted that increasing peasant piety was a positive thing because it would make peasants more obedient. Moreover, in the districts with Herrnhut congregations, rural criminality and drunkenness decreased noticeably. On the other hand, the increasing number of peasants who attended the Moravian meetinghouses rather than regular Lutheran services began to look like a opposition movement to established authority. Also, the Moravians saw nothing wrong with recruiting their clergy from among the Latvian peasants, which violated the Lutheran Church's caste-conscious recruitment procedures. There were also the Moravian preachments, which, though they firmly supported obedience to secular authority, also stressed an equality among the faithful that placed all Christian believers—nobles, burghers, and peasants, as well as Germans and Latvians—on the same level. Moravian beliefs in peasant self-education went against the grain of those Lutheran clergy who believed that peasant education should be organized and guided by the established church.[9]

As a result of these stances, but before the Livland Lutheran Consistory had reached its own conclusions, in 1743 Moravianism was forbidden by Empress Elizabeth and the brethren's meetinghouses and property confiscated. This was not the end of the story for the Livland peasantry, however, first, because the prohibition was lifted by Empress Catherine in 1770 and, second, because the pietistic spirit had become deeply embedded in the folk memory of the mid-Livland Latvian peasant. In those areas in which peasant Lutheranism had become widespread, the peasants retained a pietistic bent even without the meetinghouses and organized congregations. Furthermore, the Herrnhut encouragement of self-education appears to have spread beyond the central Livland areas and to have fueled a movement for home instruction that yielded improved peasant literacy in the second half of the eighteenth century. Beyond these short-term effects, the pietistic spirit gave Latvian thought a cultural stance that surfaced repeatedly in the nineteenth century, as Latvians developed a literature and began to identify the unique characteristics of their national culture.[10]

LATVIAN AUTHORS AND READERS

Like everything else in the Baltic littoral, the publication of books—including books in Latvian—had to recover from the disastrous effects of the Great Northern War and the plague of 1710/11. The pace of recovery is evident in the statistics of book publishing. In the decade from 1710 to 1721, only five new titles in Latvian appeared, but from 1722 to the mid-1750s, some ten to seventeen new titles were published per decade.[11] This pace continued unabated, so that in the eighty-year period from 1755 to 1835, more that seven hundred new titles were printed in Latvian. Estimating printing sizes conservatively, the total number of books in Latvian printed in the whole 1755–1835 period was upward of one million.[12]

The steady output of new titles in the second half of the century reflected to some extent the founding of Baltic publishing firms, such as those of J. F. Stefenhagen, which lasted from 1769 to 1919, and J. K. D. Miller, who published from 1789 to 1929. Publishers were especially eager to publish in Latvian when they discovered a market for books on other than religious themes. The number of titles with religious content continued to be a strong component of publishing, but secular themes—following the interests of the Enlightenment—became increasingly important. Interest in religious writings was renewed under the influence of pietism, but by the end of the eighteenth century there were nearly as many Latvian publications that were meant to entertain, inform, and criticize.

Most of the titles were written by clergymen who belonged for the most part to the Baltic German cultural world and learned Latvian later in life. During the century, however, those authors began differentiating their interests in the Latvians. Some, such as Gotthard Friedrich Stender (1714–96, known among Latvians as "Old Stender"), his son Alexander Johann Stender (1744–1819, "Young Stender"), and Karl Gotthard Elverfeldt (1756–1819), continued to work in the religious-didactic tradition, creating works of religious instruction and moral uplift.[13] Within this tradition, however, "Old Stender" introduced secular themes by inventing fairy tales and commenting at length on the problems of everyday life. Another group of authors including Garlieb Merkel (1760–1850), though writing *about* Latvians, published virtually nothing *in* Latvian. Andrejs Johansons, the preeminent historian of eighteenth-century Latvian-language culture, opines that those authors, including Merkel, "with minor exceptions remained unknown to contemporary Latvians,"[14] while religious works in Latvian were widely diffused. Thus, in 1782 in the Mazsalaca parish, which included 350 farmsteads, there were 655 hymnals, ninety-eight Bibles, and two books of biblical stories.[15] Evaluations of eighteenth-century Latvian writings judge them to be much improved over that of the previous century but still strongly influenced by German syntax, idioms, and vocabulary.[16]

For all its inadequacies, however, Latvian-language writing and the intellectual efforts that lay behind it did have one demonstrable consequence, namely, increasing literacy among the Latvian peasantry. In the districts where the Herrnhut movement had been popular, for example, peasant "brothers" and "sisters" had been encouraged to write spiritual biographies; those that survive are the earliest examples (in manuscript form) of Latvians writing about themselves. Statements about peasant literacy at the end of the eighteenth century are bound to be imprecise, but one contemporary—the pastor K. F. Watson (1777–1826), in the early decades of the nineteenth century in Courland (where the rural population was mostly Latvian speaking)—surmised that about a third of the peasants could at least read. Later historians have suggested that in Livland (where the peasants in the southern part were Latvian users) in 1790 as many as 61 percent of all young people were literate.[17] These proportions at the end of the eighteenth and the beginning of the nineteenth century reflect the influence of parents and grandparents who had earlier recognized the connection between literacy and socioeconomic betterment.

THE ANNEXATION OF POLISH INFLANTY (LETTGALLIA)

As the Russian imperial government consolidated its hold over Livland during the middle decades of the eighteenth century, the Polish-Lithuanian Commonwealth was growing weak. When August III, king of Poland, Lithuania, and Saxony, died in 1763 and was succeeded by Stanislas Poniatowski, a favorite of Catherine II (Catherine the Great) of Russia, the Russian government recognized an opportunity. Using the opening of a civil war in Poland between pro- and anti-Russian factions, Catherine agreed with Frederick II of Prussia and Maria Theresa of Austria that annexing Polish territory would be mutually beneficial. As a consequence, in 1772 Poland underwent its first partition, which reduced that state to about two-thirds of its former size. In this transaction, the Russian Empire gained some 1.8 million inhabitants east of the Daugava and Dnieper Rivers, including what had until this time been Polish Inflanty, or Lettgallia. In reorganizing its new territories, the Russian government abolished Lettgallia as a unit and subdivided it into the districts of Daugavpils (Dvinsk), Ludza, and Rēzekne (Rezhitsa) in the Polotsk *gubernia*. Henceforth, those Latvians living in the former Lettgallian districts would not have the separate territorial identity they had had when living in Polish Inflanty.[18]

Having been under Polish-Lithuanian control for more than two hundred years, the landholding elites of Lettgallia had had ample time to entrench themselves, and it is thus difficult to distinguish them by nationality. We can surmise, however, that most landholding families were Polish or of Polish ancestry, generally from the lower levels of the Polish aristocracy (*szlachta*). There was also an important minority of German nobles, some of whom also owned estates in Courland and Livonia. Because the population of Lettgallia had been severely reduced in the first decades of the century, estate owners welcomed serfs fleeing the adjoining western lands. The peasantry was almost entirely enserfed, although there was a recognizable subpopulation of *vaļinieki* (freemen) who worked mostly on estates as wage laborers or craftsmen.

In the second half of the century, according to a postpartition 1782 census, most of the farmland belonged to estates, most of which, in turn, were privately owned or privately held. Correspondingly, some 76 percent of the peasant-serfs lived on private estates, 16 percent on state-owned estates, and about 5–6 percent lived or worked on estates owned or held by religious insitutions such as churches and monasteries.[19] That the territory was overwhelmingly rural was underlined by the fact that in the three largest cities of the region—Daugavpils (Dvinsk), Ludza, and Rēzekne (Rezhitsa)—houseowners numbered only seventy-two, forty-four, and fifteen, respectively. Traditionally, political rights—that is, full participation in the higher levels of regional administration—had been guaranteed only to those landowners espousing the Catholic faith, but their influence began to diminish as the Russian government consolidated its control.

The most far-reaching consequence of the Russian annexation of the Lettgallian territories was the peasant population being subjected to sociocultural and linguistic influences qualitatively different from those that in the second half of the eighteenth century were shaping the peasantries of

Courland and Livland.[20] Catholicism remained dominant in religious life, but migration tended to be primarily from the east, bringing to Lettgallia substantial numbers of Russians and Byelorussians and enlarging the likelihood of intermarriage with and assimilation to cultural and language groups different from those in the western areas of the littoral.

THE END OF COURLAND AS AN INDEPENDENT DUCHY

After Lettgallia was transferred to Russian control, the only region with Latvian-speaking inhabitants to remain outside the empire was Courland-Semigallia, where imperial influence had grown steadily after the beginning of the eighteenth century.[21] After Duke Jacob died in 1681, the ducal Kettler family became increasingly less interested in governing and more interested in living the good life and conducting intrigues. Jacob's son Friedrich Casimir, who was duke from 1682 to 1698, initially followed in his father's footsteps through his interest in shipbuilding and economic development, especially with respect to the Courland towns. But toward the end of his rule his interest in governing diminished, and during the final decade of the century, the duchy's government began to experience financial difficulties and to borrow heavily. To repay some of its debts, Courland had to give up its colonies that, though small, had given it prestige. Moreover, the landed nobility used Friedrich Casimir's growing disinterest to strengthen its control over the peasantry.

His son, Friedrich Wilhelm, became duke in 1698, but because of his youth, his mother, Elisabeth Sofia, and his father's brother Ferdinand acted as regents. This turned out to be an inopportune moment for the duchy to have weak political leadership, however, because the Great Northern War, which began in 1700, required a strong duke to preserve Courland's neutrality. Lacking such leadership, Courland became a staging ground for battle by both the Polish and the Swedish armies in the first half of the war; as a consequence, the Russian government began to look at the duchy as an enemy to be raided and exploited.

By 1711, when Friedrich Wilhelm died, Courland had fallen almost completely under the sway of Peter the Great, though retaining nominal political independence. The ducal title passed to Ferdinand, the erstwhile regent, who was the last member of the Kettler dynasty to hold the title. His tenure was long, a quarter century (1711–37), but troubled, largely because much of the Courlandic nobility felt that a Russian sovereign would be more advantageous and because Ferdinand chose to reside outside the duchy much of the time. This state of affairs was exploited by the

Russian government, which pursued a complicated series of court intrigues to bring to power in Courland a complaisant duke. In 1737, when Ferdinand died childless, the Russians advanced as his successor Ernst Johann Biron, who had become the lover of Ferdinand's widow, Anna, the daughter of Tsar Ivan V. Anna, having become tsarina in 1730, was able to maneuver the Courlandic nobility into choosing Biron as the next duke. With the coming to power of the Biron dynasty, informal Russian domination of Courland-Semigallia was secured.

Ernst Johann Biron retained the ducal title from 1738 to 1758 but spent most of his time away from the duchy, largely at the Saint Petersburg court. The ducal title brought him an annual income of about 250,000 thalers, much of which he spent in Saint Petersburg buying influence and in Courland building and lavishly maintaining his residences. Seeking to please his imperial hosts, he permitted large numbers of Russian army officers to acquire estates in his duchy, which was still nominally a part of the Polish-Lithuanian Commonwealth. Biron's politics were opportunistic in the extreme, yet in seeking to assuage his political rivals he further weakened the powers of the ducal office.

The Courlandic nobility, no less opportunistic than the duke, continued to try to keep a maximum of independence, even though pro-Russian sentiment was growing steadily within its ranks. Toward the end of Ernst Johann's rule, his power had diminished to such an extent that the nobility deposed him and handed the ducal office to his son Karl. Karl, however, put in only a cameo appearance—1758 to 1763—and, because of his irresponsible attitudes toward power, left the affairs of the duchy considerably worse off than they had been. Ernst Johann reassumed the title of duke in 1763 and held it until 1769. In 1769 he stepped down in favor of his son Peter, who had returned to Courland in 1763 from Russia.

Peter was the last of the Biron dynasty, and his quarter-century rule concluded the Russification of Courlandic affairs that had begun during the Great Northern War. During Peter's tenure he was in constant conflict with the duchy's nobility, which by this time was divided among those who, however weakly, supported the Biron dynasty; those who thought that Courland should become part of the Russian Empire; and those who wanted to steer an independent course. (In light of the weakened state of the Polish-Lithuanian Commonwealth, that connection now seemed appealing to only a handful of Courland nobles.) The two factions that opposed the Biron dynasty won out in the end. By the third partition of Poland the Courlandic nobles were ready to pledge their loyalty to Catherine the Great, assuming that she would guarantee their rights and their commanding role in the province. When in 1795 Poland-Lithuania disappeared from the map of Europe, Catherine the Great paid Peter Biron a substantial sum for his estates and granted him a pension, allowing him to retire to Silesia. This settlement brought to an end the 233-year existence of Courland as a relatively independent duchy and extended the Russian imperial borders to the shores of the Baltic Sea.

EXPERIMENTS WITH PROVINCIAL GOVERNMENT

Early in her reign, Catherine the Great became dissatisfied with the decentralized nature of the administrative apparatus of her empire and sought ways to tighten it. She was, after all, an "enlightened" ruler interested in reform, which was nearly impossible without adequate machinery. The administrative reorganization she implemented—the so-called regency (in German, *Staathalterschaft;* in Russian, *namestnichestvo*)—was relatively short-lived, lasting from 1775 to its abolition by her son Paul in 1796.[22] Its timing meant that the Baltic area was affected unevenly: Lettgallia beginning in 1778, Livland beginning in 1783, and Courland beginning in 1795 (the dates at which Russian influence came to each area). During the years the reforms were in place, however, they went a long way toward reducing—not without considerable resistance—the political autonomy of the provincial Baltic nobilities. The price Catherine paid for these reforms—at least in Livland—was decreased control over private estates, which meant, down the line, greater freedoms for the landholders in dealing with their peasant-serfs.

Nonetheless, the reforms affected virtually all other aspects of power holding: provincial administrative positions, the court systems, urban government, the corporations of the nobilities, and the system of tax collection. They clearly demonstrated how far a determined Russian ruler could go in diminishing the "historic privileges" of landed elites in the western borderlands. At the same time, because Catherine had had to provide the Baltic nobilities with a quid pro quo for accepting the reforms, the regency period was a good index of how much Saint Petersburg had to rely on such regional nobilities for local administration. Tsar Paul's revocation of the reformed system in 1796 meant, for the Baltic provinces, a return of most aspects of the provincial administrative system to the status quo ante.

But the attention paid by the reforms to peasant representation at the lower levels of the reorganized court system, and the opportunity to be represented in urban councils of non-German property holders, was not forgotten by the provincial population, even after these openings were again closed. Moreover, the upper social orders of the Baltic area were forced to look at the conditions of the peasantry because the Crown had made this a theme of the reform. As a quid pro quo for lifting the reforms, however, Tsar Paul required the Baltic landowners to supply the Russian army with recruits, which meant that estates were henceforth obligated, when the call came, to send one per x number (the formula changed) of its able-bodied male labor force to serve in the Russian army for twenty-five years. All in all, the regency experiment as well as its revocation suggested, even to the most fatalistic Baltic peasantry, that the ways in which they lived their daily lives were not eternally fixed.

RIGA IN THE ENLIGHTENMENT

During the eighteenth century, Riga remained the metropolis of the Baltic area, but, having also become a city in the Russian Empire, it encountered new challenges as well as opportunities. Predictably, the Riga patriciate, which governed the city through a council of magistrates recruited from the leading merchant guilds, jealously guarded the city's autonomy and generally succeeded in warding off efforts at imperial control until the second half of the eighteenth century.

The magistracy's domination of the city remained almost absolute.[23] An elaborate system of controls, exercised through an expanding administrative bureaucracy, allowed the magistracy to prevent a too-rapid expansion of the Riga population and to limit the number of persons engaged in the principal trades and professions. Yet growth was inevitable. Riga had a monopoly over the empire's western trade, which made the city increasingly attractive to the ambitious and energetic. Riga's population grew from about 10,000 at the conclusion of the Great Northern War in the Baltic (1710) to about 27,800 in 1800.[24] Although the population sources of this period are ambiguous, much, if not most, of this growth was due to continuous in-migration.

In its physical appearance, in the language of its government, and in the character of its dominant culture, Riga remained a German city. Whether nationality (as conceived of in the nineteenth century) played a significant role in the city's life, however, remains a thorny question. Reliable estimates place the nationality composition of the city in the second half of the century at about 45 percent German, 31 percent Latvian, 14 percent Russian, 9 percent Polish, and 1 percent other.[25] Contemporary accounts speak of the city's population as consisting of Germans and non-Germans; the prolific use of such imprecise terms in the sources creates an opportunity for disputes. Latvian historians suggest that many Latvians had Germanized their names and were therefore counted in the German population; by this reasoning, the proportion of Latvians in the city was probably higher.

It is more likely, however, that the principal instruments of self-definition for the Riga residents were language and occupation rather than nationality in the modern sense. Even language and occupation however, produced various kinds of cleavages. Most non-Germans (including Latvians) were concentrated in occupations supporting the maritime activities of the great Riga merchants and in some nine craft guilds (of the forty or so guilds in the city). There were also Latvian-language Lutheran congregations and Latvian-language schools, for which, of course, the language distinction was of prime importance. There was also residential segregation, which was easily accomplished because the magistracy controlled the ownership of city properties. The German-speaking patriciate monopolized the private housing and business establishments in the inner city, whereas the non-Germans tended to reside in peripheral areas. But none of these cleavages was absolute because there were guilds that had both German and non-German members and because patrician residences often had large numbers of live-in non-German servants and laborers.

In light of these considerations, the famous conflict, lasting from 1747 to 1784, between the well-to-do Steinhauer brothers—Latvians and Riga businessmen—and the city council over admitting the brothers to the official ranks (*Bürger*) of property owners is instructive.[26] The council argued that the Steinhauers were not free men because as Latvians they were descendants of serfs. The Steinhauers' protracted litigation eventually resulted in their right to possess urban property, but, as even Latvian historians have observed, the upward socioeconomic mobility of Riga Latvians in the eighteenth century usually led to their being linguistically and culturally assimilated to the German-speaking culture of the Baltic world.

Despite its overall German character, however, Riga continued to be a magnet for Latvians.[27] Its large Latvian population meant that Latvian in-migrants whose German was poor or nonexistent could find supportive neighborhood networks as they searched for employment. Serfs who fled to the city could hope to receive their freedom, and the Latvian schools in Riga promised at least a primary education. These opportunities appeared especially tempting as the severity of rural serfdom increased and flight seemed to many peasant-serfs the only means of survival.

AGRICULTURAL CHANGES AND RURAL UNREST

There were many signs during the second half of the century that both the legal institution of serfdom and the estate system being implemented within it were unable to cope with changing circumstances.[28] To begin with, the rural population in all three Latvian areas of the littoral was increasing with every generation and thus rapidly expanding the number of peasants that had to be absorbed by the existing estates. The events that by the end of the century had joined Swedish Livland, Polish Inflanty, and the Duchy of Courland to the Russian Empire had not altered the institutional arrangements in the countryside, and the landowning nobility had fought hard and successfully to sustain them. In theory, the peasants' recompense for laboring on the estate's demesne was farming estate land set aside for peasant use and the landholder's patriarchal protection, but this arrangement—however justifiable it might have seemed in the medieval period—by the end of the eighteenth century had lost its rationale in the eyes of not only "enlightened" Baltic critics of serfdom but also most segments of the peasantry. Both the critics and the peasants saw such arrangements as merely the means for extracting increasingly larger amounts of labor from people legally bound to stay in place. The peasants, moreover, saw such arrangements as threatening their survival because their obligatory labor diminished the time on their own land and kept them from seeking better opportunities. (Another problem was that the judges of what constituted mistreatment of the peasantry were the same people—the landowners and their agents—who were practicing it.)

The amount of obligatory peasant labor on the estates increased during the second half of the eighteenth century, despite the fact that demands for Baltic agricultural products remained at satisfactory levels and estate incomes were generally good, with landholders surrendering up to 30–50 percent of their agricultural product for the long- and short-distance markets. Yet the personal expenses of the landholding class appear to have been on the increase, producing rising indebtedness; thus there were continuous efforts to extract additional labor from the peasantry. Contemporary records suggest that, alongside the traditional labors, new categories of "extraordinary labor" were being devised as estate owners took on new income-yielding involvements.[29] Farmstead heads (*saimnieki*) began keeping several farmhands (*kalpi*) so that personnel could be sent to the estate farms to meet both the new and the old obligations. Those peasants who could not meet their labor obligations were dispossessed and fell into the farmhand rank. Other landholders deliberately expanded the demesne (the estate portion of the arable land) at the expense of peasant land to increase the estate's agricultural yield. Some Marxist-Leninist Baltic historians have characterized the final decades of the eighteenth century as the start of a "crisis of feudalism," and there is no doubt that at that time rural unrest was greater than ever before.[30] It is not clear, however, that these events led to a systemwide crisis.[31]

In Livland, a serious incident in the Aluksne district resulted in the arrest of 120 peasants and the punishment of 49. In 1776 and 1777, unrest in Cēsis resulted in the corporal punishment or imprisonment of some seventy peasants. In 1783 and 1784, when the new imperial head tax was introduced, which some landowners wanted to pay by transferring the cost to the peasants through enlarged labor obligations, thousands of peasants sparked widespread unrest on some one hundred estates in both the Latvian and the Estonian parts of Livland. (Peasants' paying the new tax directly believed that by so doing they would become Crown peasants who, they believed, received better treatment than peasants on private estates.) Responding to landholders' requests, the imperial government expanded the number of troops in Livland and kept them in the province for the rest of the century, both as a massive show of force and to suppress incidents. In the chronicles of peasant unrest of the period, there is little mention of Lettgallia and none of Courland, suggesting that this crisis was less than systemwide. At the same time, the incidents that did occur indicate that in many locales landowner exploitation of unchecked privilege had pushed many peasants beyond their traditional fatalism.

ENLIGHTENED CRITICS OF SERFDOM

Because peasants endured the burdens of serfdom in their everyday lives, their dissatisfaction is not surprising; neither was it illogical for the landholders, especially the landed nobilities, to use their substantial powers to defend their interests and the existing system. At the same time, however, to some individuals among the Baltic elites, serfdom seemed a relic of the past and, in enlightened principles, a violation of human rights. Few, however, expressed their views on this matter publicly, for such attacks could well be interpreted as seditious in the Baltic political context. Some, such as Johann George Eisen (1717–79), a clergyman, sought to reform the serf system on their own landed properties.[32] Eisen, who tried to find ways to free his serfs, was soundly condemned by his peers. K. F. Schultz (1720–82), a nobleman, tried to introduce similar reforms on his estates at Aizkraukle (in German, Ascheraden).

Although criticism of serfdom elsewhere in Europe was not unusual in the second half of the century, in the Baltic such criticism was scattered and subdued. Perhaps because of this and because of the horror with which landed nobles everywhere viewed the events in France after 1789, Garlieb Merkel (1769–1850) attracted much alarmed attention when in 1796, at the age of twenty-seven, he published *Die Letten, vorzüglich in Liefland, am ende des philosophischen Jahrhunderts*.[33] This book displayed a youthful disgust with the Baltic agrarian regime and with the unwillingness of the Baltic elites to change it. Merkel denounced serfdom as inhumane and drew on many examples—some probably based on rumor—of how landholders' unrestricted power over the enserfed peasantry had led to mistreatment and cruelty. Because the work was written in German and not translated into Latvian until the second half of the nineteenth century, it is doubtful that it had much effect on Latvian public opinion.

What was remarkable about Merkel's work was his conceptualization of the people he was writing about: the work espoused the view that the Latvians were a *Volk*, a people with a common viewpoint whose attitudes were on a collision course with those of the German speakers of the provinces. At the end of the eighteenth century this was a radical concept, picturing Baltic provincial conflicts less in terms of the agrarian question (*Agrarfrage*) than in terms of nationality. Moreover, it seemed to be predicting a general national conflict. In *Die Letten* and its several sequels, Merkel described the Latvian past as the story of a nation under duress, thus reinterpreting Baltic history in the protonationalist terminology suggested by the cultural philosophy of Johann Gottfried Herder (1744–1803).

Figure 2. Garlieb Helwig Merkel (1769–1850), author of *Die Letten, vorzüglich in Liefland, am ende des philosophischen Jahrhunderts* (1796).

Although the hypothesis that Latvians at the end of the eighteenth century were a single people with a common consciousness is difficult to sustain, it differs radically from the notion that, because virtually all Latvians were peasants, the terms *Latvian* and *peasant* were interchangeable and that if Latvians wanted to be something other than peasants they had to assimilate to the German speakers of the Baltic area. Thus by the end of the century, at least among the enlightened critics of Baltic society, discussions of serfdom had ceased to be strictly economic and had begun to edge, hesitatingly and uncertainly, over into the national question.

THE INCIDENT AT KAUGURI AND THE PEASANT LAW OF 1804

The rural unrest that had plagued the Baltic littoral during the entire second half of the eighteenth century culminated in 1802 at the Kauguri estate near Valmiera (Wolmar), where some three thousand peasants confronted a substantial tsarist military force, including artillerists.[34] (Interestingly, the estate was in the center of the area where the pietistic movement had flourished in Livland since the first half of the eighteenth century.) The specific reason for the unrest was dissatisfaction with the methods of paying the head tax (see p. 76); in other estates of the district, peasants protested the ever-increasing number of obligatory labor days and the proliferation of obligatory tasks.

The Kauguri unrest resulted in fourteen peasants killed and eight wounded; this tragic event, however, drew the attention of the new tsar— Alexander I (tsar from 1801 to 1825)—to the Baltic area and the need for changes there. Already favorably predisposed to the idea of serf reforms, Alexander requested that the Livland nobility submit proposals to him for such reforms. (In 1802, he had approved a new peasant law for the northernmost Baltic province of Estland.) The plan submitted by the Livland Ritterschaft after twelve months of internal wrangling and efforts to sidestep the inevitable was signed by the tsar on February 20, 1804.[35] This new peasant law did not question the legality of serfdom but did change the basis of serf status. The law required that, to be classified as a serf, a peasant had to reside on land that entailed serf status for its residents; a peasant could not simply belong to a lord. Obligatory labor service was also reevaluated, not with the intention so much of lightening it as of finding a more objective basis for it.

This labor reform resulted in all labor services supplied to the lord being expressed in monetary terms; also, services and dues of all kinds now had to be defined in the *Wackenbücher* (manorial rolls) that were available to both the serf and the lord. The new law also created local courts consisting of one local noble, one farm manager, and one farmhand. Finally, the law also created committees of review for each district that were to survey peasant land and determine that labor service regulations were not being violated.

The Livland Peasant Law of 1804 was the most far-reaching measure concerning the peasantry promulgated since the Swedish period of the seventeenth century. Its provisions were meant to regulate the behavior of some twenty-six hundred landholders (not all of them nobles) in the province and thus affect the lives of some 500,000 peasants. In that the Livland nobles sought (unsuccessfully) to prevent the new law from being translated into Latvian, ostensibly to discourage sedition, we could expect that implementing the law would be uneven and take a long time. In fact, it had not been fully implemented by the end of the second decade of the nineteenth century, when the law emancipating serfs supplanted it. In the interim, imperial attention was preoccupied with the presence on the continent of Napoleon Bonaparte; further experimentation with rural reform had to wait.

6 A Century of Reforms

Persistent efforts at reform by the imperial government and the development of reform attitudes by the political and cultural elites of the Baltic littoral meant that Latvians born after passage of the Livland Peasant Law of 1804 had very different lives from those of their ancestors. In the first half of the century, the 1804 peasant law was followed in 1816–19 by the abolition of serfdom in all the Baltic provinces, though not in Lettgallia, which was not in the *baltischen Provinzen* and where serfdom continued until the imperial emancipation of 1861. With the arrival of personal freedom for the Baltic peasants, the benevolent attitudes of many Baltic German liberals toward the peasantry took a practical turn, especially in the areas of language and schooling. In the midcentury decades liberal members of the provincial nobilities fought for and obtained their peers' agreeing to allocate farmland for purchase by peasants.

The 1860s and 1870s brought the abolition of serfdom in Lettgallia, imperial reforms in law and urban government, and a substantial growth in rural-to-urban migration. In the first half of the century, socioeconomic reform created rising expectations among Latvians and a corresponding frustration with such ostensibly new practices as labor rents, which to peasants was simply corvée labor renamed. Until the 1850s, however, most Latvians (peasants and urban-dwellers alike) remained deferential to the existing distribution of political power in the Baltic provinces. But the generation coming into adulthood in the 1850s and 1860s challenged that distribution, arguing that the Latvian nation had "awakened" and that, as the majority population in the southern region of the provinces, it should be accorded proper recognition in provincial affairs. In those decades Latvians ceased to be anonymous and became fully identifiable actors in the flow of events. But they could not direct the course of the flow, which was being determined by imperial policy in Saint Petersburg.

SERF EMANCIPATION, 1816–33

The 1804 Livland Peasant Law had not yet been fully implemented when, in 1816, Alexander I approved a full-scale serf emancipation that had been presented to him by the nobility of Estland, the northernmost of the three Baltic provinces. Having returned from his Western European travels, which involved, among other things, the Congress of Vienna in 1815, the tsar was determined to demonstrate his dedication to reform. On their side, the Baltic provincial nobilities, seeing emancipation as inevitable, hoped that reform might turn out to be to their benefit. The Estland law of May 1816, containing 845 paragraphs, was the first of the series of three; in April 1817, the Courland nobility followed Estland's example and had its emancipation law, with 738 paragraphs, accepted. In Livland, where segments of the nobility remained recalcitrant to the end, the emancipation law, containing 658 paragraphs, was not signed until March 1819.[1] The Courland and Livland laws ended an institution that had structured the lives of rural Latvians in those provinces since the sixteenth century and almost immediately began to affect the daily movements of the approximately 231,000 (mostly Latvian) enserfed peasants living in the southern section of Livland and the approximately 342,000 in Courland. For the approximately 178,000 Latvian serfs living in Lettgallia, similar changes did not take place until the 1860s.[2]

Three aspects of these complicated laws need to be noted. First, they changed peasants and their families from serfs into free persons and created peasants courts in which these free persons would have a voice. But they simultaneously declared the current estate holders to be owners of the land, extinguishing even the tenuous use rights peasant-serfs had had in the old system and requiring the now-free peasants to contract with the owners for the use of farmland.[3] Moreover, the laws introduced the concept of "iron inventory," which meant that the occupants of each farmstead must keep on hand a certain amount of livestock, supplies, and equipment, reducing the peasants' rights to movable property. Thus for the next forty years actual ownership of the land was divided between the Crown, which in 1841 owned 14.8 percent of all the estates in Livland and 26.2 percent in Courland, and private owners such as nobles, retired military officers, and

Figure 3. February 19, 1819, by Johann Leberecht Eggink (1787–1867). An idealized representation of Tsar Alexander I emancipating the serfs of Livland (Vidzeme).

cities. Individuals (as opposed to corporations) owned 76.2 percent of all the estates in Livland and Courland. After emancipation, peasant-cultivators obtained the right to use farmsteads (frequently the same ones in which they had been living before emancipation) in exchange for labor rents and only infrequently for money rents.[4]

Second, implementing the emancipation law took about fourteen years, meaning that the new freedoms arrived incrementally. The peasant population in each district was classified into farmstead heads and their families, farmhands and their families, and estate serfs. Only half the persons in a given category were freed each year.[5] The impact of emancipation was further reduced by laws prohibiting immediate out-migration from districts; in Livland, these strictures were in force until 1832, and in Courland, until 1848. In practical terms, there were still serfs in the Latvian population of Courland and Livland until the mid-1820s, immobilized peasants in Courland until the late 1840s, and, until the 1860s, essentially landless peasants in both Livland and Courland whose tenure depended on obligatory labor (rent), which appeared not unlike the corvée of serfdom. The practices of the old system died hard, and the personal freedom the emancipation laws brought had to be exercised within these constraints.

Third, the introduction of contracts, agreements, and other documents created the need for precise personal identification, and thus the emancipation laws required that peasants be assigned surnames.[6] This too was a drawn-out process and in Courland did not conclude until the mid-1830s. In actuality, even before serfdom ended, free peasants and some serfs had surnames, but for the vast majority of rural people a given name and a farmstead name had been the most common form of personal identity. Although we can only guess at the significance of surname acquisition in the lives of individuals, there is no doubt that the process further encoded the cultural differences within the littoral populations. Henceforth, assimilation to a different language group, resulting from upward social mobility, would require not only abandoning the language of one's birth but also changing the surname inherited from one's parents.

CHALLENGING THE LANGUAGE HIERARCHY

Just as the emancipation laws eroded both the idea and the reality of a *Ständestaat* (a society with hierarchically organized social orders), so also, by the first decades of the nineteenth century, did trends in the German-language areas of the European intellectual world chip away at negative attitudes toward the culture of the traditional lower orders, particularly the peasantry. Reacting to the Enlightenment's veneration of reason and to cultural neoclassicism, such thinkers as Johann Georg Hamann (1730–88) and Johann Gottfried Herder (1744–1803), both of whom lived in the Baltic area for periods of time, discovered in peasant culture, particularly its language and folklore, valuable clues to deeper layers of collective existence and developed these insights into a general cultural philosophy.[7] In the Baltic provinces, where peasants spoke different languages than the upper orders, this reorientation had far-reaching consequences. Herder, who taught at the Riga Dome School from 1765 to 1769, enjoyed a particularly strong reputation among the Baltic German liberals, and many of them, adopting his cultural philosophy, began to view the Latvian-speaking peasantry as a suppressed *Volk* and the Latvian language and oral tradition as objects of substantial scientific (*wissenschaftlich*) interest.[8] In this they resembled their seventeenth- and eighteenth-century clerical precursors, but nineteenth-century attitudes tended to be less didactic and less patronizing.

Even as they maintained the distinction between *Bauernsprache* (peasant language) and *Kultursprache* (a language of high culture) and continued to discuss the desirability of and means for "Germanizing" persons of Latvian birth, the liberal Baltic German clergy began approaching all Baltic cultural products, including those emerging from the peasant order, with a new seriousness.[9] The intellectual and institutional consequences of this attitudinal change were numerous and enduring, especially in the domain of scholarly societies and publications. In 1817 the Kurländische Gesellschaft für Literatur und Kunst (Courland Society for Literature and Art) was founded in Jelgava (in German, Mitau). In 1824, twelve Lutheran pastors from Livland and two from Courland established the Lettisch-Literärische Gesellschaft (in Latvian, Latviešu draugu biedrība, Society of Friends of Latvians); its agenda included a systematic study of the Latvian language and folklore.[10] Active for the next century, the society published collections of papers (some in Latvian) from its meetings; the series eventually reached twenty volumes. In 1822, the Courland clergyman K. F. Watson founded the weekly *Latviešu avīzes* (The Latvian newspaper), the first periodical of its kind in Latvian. In 1857, the paper became the house organ of the Lettisch-Literärische Gesellschaft and as such lasted until 1915. In 1832, a Riga Lutheran pastor, Hermann Trey, began to publish another Latvian weekly newspaper—*Tas Latviešu Ļaužu Draugs* (Friend of the Latvian people), which only lasted until 1846. In 1834, the Gesellschaft für Geschichte und Altertumskunde der Ostseeprovinzen (Society for History and Antiquities of the Baltic Provinces) joined the list of new scholarly societies.

These efforts were complemented by the establishment in 1839 in Valmiera (in German, Wolmar), through the efforts of the Livland pastor Christian Ullmann, of a training institute for teachers of rural elementary schools. Jānis Cimze (1814–81), a Latvian educated in Germany, was its first director; under his guidance and initially with German as the language of instruction, over the decades of its existence the school graduated some four hundred rural schoolteachers—mostly Latvians of rural parentage.[11] Amid this outpouring of literary and scholarly activity were several writers of Latvian birth; Ansis Liventāls (1803–77), Ansis Leitāns (1815–74), Jānis Ruģēns (1817–76), and Ernests Dinsberģis (1816–1902), unassimilated to German culture, produced, in Latvian, poetry, prose, and translations.[12] These writers were not a major presence in the world of Baltic letters, but the acceptance of their work signaled not only a new receptivity among Baltic Germans but also a psychological shift among educated Latvians in the matter of national identity.

These attitudinal changes did not carry over into domains of Baltic life. The Lutheran churches in Courtland and Livland observed a policy of noninterference in decisions made by political authorities, even when Tsar Nicholas I proclaimed a church reform in 1832 that placed both of the Baltic provincial church organizations under a General Consistory that would regulate the religious life of all Lutherans in the empire and be answerable to the Interior Ministry and the Imperial Senate in Saint Petersburg. The Courland and Livland landed nobilities (in German, *Ritterschaften*) did not see this reform as threatening their control over local church matters. Even after 1832, and in fact until the introduction of Russification policy in the 1880s, the seventy Lutheran congregations of Courland and the ninety-nine congregations of Livland remained under the influence of the nobilities, which maintained throughout the period a general veto on clerical appointees from the Latvian population. Because in the 1830s and 1840s the Baltic German clergy were quiescent on these matters, so too were the handful of Latvians whom the clergy had helped into positions of prominence in the rural areas.

LAND REFORM AND THE
END OF LABOR RENTS

The middle decades of the century revealed that the provisions of the emancipation laws that redefined land tenure were feeding rather than quelling rural dissatisfaction. Exploiting their enhanced power, landowners not only regularly raised the amount of labor rents but also frequently sought to reduce the total size of the peasants' land on the estate by evicting farming families and adding their holdings to the demesne. From the landowners' viewpoint, it was becoming more advantageous to have their land worked by paid agricultural labor than by resident peasants. For Nicholas I, who succeeded Alexander I in 1825, the unsettled agrarian situation in the Baltic provinces was particularly nettlesome during the 1840s, when in Livland (and to a lesser extent in Courland) there were a series of bad harvests and repeated incidents of peasant unrest.

Less displeasing from the Crown's viewpoint but still troubling was the growing belief among Livland peasants that they could obtain land in the southern parts of Russia (the "warm lands") by converting from Lutheranism to Orthodoxy.[13] In the period from 1840 to 1852, an estimated 12 percent of the Livland Lutheran congregations converted in the vain expectation of improving their lot. In 1846, amid these disturbances, Tsar Nicholas I created a Baltic committee (in Russian, Ostzeiskii *komitet*) to review agrarian relations in Livland and propose further reforms. Among the committee members was Hamilcar von Fölkersahm (1811–56), a liberally inclined member of the Livland nobility who had become identified with agrarian reform in the numerous debates over the question in the Livland Landtag.[14]

The committee's work resulted in the 1849 "temporary" regulation that kept ownership of estate land in the hands of the estate owners but forbade them disposing of it except by selling or leasing it to the peasants who worked it. Land could no longer be paid for with obligatory labor. The liberal Livland nobles' intention was to create peasant smallholders; von Fölkersahm contributed to this goal by organizing a peasant land bank from which peasants could borrow (at 4 percent interest) to buy the land they were working. Although many in the Livland nobility opposed these new arrangements, a certain momentum had been created.

When, in 1861, another reform-minded tsar, Alexander II (1856–81), promulgated the inclusive Russian agrarian reforms that emancipated the serfs and gave them land, the Baltic nobles ended their opposition to change and during the 1860s accepted what, from the viewpoint of the peasantry, was a new agrarian order. The peasants of Lettgallia were covered by the 1861 imperial emancipation law and thus acquired personal freedom as well as the opportunity to acquire land.[15] After 1861, the Livland nobility began releasing increasingly larger amounts of estate land for peasants to buy and, after 1863, so did the Courland nobles. Moreover, in 1866, as a consequence of further imperial reforms, the role of landowning nobles in Baltic rural affairs was further reduced when institutions of local government were created; rural communities (*pagasti*) could elect their own governing councils, as well as the presiding officers of such councils, and judges to rural courts.

Peasants in Courland, Livland, and Lettgallia responded by seizing the moment but at different speeds in each area. By 1877, in Livland 41.4 percent of the rural properties were owned by peasants, with the proportion in Courland standing at 36.9 percent and in Lettgallia at 38.6 percent.[16] Thus von Fölkersahm's goal of rural smallholderships had been realized, though only after his death and largely as the result of pressures outside the Baltic provinces. Yet these reforms did not so much solve the agrarian problem in the Baltic littoral as transform it. Its new components, which forced their way into public debate during the next three decades, consisted of landlessness caused by a growing rural population and insufficient amounts of available land, dislocations caused by a swelling rural-to-urban migration that was not large enough to reduce the pressure on available land,[17] insufficiently remunerated agricultural labor, and the growing indebtedness of those peasants who had become landowners.

MIDCENTURY POPULATION TRENDS

Although the Latvian territories of Courland, southern Livland, and Lettgallia were severely overpopulated at midcentury (1800: est. 873,000; 1863: 1,240,000, see table 1),[18] it would have been worse had the attitudes toward marriage and childbirth exhibited in many other provinces of European Russia prevailed in Latvia. In European Russia, marriage was nearly universal for all, age at first marriage tended to be low (in the late teens and early twenties for both men and women), and childbirth within marriage was virtually uncontrolled.

In contrast, Latvians of both sexes tended to marry late—after age twenty-five—and large proportions of them did not marry at all.[19] Because rural illegitimacy rates in the Baltic were low, we can assume that care was taken to ensure that childbearing happened mostly within marriage. Latvian women, therefore, entered the childbearing process later in life than did Russian women in the interior provinces; with many Latvian women not entering the process, the aggregate number of children produced was lower than it would have been with early and universal marriage. On average, Latvian women had fewer children during their marriages, but the manner in which this was obtained—spacing births, infrequent intercourse, prolonged breastfeeding, or some combination—is not known. Because overall mortality in the Baltic area was not higher than elsewhere in the empire and, indeed, may have been somewhat lower, the slower growth rates were probably a result of the way in which Latvians practiced marriage and childbirth within marriage.

Such societywide practices are less difficult to identify than to explain.

TABLE 1:
LATVIAN POPULATION, 1550–1992

Year	Total Population of Latvia*	Latvians (in percent)	Number of Latvians outside Latvia	Total Number of Latvians (minimum)
ca. 1550	404,000			
ca. 1700	465,000			
ca. 1800	873,000	89.8		
1863	1,240,000			
1897	1,929,387	68.0	149,000	1,461,000
1914	2,552,000	60.0	230,000–260,000	1,761,000
1920	1,596,000	72.6		
1925	1,845,000	73.4		
1930	1,900,000	73.4		
1935	1,950,000	75.2	215,000–225,000	1,681,000
1943	1,803,104			
1959	2,093,000	62.0	262,000	1,559,000
1970	2,364,000	56.8	228,000–238,000	1,570,000
1979	2,521,000	53.7	230,000–240,000	1,583,000
1990	2,670,000	52.0	201,000–211,000	1,589,000
1992	2,657,755	52.5	195,000–205,000	1,590,320

*That is, the territory of present-day Latvia
SOURCES: Dunsdorfs and Spekke, *Latvijas vēsture 1500–1600*, p. 218; Dunsdorfs, *Latvijas vēsture 1600–1710*, pp. 181, 282; Skujeneeks, *Latvija: zeme un eedzīvotāji*, pp. 208, 284; Švābe, *Latvju enciklopēdija*, vol. 1, pp. 769, 773; Jerāns, *Latvijas padomju enciklopēdija*, vol. 2, p. 117; *Latvia: Transition to a Market Economy* (World Bank), p. vii; Dunsdorfs, *Latvijas vēsture 1710–1800*, p. 306; Zvidriņš and Vanovska, *Latvieši: statistiski demogrāfisks portretējums*, pp. 7, 23, 51, 138; Ilmārs Mežs, "Analysis of the Population Geography of Latvia after Independence," paper presented at the Association for the Advancement of Baltic Studies Conference, Chicago, June 1994.

Evidence gathered by the Princeton Project of European Fertility suggests that the Baltic area may have been among those scattered regions of Europe where the so-called demographic transition—a sustained decrease in fertility and mortality rates—had already begun in the middecades of the nineteenth century, a generation earlier than in surrounding areas.[20] Because the demographic transition is usually associated with socioeconomic modernization (industrial and technological growth, urbanization, high literacy rates), the Baltic area, by showing transition characteristics earlier, may have been an anomaly.

It is conceivable that the farmstead system on landed estates—the dominant organizational form of Baltic rural society even after emancipation—provided few incentives for having large numbers of children. Latvian peasants generally could not practice partible inheritance (dividing land among heirs) because landowners did not permit breaking up established farmsteads. Heirs other than the one son who inherited the farmstead headship were on their own, perhaps with some compensation in money or kind, and normally entered the ranks of landless farmhands. The farmhand population in turn—both males (in Latvian, *kalpi*) and females (in Latvian, *meitas*)—was highly mobile, moving from farmstead to farmstead every few years. This discouraged large families because the children of farmhands had limited work opportunities. Elderly peasants could seldom count on the support of their children because, except for the few sons who became farmstead heads, children were not in a position to render such support. These characteristics had been part of the Baltic scene since the eighteenth century, and their overall effect could have been to lower the desire for large families. Once established, however, such preferences are hard to change, and the question of why Latvians refrained from having large families continued as a theme of sociocultural commentary among Latvians as changes in the 1860s began to transform the society in which they were living.

THE LATVIAN NATIONAL AWAKENING

The agrarian problem and other significant questions in the Baltic area were discussed in very different terms in the 1860s and 1870s than they had been earlier. Simultaneously with the midcentury reforms and intertwined with them in complicated ways, the Latvian national awakening changed the terms of public and private discourse, as did the "Lithuanian awakening" to the south and the "Estonian awakening" to the north. In the Latvian case, the intelligentsia are to be found in the first, rather than the second, half of the nineteenth century. But the activists in the generations that came to maturity in the decades after 1850 were a new breed. First individually and then collectively, the post-1850 Latvian writers began to break the Baltic-German near monopoly over Latvian-language texts. According to one estimate, in 1844 only 3 percent of the authors of original works in Latvian were Latvian; by 1858, that proportion had grown to 6 percent; and by 1869 it had swelled to 51 percent.[21] The first such publications by individual Latvians included a book of original and translated poems, *Dziesmiņas* (Poetry) (1856), by the Tartu- (Dorpat)-educated Juris Alunāns (1832–64); then regularly published collections of writings such as the periodical *Mājas viesis* (Home visitor) (from 1856), edited by Ansis Leitāns, began to appear. These early publications were by no means controversial (they went through the hands of the censors, after all), and their subject matter was largely nonpolitical. But what appeared presumptuous to many Baltic German liberals was the Latvian authors' insistence that making an issue of their Latvianness made them more authentically Latvian than the Baltic German authors.

The debate sharpened in 1862 when there appeared in Saint Petersburg a weekly Latvian-language newspaper called *Pēterburgas avīzes* (Saint Petersburg newspaper), which mocked, parodied, and criticized Baltic German claims to cultural and, by implication, political superiority.[22] Seen by many liberals (as well as by the Baltic German landed nobilities) as a challenge to their political position, *Pēterburgas avīzes* was suppressed in 1865. The newspaper, which was edited by Juris Alunāns (author of *Dziesmiņas*), Krišjānis Barons (1835–1923), and Krišjānis Valdemārs (1825–91), was in a sense the house organ of the increasingly nationalistically inclined Latvian students at the university in Saint Petersburg whom Valdemārs had welded into a discussion club. The wide group of the paper's correspondents included some writers of the pre-1850 generation. The lengths to which the Baltic German authorities went to suppress the paper—charging it with sedition and its editors with creating some form of a Young Germany or Young Italy Movement among Latvians—simply goaded the Latvian activists to continued action.

Although writings could be suppressed, the attitudinal changes they evoked could not, and during the 1850s and 1860s these changes became permanent and gained momentum. Taken together, the changes constituted a new view of what the Latvian individual and the Latvian collectivity were and what role they should play in Baltic society.[23] To critics, the Latvian activists were nationalist ideologues, seeking to implement in the Baltic area the same destructive philosophy that Clemens von Metternich, the Austrian statesman, among others, had warned against and that had created so much turmoil in central Europe in the revolutions of 1848. The activists, in contrast, saw themselves not as mongering ideology but as putting forward new answers to such questions as why should landownership remain so unevenly distributed? why shouldn't Latvians play a greater role in Baltic affairs? why should economically and professionally successful Latvians be expected to assimilate to the German community? and why should Latvian continue to be regarded as a peasant tongue? The activists' writings were unphilosophical and unreflective; any philosophy of Latvian nationalism was embedded in attacks on and extended polemics against perceived injustices.

To these Latvian nationalists, the population of the Baltic littoral was a collection of *Völker* (in Latvian, *tautas*), with the language of each *tauta*

Figure 4. Krišjānis Barons (1835–1923), an editor of *Pēterburgas avīzes* and the founder of the modern study of Latvian folk songs (*dainas*).

(*Volk*) being the indicator of group membership. In this view, the long-term German-speaking dominance over Baltic affairs and institutions was a historic injustice in need of reversal and the continuing vernacular (i.e., low) status of the language of the great majority, an indicator of the maldistribution of power generally. Language could be used to stereotype, exclude, and define the status quo; the Latvian activists therefore saw their struggle as needing to be conducted on a much wider stage than just the economic one.

THE GOALS OF
LATVIAN NATIONALISM

Although influenced by German nationalist philosophy, the Latvian activists did not simply import a set formula (program), as opponents sometimes charged. The activists' attacks on the status quo were in fact multifaceted; to speak of a program or to suggest that the activists were a coherent movement is somewhat misleading. There were indeed clusters of like-minded individuals in the university cities of Dorpat (Tartu), Saint Petersburg, Moscow, and, of course, Riga, but many more persons had come to their new beliefs on their own.

Moreover, for this first generation of activists there was the problem of divided loyalties: some had benefited from the patronage of and others were married to Baltic Germans; still others because of their education expressed themselves with greater ease in German (and Russian) than in Latvian. What rankled was the continuing domination of Baltic urban and rural life by the traditional German-speaking landowning aristocracies and urban patriciates. Yet the entire Baltic German population could not be envisaged as an undifferentiated enemy because some elements of it—for example, the liberally minded Baltic German intelligentsia—were often sympathetic to the Latvian cause. On balance, in this first generation of activists, there were at least as many who wanted to coexist with Baltic Germans as there were those who wanted to displace them.[24]

A second problem, as the activists saw it, was the absence among Latvians of a consciousness of nationality. Latvian-language users lived in three adjoining provinces—Livland, Courland, and Vitebsk (the provincial location of Lettgallia). Those in the first two areas thought of themselves more as Livlanders or Courlanders than as Latvians; in Lettgallia the common consciousness was formed mostly by Catholicism. Moreover, Latvian speakers, the nationalists charged, too readily thought of being Latvian as disposable, particularly as they moved upward socially. Successful careers, especially in the Baltic cities, meant leaving behind one's peasant, and thus one's Latvian, background and assimilating to either the German- or the Russian-language culture. Geographic separatism and assimilation, however, could be overcome by accepting the notion that all Latvians were one *tauta* (*Volk*) and thus each shared in its collective soul (in Latvian, *tautas gars;* in German, *Volksseele*).[25]

To uncover this membership required, as the activists saw it, a national education in Latvian at the primary and secondary level. Rural people especially had to be "awakened" and "pulled into the light." Atis Kronvalds (1837–75), one of the most prolific early activists, urged his compatriots to view their use of Latvian as evidence that they were participants in a national consciousness that linked them regardless of where they lived or their status in life.[26]

The Latvian language was at the same time a repository of ancestral wisdom and a means of (potentially) effective communication. Even if, when compared with German, Russian, and other cultural languages (*Kul-*

tursprachen), Latvian seemed clumsy, its potential for development was great if those who spoke and wrote it adapted it to their increasingly diverse socioeconomic situations. Latvians' believing that education and prestigious occupations required them to speak another language was a grave mistake because they would not be fully accepted in the other language communities, especially those whose members occupied the higher orders.

Instead of thinking of themselves as members of a peasant order (in Latvian, *kārta;* in German, *Stand*) speaking a peasant language, Latvians needed to think of themselves as members of a nation that, with effort, could develop along the same lines as other cultures. After all, Latvian folk songs (*dainas*) amply demonstrated that the language was capable of conveying subtle understandings of nature, emotions, and human relation-

Figure 5. Atis Kronvalds (1837–75), a principal figure of the Latvian national awakening of the nineteenth century.

ships; it was only necessary to adapt the Latvian vocabulary to the modern world. Latvians needed a national culture and vocabulary in which all genres of intellectual creativity—newspapers, poetry, novels, science, philosophy, history, the law, the theater, literary criticism—could be pursued. Ironically, the activists frequently wrote their most important polemics in German and Russian because they wanted to address their arguments to the widest possible influential audience; for example, Kronvalds's best-known pamphlet, *Nationale Bestrebungen* (National currents), which he wrote in 1872, was not translated into Latvian until 1887.[27] As educated persons, the nationalists moved easily between the three languages of the southern Baltic littoral (Latvian, German, Russian), but the cultural boundaries they were seeking to draw were not easy to achieve.

What made the nationalists' job more difficult in the 1860s and 1870s was that the Latvian population was becoming increasingly differentiated socially and economically. Latvian peasants continued to purchase farmland through these decades, peaking in the late 1880s, by which time there had developed considerable friction in the Latvian countryside among the well-to-do farmstead owners ("gray barons"), the smallholders, the agricultural laborers, and the rural landless.

The better-off Latvian farmers in the countryside ceased to be tempted by assimilation of any kind and, having public institutions—rural courts and councils—in which to exercise their weight, became a force to be reckoned with. The period from 1850 to 1890 also witnessed increases in rural-to-urban migration, which not only swelled urban populations but also changed their composition. Riga, for instance, in 1867 had a population of 102,000 persons, 23 percent of whom identified themselves as Latvians, 43 percent as Germans, and 25 percent, Russians; by 1897, the total population of the city had grown to 282,000, 45 percent of whom professed a Latvian national identity, 24 percent, German, and 15 percent, Russian.[28] To the Latvian nationalists, urban Latvians constituted a growing market for their cultural program. There was also the possibility, however, that the recent in-migrants would be more concerned with issues of survival than with maintaining their nationality.

How influential were the "national awakeners"? Although it is customary to talk about a Latvian nationalist "movement," such a formulation may overestimate the number of people involved as well as overstate their influence. The number of activists who produced writings was perhaps fifty or so, depending on definitions, and there is no way to demonstrate that the widening of consciousness among Latvians was solely the result of the nationalists' efforts. At the same time, interest in their writing was brisk. Subscribers to *Pēterburgas avīzes*, the most nationalistic periodical of those decades, numbered about four thousand, most of them rural; the number of actual readers was probably substantially greater because individual issues were circulated among many readers. Literacy skills among Latvians were spreading rapidly, so that by 1897 the proportion of literate Latvians in the Baltic provinces (as compared with those in Russia proper) was relatively high—79.1 percent in Livland and 76.1 percent in Courland, compared with 21.0 percent in Russia.[29]

CONSOLIDATING A PRESENCE

In urging that Latvians transform their numerical preponderance into a dominant cultural and economic presence, the nationalist activists had to avoid appearing to be attacking the autocratic political system, which the Crown would not have tolerated, especially after the insurrection in the Polish provinces in 1863. And, by and large, they did manage to keep their attacks on the Baltic status quo compartmentalized. In addition to the cultural critiques, there were numerous writings on how to reform the Baltic agrarian system, exemplified by such pamphlets as Andrejs Spāģis's *Die Zustände des freien Bauernstandes in Kurland* (1860), as well as many writings urging new economic ventures for Latvians, such as Krišjānis Valdemārs's *Über die Befähigung der Letten und Esthen zum Seewesen* (1857), in which he recommended the establishment of maritime schools.

Valdemārs represented the practical side of activism in which Latvian economic self-improvement was of greater concern than questions of culture and language.[30] As a pragmatist and perhaps the best-connected of the Latvian activists (he had worked in the Ministry of Finance in Saint Petersburg), Valdemārs gained considerable support for Latvian economic development in the capital and in Moscow, where he established a working relationship with the Slavophiles. No less national in his thinking than others, in his Latvian-language writings he criticized those who were ashamed to admit to being Latvian and he continued to hold discussion evenings in Moscow for Latvian university students.

Although the German speakers enjoyed a monopoly of political power in the Baltic provinces, this situation seemed increasingly incongruous after the mid-1850s, as the Latvian language changed from a peasant tongue to an instrument of general communication within an increasingly differentiated population. The emergence of Latvian as a language of interaction and record in many different workday settings revealed its flexibility and potential for development, just as the Latvian nationalists had claimed.

Before the 1850s, the emancipation laws had created a system of county (*pagasts*) councils and courts throughout the southern Baltic territories, and the recording secretaries of these institutions for the most part used Latvian to keep minutes and prepare permanent documents. Also in the pre-1850 period, each peasant farmstead was required to have in its household records a statement in Latvian (a translation of a document in German that was held by the estate owner) of the obligations owed by the farmstead to the estate. Similarly, many of the labor-rent agreements that replaced the manorial corvée after emancipation were also in Latvian.

To these usages, the nationalist activists added new dimensions. As educated professionals in a linguistically diverse area of the empire, they knew how inadequate Latvian was with respect to the specialized terminologies contained in German and Russian. Hence they began to create neologisms for objects and ideas for which contemporary Latvian did not have words. Such an effort was already pronounced in the writings of Juris

Figure 6. Krišjānis Valdemārs (1825–91), an editor of the outspoken Latvian nationalist newspaper *Pēterburgas avīzes* and one of the main activists of the Latvian national awakening.

Alunāns, the author of *Dziesmiņas* (1856); after him, Atis Kronvalds and others worked diligently to develop new vocabularies for humanistic fields. In the more specialized areas, such as botanical knowledge was Jānis Ilsters (1851–89); jurisprudence, Andrejs Stērste (1853–1921); and maritime affairs, Ansis Bandrēvičs (1850–1935).[31] The fate of the neologisms created in this period varied greatly, with their acceptance or rejection depending on their fit with popular usage. Thus, the Baltic German argument that assimilating to the German language (and the culture based on it) was mandatory for Latvians who wanted to advance themselves sounded increasingly like defending an artificially sustained privilege.

The language renovators also contributed to the rapid growth of Latvian-initiated and Latvian-sponsored organizations that began in the late 1860s. All such organizations were suspect in the eyes of the Saint Petersburg government, especially in the non-Russian western borderlands; to receive official permission to exist, Latvians declared that their groups were overtly nonpolitical. Thus, for example, in 1868 the Riga Latvian Association—henceforth the largest, wealthiest, and most influential Latvian organization in the Baltic provinces—was described as a relief organization to help famine victims; in 1873 the planners of the Latvian Song Festival—the first in a long series of festivals with deep nationalistic overtones—described it to the authorities as a purely cultural event.[32]

These organizations inspired others, particularly agricultural societies, of which, by 1913, there were 192 in the Latvian area of the Baltic provinces. Each organization, regardless of purpose, created yet another microenvironment where the Latvian language would be used, and each cultural event signaled, at least to the Latvians gathered from various parts of the Baltic provinces, that they had a common cultural heritage (and language) to celebrate. Nationalist activists did not need such reminders, but most Latvians benefited by any occasion that signaled their presence in public affairs. By 1887, Livland alone had some 231 Latvian organizations, ranging from local literary groups to fire insurance societies.[33]

By the mid-1880s, then, a Latvian presence—an "awakened nation"— had become a force to be reckoned with. For most of the nineteenth century, scholars outside and in the Baltic area had praised the Latvian oral tradition—folk songs (*dainas*), stories, legends, and proverbs—viewing it as worthy of systematic investigation; from the 1850s onward, Latvian nationalists had convincingly argued for the language's centrality to the experience of being Latvian. The Latvian-speaking population in the Baltic was using the language in a host of new practical circumstances (including polemics) requiring all manner of written expression, and Latvian literary artists were adding to these an increasingly diverse popular culture. The durability of this popular culture was occasionally questioned, but even the

Figure 7. The choirs in the first national Latvian Song Festival, June 28, 1873, parading from the Riga Latvian Association headquarters to the festival grounds in the city's Emperor's Garden.

Baltic German liberals, after some intensive institutional skirmishing that lasted into the early 1880s, were generally reconciled to living in a cultural atmosphere—certainly in the cities—that was increasingly multilingual.

At the personal level, the situation was more ambivalent. Many nationalists had married women of German background, only to witness their offspring losing all contact with Latvian-language culture. Those who assimilated could be seen as abandoning an "awakened" nation rather than just moving upward socially. Švauksts, a caricature in the first Latvian novel, *Mērnieku laiki* (Time of the surveyors; published in 1879 by Reinis and Matīss Kaudzīte), was a stereotype of a jumped-up Latvian behaving and speaking as if he were a Baltic German (i.e., of the upper class).[34] That kind of social self-criticism suggests a growing self-confidence among writers who were finding that writing in Latvian was normal, rather than an experiment.

Figure 8. An illustration by E. Brencēns from the first Latvian novel, *Mērnieku laiki* (1869), showing Švauksts, the rural Latvian trying to dress and act like a Baltic German.

By the mid-1880s, the Riga Latvian Association had been active for some twenty years, implementing a broadly based program of cultural development through its various committees. Another Latvian literary magazine—*Austrums*—was founded in 1885, and Latvians were able to subscribe to such newspapers as the *Latviešu Avīzes* (est. 1824), the moderately nationalistic *Baltijas Vēstnesis* (est. 1868), *Balss* (est. 1878), *Baltijas Zemkopis* (est. 1875), and *Tiesu Vēstnesis* (est. 1880).[35] Thus for Latvians born in the 1850s and early 1860s, a quarter century of socioeconomic transformation and culture building was demonstrable proof that Latvians were not simply an undifferentiated mass of peasants.

THE ADVENT OF RUSSIFICATION

Changes begun during the 1860s and 1870s took a different turn in the 1880s, when the Latvian nationalists' flirtation with the Slavophile movement in Moscow and Saint Petersburg bore unexpected fruit. In the hope that the imperial government would help diminish Baltic German privilege, in 1870 Latvians tried to present special petitions of grievances to Alexander II asking for further reforms; subsequently the Latvian nationalists Krišjānis Valdemārs, Fricis Brīvzemnieks (1846–1907), and Kaspars Biezbārdis (1806–86), who wrote for the Slavophile press, made it clear that they would welcome an expansion of imperial influence in the Russian provinces.[36] But the imperial government was forming its own plans for the non-Russian Baltic borderlands, particularly after the assassination of Alexander II and the ascension to the throne of Alexander III (1881–94), a conservative monarch who generally distrusted the Baltic Germans.

In 1882, during an inspection of conditions in the Baltic provinces, the delegation located in Riga and led by Senator Nikolai Manasein, permitted petitions to be sent to it from the Latvian countryside. Some twenty thousand such petitions—the result of a drive organized by the Riga Latvian Association—arrived in Riga, laying out a host of grievances. Among other things, the petitions asked that the Baltic provinces be changed from three (Estland, Livland, Courland) to two, reflecting the linguistic distribution of the majority populations (Estonians and Latvians); that the provincial parliaments (*Landtage*) be replaced by the zemstvo form of government, as in Russia proper; that the judicial system be reformed and its Baltic German officials replaced with Russians; and that Latvian (Estonian in northern Livland) become the language of instruction in all urban and rural schools and that Dorpat University establish chairs in those languages.[37] The outcome was not what the Latvians expected, however, for Manasein proposed a generalized Russification program to the tsar that cut at least as much against Latvian nationalist aspirations as against Baltic German privilege. In this political game, the Latvians had been naive.

Beginning in 1885 and continuing for the next decade and a half, there were several waves of Russification decrees. One directed that the German and Latvian languages be replaced with Russian in the legal and educational systems of the Baltic area. Other directives sought to enlarge the Russian Orthodox Church by mandatory conversions of partners of mixed marriages. Despite the cultural threats embodied in those Russification directives, however, and the harm done to the careers of many non-Russian speaking schoolteachers and other professionals, the entire Russification effort did not have the intended results, at least as far as the Latvian population was concerned. For though these measures lay like a pall over Baltic cultural life for the next three decades, they were stringently enforced only from 1885 to 1895.[38] Even during that period, however, there was no diminution of Latvian-language writing, either in belles lettres or in practical sorts of writings. Indeed, judging by quantity, the total volume of Latvian-language writing increased; in terms of quality, that writing became differentiated across all literary genres and included more individual works. The number of new titles published in Latvian rose from 181 in 1884 to 822 in 1904; the total print runs rose from 168,000 units in 1884 to more than five million in 1904.

The generation that came of age and entered professional life in the 1890s learned Russian, as they were required to do, and German because it was still a necessity for virtually all professional education. But there is no sign in that generation's memoirs that learning the "culture languages" diminished their attachment to, or ability to use, Latvian, and the nationality statistics of the period do not suggest any appreciable increase in assimilation to the Russian population or Russian culture. If anything, among Latvians coming of age in the 1890s, obligatory Russian in the education and judicial systems intensified their dislike of tsarist autocracy, which joined Baltic German socioeconomic hegemony as a target for a new generation of critics.

OTHER AWAKENINGS

The concept of *tauta* (in German, *Volk*) remained prominent from the mid-1850s onward, but the population it was meant to refer to changed substantially. As we have seen, over the centuries Latvians had never been *only* a peasantry, but by the mid–nineteenth century the notion that the Latvian *tauta* had a shared outlook made a good deal of sense. Even then, of course, the Lettgallians tended to be left out of the Latvian *tauta* because virtually all the "national awakening" activists came from the Latvian populations of Livland and Courland, especially the latter.

By the 1880s, the concept had become less clear, producing disagreements about what the real interests of the Latvian *tauta* were and who could best articulate them. In the 1870s, there had been a division of opinion within the Riga Latvian Association about how best to use its resources—whether for economic development or for cultural institutions.[39] In the same decade, the writer and journalist Juris Māters (1845–85) charged urban Latvians with willfully ignoring Latvian farmers; in the 1880s the short-story author Jēkabs Apsītis (1858–1929) began publishing dour accounts of the evils of urban life in contrast with the purity of rural Latvian folkways. But in the 1890s, the questions of who belonged to the *tauta* and who was entitled to speak in its name began to receive more radical answers, as a new generation of Latvian intellectuals discovered—or awakened to—Marxist thought and as the first signs of an "awakening" appeared among the Lettgallians.

The segment of the 1890s Latvian intelligentsia that began to reject nationalist ideas contained many subgroups, even though it was usually assigned a collective identity (in part through self-description) as the *jaunā strāva* (new current).[40] The members of *jaunā strāva* were all receptive to late-nineteenth-century progressive ideas—historical materialism, Darwinism, feminism, realism, democracy, and the like—but manifested their modernity in different ways. Eduārds Veidenbaums (1867–92) and his fellow students at Dorpat University wrote irreverent and critical poems and published a multiauthored collection of writings (*Pūrs* [Dowry], 1891–94, in three volumes) to introduce the general public to the new ideas. Others, such as Jānis Jansons (Brauns) (1872–1917), attacked Latvian literature as irrelevant to the social realities of Latvian life. Jānis Pliekšāns (Rainis, pseud.) (1865–1929) and his brother-in-law Pēteris Stučka (1865–1932) edited the newspaper *Dienas Lapa* (Daily paper), which after 1893 became a house organ for the *jaunstrāvnieki* (adherents of the new current) and the first major Latvian outlet for Marxist criticism of Baltic socioeconomic conditions. Their Marxism came from German social-democratic writings, especially from Austria-Hungary, where the nationality question also loomed large in both theory and practice.

The *jaunstrāvnieki*, given their ideological bent, focused on cleavages in the Latvian population: the fact that in the late 1890s there were in the Latvian countryside more agricultural laborers (591,000) than landed peasants (approx. 418,000), according to the 1897 census; the fact that, from 1864 to 1894, the number of factory laborers in Riga alone had grown from 6,114 to 24,920, while the Riga Latvian Association, it was charged, represented only the Riga Latvian merchants and property owners;

and the fact that income differentials among Latvians in both the country-side and the urban areas were immense.[41] All those aspects of Latvian life were attributed to the Marxist theory of class warfare, with progressive activists championing of the landless, the proletariat, and the poor generally.

By 1897, the *jaunstrāvnieki* had established cells in Riga and other major cities and had participated in meetings calling for strikes and labor stoppages. That year, the authorities moved against them, arresting eighty-seven and bringing most to trial in 1899. Their sentences varied from imprisonment to exile from the Baltic provinces to police supervision. As a result, the movement lost its immediate efficacy, but its activists became even more radicalized. The *jaunā strāva* denied the right of "conservative" organizations like the Riga Latvian Association to monopolize the concept of *tauta* but took the existence of a Latvian *tauta* for granted and used Latvian to express the "new" ideas. Its radicalism took for granted what the "national awakeners" of the 1860s and 1870s had had to persuade Latvians to believe in. By staying inside the Latvian-language world to sharply attack Latvian nationalism, the *jaunā strāva* demonstrated that the Latvian intelligentsia could sustain deep cleavages without diminishing the Latvian presence in the Baltic littoral.

The 1890s witnessed another challenge to that presence when nation-ally minded activists appeared among the eastern Latvians—the Lettgalli-ans.[42] As noted earlier, because of their location, the Latvian serfs in the westernmost districts (total population in 1897 of 502,000) of Vitebsk that adjoined Livland had not been emancipated until 1861 and thus experi-enced much slower rates of socioeconomic differentiation. Throughout most of the 1860–1900 period Lettgallia was the least urbanized of the Latvian territories and its population the least literate. The nationalist activists in Courland and Livland were aware of the Latvians in Lettgallia and wrote about them occasionally, but their "awakening" efforts were directed at the Latvians in the Baltic provinces proper.

Not until the late 1890s did there emerge among Lettgallians a nation-ally minded intelligentsia that began to explore their folklore and language and to announce Lettgallian as an important variant of the Latvian lan-guage. That first generation was divided on the question of its exact ties to the western Latvians. Francis Trasūns (1864–1926) and Pēteris Smelteris (1868–1952), among others, argued that Lettgallians were part of the Latvian *tauta* and urged that publications emerging from and aimed toward a Lettgallian reading public use the conventions that had been worked out for the language by the Riga Latvian Association's committees.[43] By con-trast, Francis Kemps (1876–1935) stressed the importance of the Lettgallian dialect and argued that the Lettgallians should strive to preserve their regional uniqueness.[44] In these decades, calls for cultural separatism in the Lettgallian intelligentsia remained muted; such calls suggested, however, that merging western and eastern Latvians would require far more attention than that process had needed in Courland and Livland.

THE REVOLUTION OF 1905

In the opening years of the twentieth century, the population of the Latvian territories of the Baltic littoral (including Lettgallia) was the largest it had ever been—some 1.9 million according to the 1897 census—as was the proportion of Latvians within it (68.3 percent, or about 1.3 million persons). Latvians had always had an impressive numerical presence, but now they also possessed undeniable weight in socioeconomic and cultural life.[45] But their political influence was weak: they were excluded from provincial government, had only minimal representation in the Riga city council, and by 1905 had gained majorities in the city councils in only four small towns. The dedication of the *jaunstrāvnieki* to reform and the increased radicalization of many in their ranks after the 1897–99 crackdown were symptoms of the frustrations that were felt throughout the Latvian population.

Those frustrations came to a head in the events of 1905, a revolutionary year in the rest of the empire as well as in the Baltic provinces. In the Latvian territories of the Baltic littoral, however, the impulse to revolution was filtered through local conditions and therefore directed not only against unemployment, substandard labor conditions and imperial autocracy in the major cities but also against the Baltic German baronial regime in the countryside. What transpired in 1905 in the Latvian territories was a culmination of continuous illegal organizational activity in the preceding half decade, principally by social democrats. They continued to establish cells even after the 1897–99 crackdown, printed and distributed antiwar leaflets during the Russo-Japanese War, agitated for the restoration of university autonomy, and participated in industrial actions of various kinds, including strikes in the major factories. In June 1904, representatives from various social-democratic groups had met illegally in Riga in what became the first congress of the Latvian Social Democratic Workers' Party (LSDWP). At that time, the party reportedly had about twenty-four hundred members, eighty-five of them living outside Latvia.[46] The party decided at this point to admit only Latvians but established a federative committee to further collaboration with similar non-Latvian groups in the Latvian territories.

It was the federative committee that, a few days after Bloody Sunday in

Saint Petersburg (January 22, 1905, when the tsar's troops killed seventy demonstrating civilians), called for a general strike in Riga and the other large cities in the Latvian territories, triggering a series of strikes, demonstrations, meetings, and more violent actions throughout 1905. Spreading quickly to the countryside, these actions came to involve persons who did not adhere to a social-democratic ideology. Provincial authorities called for a military alert in March and April in both Livland and Courland, requesting additional units of the Imperial Army. The LSDWP held its second congress in June, urging continued action in cities and rural areas. In August, martial law was proclaimed in Courland. In October, the federative committee called for a meeting in Riga of representatives of all opposition groups, ranging from conservatives to the moderate left. In early November, some one thousand persons met in Riga for the first congress of Latvian schoolteachers; in mid-November, also in Riga, there was a congress of about nine hundred Latvian county (*pagasts*) representatives.

Paralleling such meetings were strikes as well as violence directed against symbols of Baltic German landowner power. It is estimated that in 1905 some 316,000 persons participated in strike activities in Livland and Courland. In the countryside, in the Latvian areas of Livland, 183 estates and seventy-two manorial residences were partially or completely put to the torch; a similar fate met 229 estates and forty-two manorial residences in Courland. Rural destruction was estimated to be about 3.8 million rubles in Livland and 5.0 million rubles in Courland.[47]

By the end of November 1905 martial law had been proclaimed in Livland as well, and by early December, in the third Baltic province of Estland; in mid-December the reaction by imperial and provincial authorities began, lasting until April 1907. In rural areas the so-called punitive expeditions, made up of units of the Imperial Army as well as privately organized, baronial self-protection (*Selbstschutz*) squads, seemed less interested in restoring order than in exacting revenge. Totals for the various categories of killed and punished persons vary: one estimate is 2,596 executed revolutionaries; 713 sentenced to prison or hard labor, 2,656 resettled to the northern regions of Russia or subjected to corporal punishment; and 1,817 expelled from the Baltic provinces. All told, perhaps as many as nine thousand persons were punished in some fashion; in addition, an estimated five thousand fled westward, with some four thousand ending up in North America.[48]

The events of 1905, as well as the numerous trials and executions that continued throughout 1906 and the first half of 1907, had a galvanizing effect on the Latvian intelligentsia, regardless of political disposition and post-1905 residence. The most radical revolutionaries were dead or living abroad, rededicating themselves to the revolutionary cause. The rhetoric of

class warfare became more pronounced in their writings about their homeland, and the revolutionary socialism of Vladimir Lenin, increasingly attractive.

Moderate Latvian socialists—abroad and in the Baltic area—searched
for unifying ideas and began to articulate, however, hesitatingly, the notion
that there should be a Latvian state, perhaps autonomous, perhaps independent. Although not participants in the 1905 actions, liberals and centrists,
appalled by the harshness of the punitive expeditions and disillusioned
with both the imperial system and the Baltic Germans, became active in
provincial- and imperial-level politics. In these bodies they argued for
decentralized imperial power and increased power to the indigenous peoples of the Baltic area.

Although using the printed word as an indicator of activism is a crude
measure, it is telling that in the 1905–7 period there were 107 periodicals
in Latvian, 63 of which were daily or weekly newspapers; by 1910 there
were forty-five publishing firms in Riga alone and seventy-nine in the
Latvian territories,[49] more than at any time in the past. The Latvian-run
Central Agricultural Society, founded in Riga in 1906, opened 106 local
societies throughout the Latvian territories; the largest union of coopera-
tives (called *Konsums*) had seventy-four constituent societies. By 1914,
there were in the Latvian territories some 860 different agricultural organizations with an estimated sixty thousand members. Thus, the events of
1905 and their aftermath seem to have given organizational momentum to
Latvian activism, fueled by the ferocious images those events had planted
in the Latvian imagination.[50]

The poet Jānis Rainis contributed one very powerful image of the 1905
turmoil in his dramatic play *Uguns un nakts* (Fire and night), which was
published in 1905 but not performed until 1911.[51] Rainis, a member of the
jaunā strāva in the 1890s and a well-known social-democratic literary
figure, had been imprisoned in 1897 for participating in strikes and then
exiled from the Baltic provinces to Russia proper. In prison, Rainis translated Goethe's *Faust* into Latvian, thus advancing Latvian literary language.
Returning to Latvia in 1903, he continued his impressive literary output
and in early 1905 announced his support for revolutionary activity in a
collection of poems called *Vētras sēja* (Reaping the storm). Later that year,
in *Uguns un nakts,* Rainis reached into the literary legacy of the national
awakening for the symbol of Lāčplēsis—the Bearslayer.

Lāčplēsis was not new to Latvian thinking. In 1888 the poet-soldier
Andrejs Pumpurs (1841–1902) had published a long poem called *Lāčplēsis*
to provide Latvians with a national epic, as Elias Lönnrot had done for the
Finns in the *Kalevala* and F. R. Kreutzwald for the Estonians in the
Kalevipoeg.[52] In Pumpurs's popular epic, Lāčplēsis—one of many indistinct
figures in Latvian folklore—was raised to national stature, clothed with

heroic attributes, and—as a symbol of the Latvian *tauta*—depicted in an eternal struggle with the Black Knight, who embodied the rapacity of the Baltic German overlords.

In Rainis's drama the protagonists are the same but their symbolic meaning, in light of Rainis's political beliefs, more ambiguous. In *Uguns un nakts,* Lāčplēsis could be seen as both the proletariat and the Latvian *tauta* and the Black Knight, as both the Baltic Germans and the Russian autocracy. At the end of both the poem and the play, the conflict between Lāčplēsis and the Black Knight is unresolved; they are locked in an unending conflict. Because the 1905 revolution had not appreciably changed the distribution of political and socioeconomic power in the Baltic area, the play's ending corresponded to reality and the penultimate lines—"the battle's ongoing and will not end" (*vēl cīṇa nav galā un nebeigsies*)—promised future conflict.

The strong staying power of these images added to the popularity of the play, which in the space of four years (1911–14) was performed 112 times in the New Theater in Riga. Fifteen years later, the new Latvian government would create the Lāčplēsis Order as an award for heroism in the Latvian war of independence (1919–20). Eight decades later, during the perestroika period in Latvia, the poet Māra Zālīte (b. 1952) and composer Zigmārs Liepiņš (b. 1952) used the theme and the protagonists in their rock opera *Lāčplēsis,* which adroitly linked the "stagnationism" of the Soviet period to the 1905 revolution as well as to the nineteenth-century national awakening.[53]

RIGA: EMERGENCE OF A METROPOLIS

The city of Riga was both a recipient and an agent of the radical socioeconomic changes of the second half of the nineteenth century. For one thing, it received the lion's share of the rural-to-urban migration that became particularly heavy after the imperial reforms of the 1860s made it easier to move across external and internal provincial boundaries (see table 2). If in 1867 the Riga population was almost four times larger than it had been at the beginning of the nineteenth century (1800: 27,894; 1867: 102,590), by 1913, when its population stood at 517,264, it was more than five times larger than it had been in 1867 and more than eighteen times larger than it had been in 1800.[54] This expansion totally altered the city's physical appearance. The old city walls were torn down in the 1860s, and the city limits rapidly moved outward with the annexation of erstwhile suburbs. With every generation, medieval structures disappeared and were replaced by modern buildings, main thoroughfares were expanded and

TABLE 2:
THE URBAN POPULATION OF LATVIA AND THE
POPULATION OF RIGA, 1862–1989

Year	Urban Population of Latvia (%)	Population of Riga	Urban Population Living in Riga (%)	Total Population Living in Riga (%)
1862	14.8	102,590	55.9	8.2
1881		169,329		
1897	28.3	282,230	51.6	14.6
1913	40.3	517,522	50.3	20.2
1925	32.8	337,699	55.8	18.3
1930	34.9	377,917	57.5	19.8
1935	34.6	385,063	56.2	19.7
1959	53.0	580,423	52.3	27.7
1979	68.0	731,831	42.6	29.0
1989	70.8	915,000	48.4	34.2

SOURCES: Andersons, *Latvju enciklopēdija 1961–1982,* vol. 4, pp. 78–87; Skujeneeks, *Latvija: zeme un iedzīvotāji,* pp. 211–13; Asaris, *Latvijas pilsētas,* pp. 156–60; Zvidriņš and Vanovska, *Latvieši: statistiski demogrāfisks portretējums,* pp. 56–67; Švābe, *Latvju enciklopēdija,* vol. 1, pp. 770–71; Drīzulis, *Rīga socialisma laikmetā,* pp. 347–52.

paved, and working-class residential areas proliferated. The narrow, inward-turning medieval heart of the city became a "historic" part of an expanding city center, and the nearby small rural estates to which the urban patriciate had repaired to escape the summer heat of its urban dwellings became neighborhoods within the city's borders.

Riga also received the lion's share of Latvians who decided to move during the 1860s and after.[55] In 1867, the four largest language groups in Riga were Germans (42.9 percent), Russians (25.1 percent), Latvians (23.6 percent), and Jews (5.1 percent); by 1913 the proportions had changed dramatically, diminishing all (Russians, 21.2 percent, Germans, 16.7 percent, Jews, 4.5 percent) but the Latvians (39.6 percent). Indeed, by 1913 two new language groups—Lithuanians, 5.5 percent, and Poles, 5.5 percent—had made a strong appearance, increasing the dominant groupings to six. The absolute numbers of all language groups in 1913 of course were larger than in 1867, and in these terms the Latvians, with a population of 187,135, outdistanced by far the next-largest grouping—the Russians—who stood at 99,985.

To Latvians, and especially the nationalistically inclined Latvian intelligentsia, these population shifts were just and proper: Livland's largest city, surrounded as it was by a veritable ocean of rural Latvian-speakers, should also be *Latvian*. To the Baltic Germans, however, who continued to monopolize Riga's municipal government, Latvians flooding into Riga threatened their traditional privileges and therefore required vigilance. To the Saint Petersburg government, whose officials and military personnel constituted a large proportion of Riga's Russian population, the city was an economic dynamo, yielding substantial tax revenues from industrial enterprises and serving as an important center for a burgeoning import and export trade. In this view, Riga's traditional Baltic German elite and its clamorous Latvian population could be controlled by Russification. After all, in most important respects the Baltic Germans were already loyal to the Crown,[56] and the Latvians, with a number of their leading nationalists seemingly cooperating with Russification, were not thought of as being a threat to imperial control. Latvian nationalists, whose agenda was to increase the socioeconomic and cultural weight of Latvians in the city, saw the Baltic German and Russian power wielders as increasingly alien presences.

Imperial reforms of urban government during the 1860s and 1870s reduced the power of the traditional urban patriciate in Riga and opened the city council elections to property holders regardless of language or nationality. Linking the vote to property holding disadvantaged Latvians, however, because their principal sources of income were industrial wages and small commercial enterprises. The number of Riga residents with electoral privileges remained small in any event, reaching only 4,535 in 1913 when the city had almost half a million inhabitants. Hence Latvian representation in the Riga city council remained negligible before the turn of the century (two places out of seventy-two in 1878, eight of eighty in 1901) and increased slowly thereafter (fourteen in 1905, twenty-six in 1909, twenty-three in 1913).[57]

Moreover, despite the solidarity that nationalists urged on all Latvians, the Riga Latvians had had fundamental disputes from the first. The Riga Latvian Association, founded in 1868, divided over whether the national cause would be best served by wise economic investments or by its support of cultural activities. The Riga Latvian leadership was accused of arrogance toward rural Latvians, and the socialistically inclined *jaunstrāvnieki* criticized all nationalist undertakings as a front for moneymaking.

At the same time, none could gainsay the Riga Latvians as the force behind continued Latvian cultural growth. After the closing of *Pēterburgas Avīzes* in 1865, the most important newspapers—notably *Baltijas Vēstnesis* (from 1868) and *Dienas Lapa* (from 1886)—were published in Riga; Riga was the site of the Polytechnic Institute, where an increasing number of Latvian students received a higher education with every decade. The thousands of Latvian in-migrants attracted by Riga's expanded industry provided a readership for not only the Latvian periodical press but also Latvian authors. By the early 1900s, then, Riga had joined the ranks of the cosmopolitan capitals of northern Europe, making the city that much more attractive to Latvians.

LATVIANS IN THE RUSSIAN EMPIRE

Although from the mid-1880s onward imperial policy—in the form of Russification, the arrests and expulsion of the *jaunstrāvnieki,* and the punitive expeditions of 1906–7—seemed designed to weaken the loyalty of Latvians to the empire, that result, when it surfaced, was more of an individual than a collective response. Even after the events of 1905, Latvians continued to make use of the opportunities the empire offered, as statistics concerning emigration from the Baltic area suggest.[58] By 1897 (the year of the first imperial census), an estimated 115,000 Latvians (or about 8 percent of all Latvians in the empire) had taken up residence within the empire but outside the Baltic provinces proper, most of them (about 95.7 percent) in the ten provinces of European Russia. Yet most did not move far: the non-Baltic provinces containing Latvian populations above ten thousand were Kovno (35,188), Pskov (11,127), Vitebsk (10,270), and Saint Petersburg (10,251). These numbers continued to grow in the post-1905 period; by the beginning of World War I an estimated 220,000 Latvians (or about one-eighth of all Latvians) were living in non-Baltic Russia. The vast majority of these—in both the pre- and post-1905 period—left the Baltic area in search of land, but a not insignificant portion sought employment in developing industry. Thus, in 1897, 3,044 of the Latvians in Saint Petersburg, Pskov, and Kovno Provinces were factory workers.

A smaller proportion left the Baltic to pursue higher education in the universities, academies, and institutes of Saint Petersburg and Moscow. Although most Latvian young people in search of higher education took their degrees at the university in Dorpat (Tartu) and the Riga Polytechnic Institute (where Latvian matriculants increased from 1,037 in 1894 to 2,088 in 1913),[59] there was nonetheless a constant drain to the Russian university cities. It is likely that a high proportion of those educated in Moscow and Saint Petersburg found employment outside the Baltic provinces, some as teachers and docents in institutions of higher learning. Also, Latvians with appropriate professional degrees were still viewed with suspicion by the dominant Baltic Germans: of the 150 Latvians who by 1905 had theology degrees from Dorpat (Tartu), only about half found work in the Lutheran churches in the Baltic (thirty in Courland and forty-five in Livland).[60] The extent to which this "brain drain" would have become permanent is impossible to calculate because many returned to the Baltic region after the founding of the Latvian state in 1918. But the pre-1914 figures suggest that the geographic movement of energetic and ambitious Latvians was not constrained by such policies as Russification. Those policies, by and large, tended to convert educated Latvians into reform-minded opponents of autocracy rather than enemies of all things Russian.

That reformist strain was also evident among the Latvians elected from the Baltic area to the Duma, which, after 1906, became the first imperial-level parliament. There were six Latvians in the first Duma, seven in the second, and two apiece in the third and fourth.[61] Most of them were oriented toward the Constitutional Democrat (Kadet) bloc in the Duma; their numbers included not only Jānis Čakste (1859–1927), who would later become the first president of independent Latvia, but also F. Grosvalds, F. Trasūns, and J. Goldmanis, who remained active in post-1918 Latvian politics. The presence of these Latvians—however small their numbers and however ineffectual the institution to which they had been elected—nonetheless symbolized a willingness by the Latvian elite to engage with the Russian political system and seek reforms. In the immediate pre–World War I years, the spectrum of Latvian political opinion included a right wing (e.g., Fricis Veinbergs, editor of *Rīgas Avīze*, which opposed the existence of the Dumas), a moderate center (the Duma deputies and their supporters), and a left (the Latvian Social Democratic Party and those in it who leaned toward Vladimir Lenin and the Bolshevik movement). Only on the left and the right was it possible to find uncompromising ideologues; most Latvians who were involved in politics at the local, provincial, and imperial levels tended toward flexible, centrist positions. Latvian public opinion, by contrast, was more protean than the positions assumed by these political leaders.

7 The Latvian Nation Acquires a State

In the Latvian territories of the Baltic littoral, the decade after the 1905 revolution saw a mix of the old and the new. The Latvian-language literary culture continued unabated, putting to rest the question of whether the language could sustain a high-quality cultural life. Although Russification laws were on the books, their implementation was ineffective. The number of Latvians who attended and graduated from institutions of higher learning, entered such relatively prestigious professions as law, medicine, and finance, and became successful urban businesspeople rose steadily, expanding the Latvian middle class. The opportunities for upward mobility were becoming greater, as economic growth moved the Baltic provinces into the ranks of the most developed parts of the empire. This was reflected in demographic statistics: in the period from 1897 to 1914, the population in Latvian territories in the Baltic littoral (including Lettgallia) increased from 1.9 million to 2.5 million, with that of Riga going from 282,000 in 1897 to 517,000 in 1913 (see table 1, p. 88).[1]

Among the Latvian intelligentsia the existence of a Latvian *tauta* (nation) was now taken for granted, even on the political left, where it was conceived of as a cluster of antagonistic classes. That the Latvian *tauta* was an important presence in the Baltic area was not questioned, but there was concern about its future. The *tauta* had relatively low rates of natural growth as the result of a low birthrate and thus was not expanding as a proportion of the total Baltic population.[2] Continuing high out-migration by Latvians, despite Baltic economic growth, was particularly worrisome.

One estimate held that, not counting the political exiles of the 1905 upheaval, some five thousand Latvians (including Lettgallians) left the Baltic area annually for other parts of the empire, so that, by 1914, an estimated 14.8 percent of the Latvian *tauta* was not living in what the Latvian intelligentsia now saw as Latvian "home territory."[3]

The most pessimistic assessment with respect to national survival was that, in the years just before World War I, only some 60 percent of the population of the Latvian territories was Latvian, with other nationalities being more prominent in such nonagricultural domains as politics (Germans and Russians), business (Germans and Jews), and the professions (Germans and Jews). Even in agriculture, only an estimated 39.5 percent of all arable land in the Latvian territories was owned by Latvian farmers; 90 percent or so of the rest was the property of some 1,300 private estates, owned or leased for the most part by Baltic Germans and, in Lettgallia, by Russians and Poles.[4] But the Latvian political elite had an opportunity to rectify those injustices after 1914, when Russia's participation in World War I caused imperial power to wane. It was at this time that the idea of self-determination gained in appeal, though by no means among all Latvians.

OPPORTUNITIES DURING WORLD WAR I

Germany declared war on Russia on August 1, 1914, and within six months the southern part of the Baltic littoral (East Prussian, Polish, and Lithuanian territories) had become a war zone. Among Latvians in the Baltic provinces, the intelligentsia enthusiastically supported the Russian war effort, grouping the Baltic Germans with the German Reich as enemies of the empire and attacking the few Latvian voices that warned of Russia's long-standing antinational policies.

In the early weeks of the war, some 20,000–25,000 soldiers mobilized in the Latvian territories had been sent to East Prussia, and more followed in later months.[5] The Imperial Army, however, was defeated by the eastward-moving German forces in the battles of Gumbinnen, Tannenberg, and Masurian Lakes during the autumn and winter of 1914; by the autumn of 1915, after repeated Russian failures, the Germans occupied the whole of Courland south of the Daugava River. By that time, an estimated 10,000–15,000 Latvian soldiers had fallen in battle, most of them fighting in the Third and Twentieth Corps of the Russian army.[6]

Moreover, the Germany army in the southern Latvian territories brought about an unprecedented dislocation of the Courland rural population. Approximately 570,000 refugees fled or were evacuated from Cour-

Map 5. Independent Latvia, ca. 1930

land as the German army consolidated its hold over that province and established a new military-civilian government there. Most of the refugees went to Livland and Lettgallia, but an appreciable number moved north to Estonia and east into Russia proper. The flow of refugees (Latvians and others) northward and eastward continued for the next two years; one estimate suggests that, by the time the flow had abated, some 760,000 persons had left the Latvian territories of the littoral.[7] To the invading Germans, however, the Baltic seemed not so much Russian-occupied territory as land that had been German and now needed to be taken back permanently. Although public opinion among Baltic Germans was by no means uniformly on the side of the Reich, an appreciable number of prominent persons thought exactly in that revanchist fashion.

To those Latvians for whom the war had a political as well as a military meaning, the German army's rapid arrival in the Baltic area underscored the Russian political and military leadership's incompetence. In August 1915, a strong argument was made to, and accepted by, the Russian high command that separate units of Latvian infantry *(strēlnieki)* should be created within the Russian army. By early 1916, eight such battalions with about 130,000 soldiers had come into being.[8] Largely a volunteer force, predominantly but not completely Latvian, they joined the many thousands of Latvians who had been and continued to be conscripted to units of the Russian army that were fighting on the eastern front.

Because the volunteers in the Latvian units came from all ranks of society, they were the core of a potential Latvian "national" army, a phenomenon much feared by the Russian high command and by the Baltic German political leaders. There is little doubt that the Latvian population tended to view them as precisely that from the moment of their formation. From 1915 to 1917 the Latvian units fought on the Courland front and around Riga, suffering some thirty-two thousand casualties that seemed to many a waste of Latvian life in that the German military position improved somewhat during that period. The considerable demoralization that ensued among the Latvian *strēlnieki* after the military leadership turned out to be incompetent caused them to greet the 1917 February revolution in Russia with considerable hope. Having fought the enemy as loyal subjects of the tsar, Latvian soldiers demonstrated widespread support for some kind of definitive change.[9]

While the Latvian *strēlnieki* were engaging the Germans on the Riga-Daugava front, immense numbers of refugees in unoccupied Livland (Vidzeme) confronted tsarist authorities with a seemingly intractable problem. All told, some 2.6 to 3.0 million refugees flowed into Russia proper from the Polish, Lithuanian, and western Latvian territories. The Russian government was therefore grateful when the Latvians began organizing refugee relief efforts, beginning in September 1915 with a congress of representatives of eighty-three Latvian relief organizations that established the Central Committee for Refugee Relief.[10] By early 1916, the committee had registered 730,000 Latvian refugees; by March 1917, some one million Latvians had taken up life outside the Baltic area.

The revolution in Russia did not disturb this organizational activity; if anything, it gave the Latvian relief organization leaders reason to believe that they would be moving into positions of greater authority and thus shaping their own future. In mid-March Prince Lvov, head of the provisional government, replaced the Russian governor of Livland with a Latvian, Andrejs Krastkalns (1868–1939). Later in March the first of a number of meetings of representatives of various Latvian organizations was held in Riga to prepare for elections to new local and regional political councils meant to replace the crumbling structures of the imperial state. A new political party, the Agrarian Union, was founded in May under the leadership of Kārlis Ulmanis (1877–1942) and Miķelis Valters (1874–1968) to represent the interests of rural Latvians; in the same month, in the city of Valmiera, a congress of landless rural people and day laborers met.[11]

Paralleling these efforts, and as the result of relentless organizing activity by the Latvian Social Democrats (especially the increasing number of Bolsheviks in their midst), the first *soviets* (councils) appeared in cities, factories, and Latvian units of the army. The soviets drew their support from the less wealthy, the landless, and the not inconsiderable number of soldiers in the disillusioned Latvian infantry units.[12] In this new, heady, and rapidly changing atmosphere, all public discussion became politicized and a great variety of plans were put forward about the Latvian future. With organizational activity riding the wave, virtually every person in the Latvian population had a point of view, ranging from the most conservative (collaborating with the Baltic Germans to oppose the Bolsheviks) to the most radical (Bolshevik revolution). The notion of a free Latvia was conceived with many permutations: partial autonomy, complete autonomy, complete independence, all along the political spectrum. Yet given that Courland was under German occupation and that much of the Latvian population was scattered and struggling to survive, it was not clear who the various self-styled representatives at the various meetings truly represented. Anyone with a vision of the Latvian future could claim to be speaking on behalf of the Latvian people without much fear of contradiction.

ALTERNATIVE FUTURES

The fall of 1917 brought two major turns of events: in September, the German army attacked Riga, took the city, and headed northward into Livland (Vidzeme); in late October Lenin and the Bolsheviks came to power in Petrograd, replacing Alexander Kerensky and the Provisional Government. The German victory marshaled support for the "national" cause (in which Kārlis Ulmanis, the leader of the Agrarian Union, was becoming increasingly prominent) and convinced some (including the Lutheran pastor and popular novelist Andrievs Niedra [1871–1942]) that the Germans, including the Baltic Germans, were likely to be victorious and thus had to be compromised with. The successful Bolshevik coup in Saint Petersburg (now Petrograd) enhanced the popularity and influence of the Latvian Bolsheviks, headed by Pēteris Stučka (1865–1932), but their cause—to bring about a proletarian revolution among the Latvians—was weakened because not all Latvian socialists were Bolsheviks and therefore the Latvian left was in a fragmented state.

These different visions of the Latvian future competed during the next three years, though compromise with the Germans—Reich or Baltic—never had much popular support. The national cause began consolidating its position in mid-November 1917 with a meeting in the city of Valka of the first Latvian National Assembly, which proclaimed itself a provisional national council and announced, first, that *Latvia*—consisting of Vidzeme (Livland), Kurzeme (Courland), and Latgale (Lettgallia)—was an autonomous unit in the Russian state and, second, that Latvia's future would henceforth be determined by a constitutional assembly elected by the Latvian people.[13] On their side, the Latvian Bolsheviks retained widespread support among the Latvian *strēlnieki*, as well as in such German-unoccupied cities as Cēsis, Valmiera, and Valka. But during 1918, their power in the Latvian territories waned, as many of the *strēlnieki* units and civilian Bolsheviks left for Russia (after Russia's withdrawal from the war in March) to become defenders and builders of the embryonic institutions of the new Russian Bolshevik government.[14]

Thus, during 1918 the supporters of the Latvian national cause gained time in which to strengthen their position and to undergo their own radicalization—shifting from support for an autonomous to an independent Latvia. After the general armistice of November 11, 1918, representatives of all the major political parties (including the Latvian Social Democrats but not the Bolsheviks) met in secret in Riga on November 18 and formed a national council, which then publicly proclaimed the existence of a Republic of Latvia and a Latvian Provisional Government.[15] The provisional government was headed by Kārlis Ulmanis, leader of the Agrarian Union, who was unanimously chosen to be prime minister (see appendix). Riga, of course, was still occupied by the German army and lay entirely within the Latvian territory under German control. Despite the armistice, the participants in the November 18 meeting were taking a risk because the leaders of the German forces showed no signs of withdrawing and in fact were formulating plans for colonizing the Baltic area. Nonetheless, in December the provisional government began to turn into a potentially effective political structure, as—at least on paper—ministries were created, ministers assigned to them, and staffs recruited. In this embryonic bureaucracy, there was a handful of talented Baltic Germans, though most did not believe that the provisional government would survive.

INDEPENDENCE WARS

The skeptics, who were not limited to Baltic Germans by any means, were right in the short run because, during the two years after November 1918, it did not look as though the Latvian Provisional Government would survive. The Baltic area was strategically and economically important to outsiders, and they would not surrender their hold without a battle. A large segment of the Latvian *strēlnieki* had pledged its loyalty to the Bolshevik cause and, even before the November proclamation of independence, was being readied by the Russian Bolshevik government to help keep the Latvian territories part of Russia. The *strēlnieki* who remained in Latvia and on whom the provisional government relied for its military protection, although small in number, became the core of a new national army. Creating such an army was difficult, however, given the continuing German occupation and the provisional government's lack of resources and international recognition. The Latvian Bolsheviks returned in December 1918, and from then until May 1919, the Latvian territories not under German occupation (most of Vidzeme and all of Letgallia) had a provisional Latvian Soviet government headed by Pēteris Stučka.[16]

This short-lived government was created over the objections of the Latvian Bolsheviks, who argued that a separate state in Latvia was unnecessary and that the proletariat wanted to be part of a Sovietized Russia. Lenin thought otherwise, believing that the recently proclaimed national governments in the Baltic area needed to be countered by Soviet governments. Although he was directed by Lenin to take charge of the Latvian Soviet government, Stučka felt that such a government was likely to be temporary; consequently, the months of his rule were marked more by a settling of scores than by a serious effort to launch a new state. Stučka's manner of governing, patterned on that of the nascent Bolshevik government in Russia, included imprisoning and executing real and potential "bourgeois" and "counterrevolutionary" enemies, thus squandering much of the grassroots support the Bolsheviks had had in the Latvian population before the end of 1918.

During these months, the Ulmanis government, having fled from the Bolsheviks to the western Latvian port city of Liepāja (Libau) in German-occupied Kurzeme (Courland), was in a sense under German protection. Despite their precarious position, Ulmanis and his government ministers retained considerable freedom of movement and action and were thus able to continue to seek resources and support both in Latvia and abroad.

On the battlefield, the Latvian soldiers were joined in an uneasy alliance with the German armed forces against a common enemy: the armed Latvian Bolsheviks. The considerable pessimism that existed about the ultimate success of the Ulmanis government even in Latvian circles and the Germans' own agenda were revealed when a Latvian countergovernment was created in mid-April 1919 by Andrievs Niedra, who favored extensive cooperation with the Germans.[17] This government was supported by Rüdiger von der Goltz, a German military commander who wanted to destroy the Ulmanis government's credibility. But the recapture of Riga from Bolshevik control by German and Latvian troops at the end of April 1919 changed the balance of forces. The Niedra government had supposedly replaced the Ulmanis government by this time, and the freeing of Riga was expected to raise Niedra's prestige and grassroots support. In reality, it demonstrated his utter dependence on the Germans, and, as Latvians reestablished themselves in Riga, Niedra and his cabinet quickly faded from view, becoming an appendage to further German intrigues. With the Latvian Bolsheviks in retreat toward the Russian border, with the Niedra government having lost what little popular backing it had, and with the idea of an independent Latvian state becoming popular, Ulmanis's difficulties in enlarging the national military force diminished. Joint military operations with the Germans during the late spring succeeded in pushing the Bolshevik armies into easternmost Latvia—Lettgallia—where they remained until the spring of 1920.

In the meantime, there appeared on the scene one Pavel Bermont-Avalov, a brazen military adventurist who imagined himself a Russian count, together with some divisions of the Russian White Army. Von der Goltz and Bermont-Avalov formed an alliance that also involved a handful of Baltic German barons, with Bermont-Avalov commanding this joint German–White Russian–Baltic German army, which was about thirty thousand soldiers strong. By October 1919 the Ulmanis government had raised a fighting force of about 11,500 soldiers, a national army strongly supported by the population.[18] By early December, the so-called Bermontians *(bermontieši)* had been defeated, and the only threatening presence remaining on Latvian soil were fragments of the Bolshevik army in Lettgallia. These were driven out of Latvian territory by mid-January 1920, after the Ulmanis government had negotiated for military assistance from Poland for the action and Lenin's Bolshevik government had decided not to support further military efforts in the Baltic area.

The victorious Ulmanis government signed an armistice with Soviet Russia on February 1, 1920, and a peace treaty on August 11. At that time Soviet Russia also recognized Latvia as an independent state, thus becoming one of the first of the "great powers" to do so. (The United States did not extend such recognition until 1922.) The Soviet government's diplomatic recognition of Latvia, however, did not preclude continuing propaganda attacks, in and through the Comintern, on Latvia's government as an instrument of the "bourgeoisie" that had robbed the Latvian proletariat of its birthright. Be that as it may, by the summer of 1920 Latvian territory was free of all foreign military forces and the Ulmanis government could begin to rebuild. The First World War had enlarged the Latvian *tauta*'s presence in the Baltic area, resulting in a state in which the Latvian *tauta* had the dominant voice.

LATVIANS IN THE SOVIET UNION

The 1920 treaty with Soviet Russia signaled that there was indeed a Latvian state with a Latvian government, and this recognition meant that a number of wartime refugees felt it safe to return. In the period 1919–27 an estimated 223,000 Latvians returned from Russia (12,000 returned from other countries).[19] Still, in the 1920 *Soviet* census, 151,400 respondents gave Latvian as their nationality; in 1927 6.6 percent of those Latvians said they were members of the Communist Party. Thus, to a substantial number of Latvians living in the Soviet Union, the prospect of life in an independent Latvia did not seem enticing, and they chose not to return.

It would be a mistake, however, to believe that all the Latvians who remained in Soviet Russia (after 1922, the Soviet Union) adhered to the Bolshevik cause. There were Latvian Lutheran congregations in the Soviet Union until the 1930s, and large numbers of these non-Bolshevik "Soviet Latvians" had migrated to Russia before World War I and the Bolshevik revolution of 1917. At the same time, however, other Latvians had played an important role in the Bolshevik movement in Russia, especially during the 1917–22 period.[20] The veterans of the revolutionary years remained active in the party after the Russian civil war, and, though in 1922 Latvians were only 0.15 percent of the population of Soviet Russia, 2.53 percent of Communist Party members were Latvians. At the Thirteenth Party Congress in 1924, some 7 percent of the delegates were Latvians.[21]

Lenin's variant of revolutionary communism had attracted significant numbers of Latvian political activists from the beginning, and a large proportion of the early adherents remained faithful to Bolshevism throughout the turmoil of the revolutionary and civil war years. Others, such as the *strēlnieki*, came to support the Bolshevik effort during the war years. Given the large number of Latvian Bolsheviks, no single motive can be said to have been dominant. To intellectually inclined activists such as Pēteris Stučka, ideological conviction was probably paramount, for it was exhilarating to be part of a movement that billed itself as the carrier of the future. Among the *strēlnieki*—some twelve thousand of whom, having fought in the Russian civil war against the armies of the White generals, thus helping the Bolsheviks to victory, returned to Latvia—motivation grew out of increasing disillusionment with the institutions (and military leaders) of the imperial state and, subsequently, the provisional government. The Bolsheviks promised decisive action and, more important, land and political power to the "workers and peasants." But there were also opportunists who cast their lot with whatever organized movement was likely to be victorious, as well as those who saw supporting the Bolsheviks as a matter of survival in a situation that offered few good options. Returning to Latvia, where a *national* (and a "bourgeois") state was being created, would not have attracted those who had never felt a deep national identity and who therefore did not view the creation of a *Latvian* state to be of much importance. One could just as easily remain Latvian and help build a proletarian state.

During the 1920s and the first half of the 1930s, therefore, the Soviet Latvians created a flourishing Latvian subculture in Leningrad and Moscow. In 1923 in the Soviet Union there were 150 Latvian-language schools, seventy libraries, sixty reading rooms, and sixty social clubs of various kinds; by 1934 the number of schools had increased to 188 and the number of clubs to two hundred.[22] Latvians in large numbers entered the apparat of the new Soviet state at all levels. Stučka, for example, helped create the legal framework of the new state; Jānis Rudzutaks (1887–1938) helped devise mechanisms by which the party could control the pace of economic development; Valērijs Mežlauks (1893–1938) helped create the economic planning system; Dāvids Beika (1885–1946) served as commissar of heavy industry; Jēkabs Peterss (1886–1938) assisted Feliks Dzerzhinski in creating the principal organ of state security (the Cheka); and Jēkabs Alksnis (1897–1938) served from 1931 to 1937 as the commander of the Soviet air force. Note that the dates of death of these leading figures are almost all in the 1937–38 period, reflecting Joseph Stalin's purges of "old Bolsheviks" from the party cadres. It is estimated that in 1939 the number of Latvians in the Soviet Union was about 126,000, suggesting that some 74,000 Soviet Latvians had "disappeared."[23] The party sent many of those who survived the purges, or their offspring, to Latvia in 1940–41 and after 1945 to assume leading roles in the government when that country became the Latvian Soviet Socialist Republic.

THE PROBLEMS OF RECONSTRUCTION IN LATVIA

At the conclusion of hostilities on Latvian territory in 1920, the Ulmanis provisional government did not have to start from zero. In its short three-year existence it had created, partially and in many cases only on paper, some of the necessary administrative machinery of a state. Nor did political energies need to be revived: as the period of independence began, there already existed two major organized political parties—the Social Democrats and the Agrarian Union—as well as a host of smaller ones, all of them to a greater or lesser extent seasoned by years of organizing effort and political debate and brimming with ideas about how the new state should be structured and its business conducted. During the war years the embryo of a diplomatic corps had also come into being, as Latvian politicians, though having no formal training as diplomats, had had to negotiate with foreign governments for recognition and support of the provisional government.

But the government could not remain provisional much longer. A national Constitutional Convention (Satversmes Sapulce), with 150 members, was elected and convened on May 1, 1920.[24] Jānis Čakste (1859–1927), who had earned his reputation by working on refugee relief, was elected president of the assembly and of the Latvian Republic; Kārlis Ulmanis, the head of the prestate Latvian government, became premier. The Constitutional Convention now had to deal with the nation's business—primarily reconstruction but also creating a constitution and the electoral machinery for a permanent legislature—until the first parliament could take over.

The tasks confronting the convention were daunting. Before the war, the Latvian territories of the Baltic provinces had a population of about 2.5 million, but by the mid-1920s, after the refugees had returned, that number stood at 1.7 million—a decrease of 32 percent. Among those Latvians who had left permanently, in 1926 an estimated 150,000 were living in the Soviet Union, many of them Bolsheviks. A population loss of this magnitude signified all variations of human tragedies and a substantial diminution of the labor force.

Because virtually all major industrial and transportation equipment had been moved to the interior of Russia during the war, industry was paralyzed. Transportation and commercial facilities (especially seaports) were severely damaged. In the countryside, some 24 percent of all farmsteads had been destroyed or damaged, and approximately 29 percent of all arable land in the Latvian territories lay fallow. After the collapse of at least three different currencies—the Russian ruble, the German occupation currency, the currency of the brief Bolshevik government—the monetary system was chaotic, with barter widespread in most parts of the country. The natural eastern market had disappeared, western markets had been disrupted, and Latvia's immediate Baltic neighbors—Estonia and Lithuania, themselves newly established states—also faced severe economic and financial problems. Moreover, the Allied powers presented the new Latvian government with a large bill for assistance during the independence wars. Although all problems cried out for immediate and simultaneous attention, reconstruction progressed in logical order under the Constitutional Convention. The most important need was for a reliable national currency, which was created by issuing 200 million Latvian rubles—an interim currency—in treasury notes; in 1922, the Latvian ruble was replaced by the lats, at the exchange rate of fifty Latvian rubles for one lats.[25] The Constitutional Convention simultaneously addressed the problem of landlessness, the speedy resolution of which all Latvian political leaders understood to be necessary for the new state to retain its legitimacy in the eyes of the *tauta*.

Not all reconstruction activities in Latvia needed a national-level assembly to begin, for much work had been going on since the 1918 proclamation of independence, when the Latvian government was too weak to do anything but issue declarations. All this, in turn, continued the organizational impulses that in the prewar period and during the war years had created a host of Latvian economic and political organizations. Thus the Latvian governments of the 1918–20 period as well as the Constitutional Convention were products of those same organizational impulses, and the convention's work was less onerous because in many domains initiatives had already been taken to reorganize and reconstruct. A good example is the Latvian Lutheran Church, whose reorganization had been approved by the Ulmanis government in September 1919 and was well under way.

The patronage rights of the landed nobilities had been abolished, and the consistorial form of church government was being changed. The new Lutheran Church constitution of 1922 created a church with Bishop Kārlis Irbe (1861–1934) as its head; by 1936 he presided over the work of 325 Lutheran congregations (272 of them Latvian) with 288 ordained ministers (228 of them Latvians). Irbe was suceeded by Archbishop Teodors Grīnbergs (1872–1962) in 1931. The Riga diocese of the Roman Catholic Church had been renewed before the independence proclamation of 1918 and now consisted of 177 congregations. The organizational basis of the principal Latvian religious faith (in 1935, 85 percent of the population of Latvia) had thus been "Latvianized" early in the life of the new state. Even so, among Lutherans, some 30 percent remained unregistered in any congregation, possibly because the epoch when Baltic Lutheranism was presided over by Baltic Germans was still part of the recent past.[26]

THE AGRARIAN REFORMS OF THE 1920s

Population movements in the Latvian territory during the war years had, by 1920, resulted in a severe decline in the urban population (40.3 percent in 1914 to 23.5 percent in 1920). Thus, the population whose problems the Constitutional Convention was now addressing was more rural than it had been, and a higher proportion of it was ethnically Latvian—72.8 percent in 1920, as compared with an estimated 60 percent just before the war (1914). By weight of numbers alone, the problems of the Latvian rural population loomed large on the assembly's agenda. Beyond that, the proportion of rural landless persons remained high. Although a large (but unknown) proportion of the estimated 600,000 persons who were landless before the war were not in Latvia after it, rural landlessness in 1920 could have involved some 40–50 percent of the Latvian rural population. The Latvian government remembered how the landless had been attracted by Bolshevik promises of land in Latvia as well as in Russia. Moreover, by 1920 large and middle-sized landowners, the majority of them not Latvians but residents of the new Latvian state, were associated in public opinion with the now-defunct but traditionally privileged upper orders. Those chiefly Baltic German barons but also Polish landowners in Lettgallia had not only recently resisted and conspired against the creation of the Latvian state but had also benefited from a centuries-old agrarian system in which the Latvian *tauta* had been serfs.

For the assembly, notwithstanding the laws it had adopted for the protection of minority nationalities, to allow these relatively wealthy non-Latvians to continue to own or control some half of all agricultural properties would have been to commit political suicide. Thus on September 16, 1920, the convention adopted the first part of two-part agrarian reform law; the second part was passed on December 21.[27] The law required, first, nationalization of privately held rural properties (including forested land) exceeding 110 hectares in size and, second, the creation of a government land fund that would supervise the nationalized properties until they could be redistributed. The process of implementing that law, which took from 1920 to 1937, thus continued to transform the sociopolitical basis of land ownership in Latvia during virtually the entire interwar period, as reconstruction activities of other kinds were being carried out and as a parliamentary system came into being.

Expropriation resulted in 9.2 million acres of land being transferred from the previous owners to the Land Fund, most of it (81 percent) from privately owned estates.[28] The question of compensation was debated at length in the assembly, with the parties on the right proposing compensation at 1920 market prices and the parties of the center and the left opposing compensation of any kind. No compensation won by three votes. The first Saeima (Parliament) debated the compensation question again in 1924, with the same results. Understandably, large landowners—principally the Baltic Germans—objected to what to them was a confiscatory measure and appealed to the League of Nations, but without success. The most the Latvian government was willing to do was to pay off debts on the confiscated land, which came to about 1.5 million lati.

Redistributing the expropriated land had begun before the compensation issue was settled because getting land to the landless quickly was deemed necessary for political stability and legitimacy, especially because the parties on the left stood ready to blame any hesitation on the "bourgeois" composition of the government. Identifying deserving recipients and the kinds of land to which they were entitled, however, was a complex process. Broadly speaking, persons who had served in the national armed forces received preferential treatment and, after them, those rural persons who could demonstrate that they had been and were landless. Beyond these groups were people who maintained that their existing farmland was insufficient to sustain their families. The land not redistributed to individuals was put to various public uses by the national and local governments.

The redistribution process reached its peak in the mid-1920s and lessened thereafter. By the end of the 1930s, some 143,000 agricultural holdings (about 52 percent of the total number of holdings listed in the 1935 census) had either been newly created or supplemented by the reform, creating a large stratum of new farmers *(jaunsaimnieki)*.[29] About 85 percent of these holding were thirty hectares (seventy-four acres) or less in size. Ownership, moreover, was not static because nonfarmers began selling granted land to farmers almost immediately. Some 43 percent (607) of the holdings granted to decorated veterans were sold, as were some 30 percent (580) of the holdings granted to families of veterans killed in the war and some 25 percent (6,427) of the holdings granted to other veterans. Not surprisingly, the group least likely to sell its holdings had received additions to existing farms (3 percent, 812). The percentage of new farmers who sold out stood at 19 percent, or 10,814 holdings.

In the final analysis, the reforms accomplished their main goal—to distribute land to those who wanted to farm. In 1920 in the Latvian territories there were 141,723 farmsteads; by 1935 that number had almost doubled, to 275,698. Also, by 1935 the number of rural landless (most of whom were now agricultural laborers) had fallen from an estimated pre–World War I high of about 600,000 to 135,953. At the same time, however, the rapid growth in the number of smallholders had a negative side: they could not easily introduce agricultural machinery, their small farms were labor-intensive, and they tended to go into debt. By 1939, there was a high inverse correlation between size of holding and indebtedness: on holdings of less than fifteen hectares, 137 lati were owed per hectare, and on holdings of more than one hundred hectares, 37 lati.[30] Although the agrarian reform had defused the *political* problem of landlessness, it had enlarged the *economic* problems of smallholdership, which, in a democratic state, could not fail to have political repercussions.

THE CONSTITUTION OF 1922 AND THE ERA OF PARLIAMENTARY GOVERNMENT

While the Constitutional Convention was dealing with agrarian reform and a host of other reconstruction measures, a committee of the convention was drafting a constitution *(Satversme)*, which the assembly voted on and passed on February 15, 1922, after extended debate on virtually every one of its eighty-eight articles.[31] The constitution contained two parts, the first dealing with the structures of the nation and the state, the second, with the rights and obligations of citizens. In the debates, the convention rejected the bicameral legislature (with an upper house and lower house) proposed by the German Party, perceiving it as a veiled attempt to preserve the social order *(kārta)* embodied in the now-defunct Livland Landtag. It also rejected a proposal by convention members from Lettgallia, who argued for autonomous status for their region. Perceiving in this the threat of separatism, the convention remained with the basic principle of the 1918 proclamation: that Latvia consisted of four coequal major divisions: Vidzeme, Latgale (formerly Lettgallia), Kurzeme, and Zemgale (the latter two produced by dividing the old Courland Province). Latgale, Kurzeme, and Zemgale enshrined the names of three pre-Christian tribal societies (Lettgallians, Couronians, and Semigallians).

The new constitution declared that Latvia was a democratic republic with a unicameral Parliament (Saeima) of one hundred members elected for three years, a president elected by a simple majority of the Saeima also for three years, an independent judiciary, and a cabinet (responsible to the Saeima) headed by the prime minister. An exceedingly liberal election law, passed in June, permitted any group of citizens, as long as they were all over twenty-one years of age, to propose a list of Saeima candidates in any of the five electoral districts (Vidzeme, Kurzeme, Latgale, Zemgale, and the city of Riga). The constitution also added the concept of a nation of Latvia *(Latvijas tauta)* to Latvian political discourse, thus recognizing that the Latvian nation *(latviešu tauta)* was one of a number of *tautas* in the new state.[32]

By the time of the first parliamentary election in October 1922, political opinions in Latvia were running high, having been fired up by the heated debates that preceded the two earlier elections (Provisional Government, Constitutional Convention) and that characterized the deliberations of these bodies. There was a superabundance of new political ideas: the Constitutional Convention, for example, only had time to discuss 260 proposals out of 622 brought before it and passed only 200 of the 260. How to satisfy those whose ideas had not been considered or whose ideas had been rejected became a central problem for the new parliamentary system. The April 1920 election to the Constitutional Convention had revealed a strong tendency among the politically active to fragment: about 700,000 persons voted for 150 deputies from sixteen parties or groupings. The dominant parties in the convention were the Social Democrats (fifty-seven deputies), the Agrarian Union (twenty-six), and the Lettgallian Farmers Party (seventeen); the other thirteen each had less than ten deputies.

The twelve years between 1922 and 1934 witnessed the election of four Saeimas (1922, 1925, 1928, 1931) and the formation and dissolution of thirteen cabinets of ministers.[33] Over these four elections, voter participation remained high (82 percent, 74 percent, 79 percent, and 80 percent), as did the number of competing candidate lists (88, 141, 120, 103). Perhaps more ominously, the number of lists receiving no parliamentary representation in the four Saeimas remained higher (forty-two, ninety-three, sixty-six, forty-six) than the number that did (twenty, twenty-seven, twenty-four, twenty-one), signaling various kinds of dissatisfaction outside the parliamentary framework. Of the "fractions" (in Latvian, *frakcijas*) in the Saeima, long-term trends were not particularly strong: the deputies of two largest fractions tended to fall in number (Social Democrats, thirty-eight, thirty-seven, thirty, twenty-one; Agrarian Union, seventeen, sixteen, sixteen, fourteen) over the four parliaments, whereas the deputies representing

Figure 9. The house of the Livland nobility (*Ritterschaft*), built in 1867. After 1920 the building became the seat of the Latvian Saeima (Parliament) of the interwar Latvian republic and serves the same function today.

minority fractions tended to rise slightly (fifteen, fifteen, eighteen, seventeen), as did those of the centrist fractions (nine, eleven, ten, nineteen). In all four Saeimas, the coalition principle had to be followed to achieve working majorities.

Although the shifting numbers and the often extreme political speeches suggest that political opinion during the four Saeimas remained volatile, examining the relative strength of the political parties (and groups) reveals a considerable amount of continuity. Beginning in the preparliamentary period and continuing throughout the four Saeimas, the dominant parties, both of which had strong extraparliamentary organizations, were the Social Democrats (formally the Social Democratic Workers' Party) and the Agrarian Union.[34] Both parties were strongly represented (relative to other groups) in all four Saeimas, which was not surprising in that by the early 1930s both had chapters in virtually all the electoral districts in the country.

The parliamentary Social Democrats generally avoided coalitions, entering them in only two cabinets, and remained in the opposition. By contrast, the Agrarian Union dominated high political office: three of Latvia's four interwar presidents (Jānis Čakste, Alberts Kviesis, and Kārlis Ulmanis) were affiliated with it; Union ministers formed coalitions in eleven out of the thirteen cabinets; and Unionists served as prime ministers in ten of the thirteen cabinets. At the same time, two Social Democrats—Fricis Vesmanis (1922–25) and Pauls Kalniņš (1925–34)—were chosen for the position of president of all four Saeimas.

Such continuity was even stronger in the membership of the standing committees of the four Saeimas (twenty committees in each of the first three and eighteen in the fourth). They met even when the Parliament was not in session, and their members in time became deputy-specialists in the major areas of state administration (taxation, defense, education, foreign policy). Indeed, by the end of the parliamentary period there had come into being a corps of professional deputies whose nineteen members had served in every one of the four Saeimas. Perhaps the greatest continuity was in the nationality composition of the four Parliaments: Latvians were the dominant nationality group throughout the period (eighty-four deputies, eighty-four, eighty, eighty-three).

In terms of political ideas and interests, the deputies of the four Saeimas can be divided into five major groupings or blocs, all of which manifested a significant presence during the period though in different combinations of major and minor parties.[35] The socialist bloc, dominated by the Social Democrats for the whole period and receiving from 28 to 38 percent of the total vote in the four elections, also contained such lesser parties as the Socialist Jewish Bund (1st, 2d, 3d Saeima), Right Wing Social Democrats (1st, 2d, 3d Saeima), and the crypto-communist Peasant and Labor bloc

(3d and 4th Saeima). The left-center bloc, receiving from 9 to 13 percent of the total vote, had as its strongest representative in all four Parliaments the Democratic Center Party but included such minor groupings as the Economic Union, the Lettgallian Progressives, and the New Farmers (Jaunsaimnieki). The agrarian bloc, receiving from 25 to 34 percent of the vote, was dominated by the Agrarian Union but included as well such groupings as the Small Landholders, the Lettgallian Christian Farmers, and the Zemgallian Christian Farmers. The right wing bloc, receiving from 8 to 9 percent of the vote, had no dominant party but was represented in all four Saeimas by no less than three small parties, the Christian Union, the Lettgallian Union, and the Christian Nationalists. The national minorities bloc, receiving from 15 to 19 percent of the vote throughout the period, had as its strongest member in all four Saeimas the German Party, but this group had to share the spotlight with five different Russian groupings (including the Old Believers and the Russian Farmers Union), three Jewish parties (Agudas Israel, Misrachi, Ceire Zion), and the Polish Party.

Most small parties did not have organizations to rival those of the Social Democrats and the Agrarian Union, yet they played important roles in cabinet coalitions and not infrequently provided swing votes for crucial pieces of legislation. With the strength of the Social Democrats and the Agrarian Union, Latvian politics contained the seeds of a two-party system. Yet the electoral laws and perhaps the tradition of "no compromise on principles" left even the major parties vulnerable to their constituencies' periodically fragmenting. Even the nationality-based parties were not immune to this tendency, as shown by the Russian and Jewish splinter parties.

Although coalitions and majorities were difficult to create in the four Saeimas, the lawmaking of the parliamentary period did succeed in some basic state building. As happened in the governing institutions of the preparliamentary period, there were many more legislative proposals (3,267) than the four Parliaments had time to debate, and many more debated (1,685) than transformed into law (1,390). The laws that were passed, however, normalized the machinery of government at the national and local levels, created a judicial system, established regulations for acquiring citizenship and safeguarding civil rights, created border security and a system of military conscription, transformed the criminal law of the tsarist period into a workable system for the republic, established primary and secondary schools, ratified treaties between Latvia and other countries, worked out agreements on the handling of human and economic problems, and regulated the cultural and educational rights of the national minorities. Implementing these laws required an army of civil servants who in 1925 worked in eleven ministries and constituted 1.3 percent (about 14,600 persons) of the total labor force.[36]

POPULATION TRENDS

In 1914 the total population of the Latvian territories (Courland, southern Livland, and Latgale) was about 2.5 million; in 1920 the same territory—now independent Latvia—had 1.58 million inhabitants.[37] A large number of refugees (upward of 750,000; the precise figure is not known) had fled during the war years; approximately 7,100 Latvian soldiers were killed or wounded in the independence war (1919–20); and about 60,000 Latvians were excluded by the eastern border settlement as mandated by the 1920 treaty with Soviet Russia.[38]

Consequently, population questions were high on the new government's agenda in the early 1920s, first with respect to repatriation and then in connection with promoting natural population growth. The Latvian government, of course, could not force people to return to Latvia, but it could and did institute procedures to make repatriation easier. A substantial proportion of the wartime refugees had returned to their home areas before 1920, and in the period 1919–27 another 236,000 returned from Soviet Russia and other (mostly European) countries. In 1920 the returnees numbered about 88,000; in 1927 there were about 400.

The censuses of 1925 (1.84 million) and 1930 (1.9 million), however, suggested that rebuilding the population to its 1914 size would be an arduous task. Not surprisingly, all the interwar governments followed a pronatalist policy, using subsidies of various kinds and appealing to Latvians' patriotism to promote marriage and large families. These pronatalist policies, however, were seeking to reverse behavioral trends that predated the demographically destructive World War I period.

In the second half of the nineteenth century, the Latvian population of the Baltic provinces had exhibited a tendency to marry late and limit the number of children. The government's promarriage and pronatalist policies had indifferent results, with late marriage remaining a feature of the interwar Latvian population, the average age at first marriage thirty-two years for men and twenty-eight years for women.[39] Although the birthrate per 1,000 inhabitants stood at 21.9 in the 1921–25 period, it slid downward in every five-year period thereafter, standing at just over 18.0 at the end of the 1930s. The birthrate did, however, exceed the mortality rate, which went from 14.6 per 1,000 in 1921–25 to 13.9 at the end of the 1930s. As a result the total population grew but not at the rate government policy makers would have liked. By 1939 the total population of Latvia had reached nearly two million, still about half a million less than the total population in the years just before World War I.

A notable feature of the internal distribution of the Latvian population was a reversal of the pre–World War I urbanization trend. In 1914 the proportion of the Latvian population living in cities and towns of more than two thousand persons stood at 40.3 percent; by 1920 that proportion had been almost halved—to 23.5 percent—with a large portion of that drop being accounted for by the fall in Riga's population, from 520,000 to 181,000 during those years. The proportion of the urban population increased during the interwar years (34.6 percent in 1935), but it would not reach pre–World War I levels until the Soviet period. This rural population (65–75 percent during the interwar period) tilted interwar politics in an agrarian direction and underlined the importance of Kārlis Ulmanis's Agrarian Union as a political force. At the same time, describing Latvia as an agrarian state[40] in this period is overdrawn, given the continued dynamism of Riga and the other large cities such as Liepāja (in German, Libau), Daugavpils (in German, Dvinsk), and Jelgava (in German, Mitau), for what the cities lacked in numbers, they made up for in economic and cultural influence, with Riga leading the way.

The state of Latvia, however, was by no means a *Latvian* state, no matter how much Latvian ultranationalists sought to promote that perception. It is true that the proportion of Latvians in the population of Latvia increased during most of the interwar period but not by much: in 1920 Latvians constituted 72.7 percent of the population and in 1935, 75.5 percent. Correspondingly, there was a diminution of the proportions of three other nationalities in that time period: Germans from 3.6 to 3.2 percent, Byelorussians from 4.7 to 1.4 percent, Jews from 5.0 to 4.8 percent.[41] The only gainers, besides Latvians, were the "great" Russians (in Latvian, *lielkrievi*), whose proportions rose from 7.8 to 10.6 percent.

The 1940 census count was overtaken by the events of the Soviet incorporation, making it difficult to estimate nationality proportions at the end of the independence period. The fall of 1939 brought the almost total disappearance of the Baltic German population, which emigrated to Germany proper. Although the emigration of non-Latvian nationalities may have increased after 1935, it was balanced by the immigration of Jews seeking refuge from the anti-Semitic policies of Adolf Hitler's expanding Reich, especially after 1936. Throughout the interwar period and especially during the parliamentary era, the minority nationalities continued to be a significant part of Latvia's national life, their rights to autonomous cultural institutions being protected by the 1922 constitution and, after 1934, by the policies of the Ulmanis government.

THE ULMANIS COUP AND THE YEARS
OF AUTHORITARIAN GOVERNMENT

The early 1930s in Latvia witnessed the effects of the worldwide depression, with diminished industrial production, growing unemployment, and shrinking foreign trade. Correspondingly, there was an erosion of confidence in the efficacy of the Saeima. The ministries and specialized agencies were seen as doing their work relatively well, but there was a growing sentiment in much of the popular press and on the political right that the work of the Saeima was paralyzed by extraordinary political divisions that widened with every election. In 1932 and 1933 there were rumors of a pending coup, with the Social Democrats fearing such action from the right (i.e., the Agrarian Union) insofar as the right had more leaders who could count on wide public support for such action. The left also feared that Latvia would go the way of Lithuania and Poland, where strong authoritarian leaders had come to power in the 1920s, or Germany, where in 1933 Hitler had begun to erect the Nazi state.

On the right, the opinion was that the escape from governmental paralysis had to come via the actions of a strong president but that presidential powers could not be enhanced because the 1922 constitution had placed effective controls on this office. When in early 1934 the Agrarian Union proposed a constitutional change to, among other things, increase the powers of the national president, the Saeima voted it down. This action was evidently the last straw for Ulmanis and his supporters; on May 15, 1934, they launched a coup.[42] Ulmanis had the support of the leaders of the Latvian army, the *Aizsargi* (national guard) organization, as well as a handful of like-minded individuals in his own party. The coup was in fact peaceful. A substantial number of potential opponents (mostly Social Democrats) were imprisoned for a while, but no blood was spilled and only a few shots fired. Ulmanis dismissed the Parliament, disbanded the political parties—including his own Agrarian Union—and proceeded to govern as prime minister of a personally appointed cabinet of ministers. At the moment of the coup, Alberts Kviesis (1881–1944) was president; he remained in that office until his term expired in 1936, when Ulmanis merged the offices of prime minister and president in his own person.

Characterizing the years of Ulmanis's authoritarian rule as positive or negative depends on which aspects of the era are emphasized. By comparison with the other authoritarian, semidictatorial, and dictatorial rulers of interwar Europe, Ulmanis kept the worst temptations of authoritarianism under control.[43] There were no mass killings or settling old political scores through violent action, no mass long-term imprisonment of political opponents, or intimidation through the systematic use of state coercion. There was a political police, which kept people on both the political left and the right under close observation, as well as a fairly effective censorship of the popular press. Thus opposition to Ulmanis and his May 15 regime could not be expressed publicly, for fear of admonitions or perhaps withdrawal of government favors. Ulmanis's popularity and public relations skills, however, raise the question of how much opposition there actually was (with the exception of the continued, though generally silent, opposition on the political left, which had been suspicious of him even in the 1920s).

Ulmanis saw himself and was portrayed by his admirers as the *saimnieks* of Latvia: the head of the farmstead who was morally entitled to supervise and guide the lives of those under his charge and to project an image of unity to the outside world.[44] National unity, hard work, rural virtues, the belief that farming was the occupation closest to the Latvian soul and a necessity for Latvia's survival in the world economy—all these beliefs formed the basis of Ulmanis's pragmatic political philosophy.

Figure 10. Kārlis Ulmanis (1877–1942), leader of the Latvian Provisional Government, 1918–1920, prime minister in numerous cabinets of the interwar republic, and authoritarian president of Latvia, 1936–1940. Deported by Soviet authorities in July 1940.

Economic indicators during the Ulmanis years suggest that the worst effects of the depression were brought under control.[45] The gross national product increased, as did the export of Latvian goods, the government being quick to interfere with and guide the economy of the nation. The strong statism of the parliamentary period continued, becoming more pronounced after 1934. Ulmanis transformed the Latvian economy along the lines of Benito Mussolini's corporate state, with the government as the guiding and conciliating force in agriculture, labor, the arts, and welfare. The intention was to diminish and, if possible, eliminate the kind of fragmentation that, in Ulmanis's mind, had wrecked the parliamentary experiment. With the nation united, Ulmanis believed, the Latvians would be able to survive the extraordinary challenges that the Europe of the 1930s presented to the Latvian state.

The unity that he sought and that was celebrated by his supporters, however, had more than a tinge of xenophobia to it, though this was not implemented with the same kind of determination as in other countries. Gradually, after 1934, non-Latvians—Germans, Jews, Russians, and other peoples conceived of as nations *(tautas)*—were being squeezed out of positions of influence, especially in the economy.[46] What bothered Ulmanis and others on the right was the extraordinarily high proportion of capital and urban property that was controlled by non-Latvians; this, they felt, had to be corrected through the preferential treatment of Latvians.

RIGA AS THE CROWN JEWEL

Ulmanis was by no means the only interwar eastern European leader who came to power wielding a philosophy of national unification, nor was the agrarian (or peasant) base of his philosophy exceptional. By 1935 upward of 60 percent of Latvia's inhabitants were rural and Ulmanis's party—the Agrarian Union—was supposed to represent their interests. The irony was that this agrarian tilt existed side by side with an extraordinary pride in Latvia's cities, especially Riga.[47]

Riga, once one of the foremost urban centers of European Russia, was now the Latvian capital—the national seat of the government, the university, and other cultural institutions and, of course, the center of national political life. Its 1935 population of 385,063 (though substantially smaller than the 1913 count of 517,522) constituted almost 20 percent of the country's total and was almost seven times the size of the next largest city, Liepāja (57,098).[48] Riga could thus not fail to play a commanding role in a country as small as Latvia or to fascinate all who had been born and grew up in "the provinces." Consequently, the interwar years continued the pre–World War I pattern of population growth from in-migration from other parts of Latvia, rather than from a natural increase (more births than deaths).

Ulmanis repeatedly referred to Riga as an ethnic Latvian *(latviska)* city, and with respect to numerical preponderance he was correct. The 1913 population had included only 42.2 percent Latvians; by 1935 that proportion had grown to 63.0 percent. At the same time, it was the least Latvian of the four largest cities (Riga, Liepāja, Jelgava, Ventspils) outside Latgale (the largest city of which—Daugavpils—had a Latvian population of only 33.5 percent in 1935).[49] Behind Latvians, the largest nationalities in Riga in 1935 were Jews (11.0 percent), Germans (10.0 percent), Russians (8.6 percent), and Poles (4.0 percent).

The minorities were more visible because of their occupational concentration. As suggested by the 1930 census, Latvians were the majority or had a plurality in all occupation categories.[50] In agriculturally related occupations they dominated (85.7 percent), and they had commanding majorities as well in government (81.5 percent), transportation (74.3 percent), service (68.7 percent), and industrial jobs (61.2 percent). By contrast, they had only a plurality in public hygiene (52.2 percent), the professions (46.6 percent), and commerce (40.4 percent). In commerce Jews had second place (30.9 percent), followed by Germans (17.6 percent); in the professions, Germans were second (24.8 percent) and Jews third (15.5 percent); and in public hygiene Germans were second (21.0 percent) and Jews third (15.0 percent). What made the national minorities stand out even more and fed the resentment of the political right was that in 1930 Latvians ranked low as owners of the places where they worked. A ranking by status of the employed showed that Jews, Germans, Russians, Estonians, Lithuanians, and "others" were ahead of Latvians in the owner (in Latvian, *īpašnieks*) category and, in most instances, even in the manager (in Latvian, *uzņēmējs*) category. The only categories in which Latvians had a respectable showing were those of clerk (in Latvian, *ierēdnis*) and laborer (in Latvian, *strādnieks*), and there were twice as many German clerks as Latvian.

Thus Riga was and was not a Latvian city in terms of population and occupation statistics, but that did not prevent its continued expansion, which had started before World War I, as the center of Latvian-language culture. In 1919 the Stučka government had nationalized the buildings of the Riga Polytechnic Institute, converting them into the University of Latvia, which became the largest institution of higher learning in the country. Both the Latvian Conservatory and the Latvian Art Academy were also established in 1919 (after the Stučka government), and both institutions expanded their activities in the interwar years. The city saw a veritable explosion of museums and public libraries in the 1920s and by 1938 had 116 elementary and secondary schools (up from 44 in 1914). In 1931, of the country's 108 printing establishments (2,576 employees), 61 (2,170 employees) were located in Riga, and by 1936, 130 of the country's 154 leading magazines and journals were publishing there.[51] Although in all these areas of cultural production, a proportion of activities were carried out in languages other than Latvian (principally German and Russian), in most respects the public language of cultural business in cosmopolitan Riga was Latvian (see table 3, p. 108).

CULTURAL AND INTELLECTUAL LIFE BETWEEN THE WARS

The new Latvian state inherited from the last decades of the tsarist period an intellectual elite that was thinking autonomously even before political independence. Although its ranks had been thinned and scattered through emigration and war, most exiles returned to Latvia during the 1920s to join those who had not left to continue the job of culture building that had begun in the previous century. Symbolizing this healing was the return in 1920 from Switzerland of Jānis Pliekšāns, 1865–1929 (Jānis Rainis, pseud.), and Elza Rozenberga, 1868–1943 (Aspāzija, pseud.), the husband and wife who had been important figures in the *jaunstrāvnieki* generation and had continued their literary productivity (in Latvian) during their fifteen years of Swiss exile (1906–20). Krišjānis Barons (1835–1923), one of the leading activists of the national awakening period and the acknowledged "father" of the effort to collect and preserve the Latvian oral tradition (especially the *dainas*), symbolized the connection between the new state and an earlier generation.

The artists and intellectuals entering the new state as adults had received their education in the tsarist period, meaning that they had been forced to learn in Russian in school and that they remembered the resistance that the Baltic Germans had shown during the last decades of the tsarist period to sharing power with Latvians and the ideas of Latvian autonomy and independence. Hence artistic creativity—in the fine arts as well as in practical writing—throughout the interwar years had a national tone. The best artists sought to articulate universal values and forms using the Latvian language and imagery and sounds from the Latvian natural world, the Latvian past, and Latvian traditional music.[52] Assuming that the continuous production of a specifically Latvian culture depended on the appropriate national education of younger generations, virtually all intellectuals and artists in the interwar years were involved in pedagogy—at the University of Latvia (established in 1919), at institutes of music and art, and at every level of the public school system. In 1919/20, there were some 2,580 certified primary- and secondary-school teachers in the public education system in Latvia; by 1937/38 that number had more than tripled, to 9,137.[53]

The deeply felt imperative to continue to strengthen a Latvian cultural world resting on an educational system with a specifically Latvian content had had strong support in the Saeima during the parliamentary period. At the same time, the constitution of 1922 required that the cultural autonomy of national minorities be protected and subsidized, and therefore in 1935 about 23 percent of all public schools in the country were dedicated to providing primary and secondary education to children of Russian, German, Jewish, Polish, Lithuanian, and Estonian citizens of Latvia.[54] About 21 percent of the schoolchildren in Latvia in 1935 attended schools of this type. This dual character of the public education system did not change even during Ulmanis's authoritarian period, although after 1934 the slogan Latvia for Latvians became increasingly respectable and the children of mixed marriages (in which one partner was Latvian) were required to attend Latvian schools. Attendance at Latvian schools by children whose parents were both Latvian was obligatory. This nationalism in the public education system grated on some Lettgallian intellectuals, who saw it as an effort to destroy the linguistic uniqueness of the eastern part of the country. The Ulmanis government then sought to soften its hard-line official attitudes with a wide network of cultural subsidies and special grants for study and research to other European countries. Ulmanis's ideology of national unity, however, did not run its full course because of the start of World War II.

FOREIGN POLICY IN THE INTERWAR PERIOD

During the first years after the 1918 declaration of independence, representatives of the Ulmanis government—notably, Zigfrīds Meierovics (1887–1925), the first Latvian foreign minister after November 1918—had to overcome western governments' desires that Russia remain undivided as well as their suspicion that all Latvian political activists were Bolshevists. That image was furthered not only by the prominent services the "red" strēlnieki were providing to Lenin's government but also by Baltic German representatives in western countries.[55] In September 1921, Latvia was admitted to the League of Nations and thereafter used the league's principles to guide its foreign policy. Latvian political leaders believed that an effective League would offer small states the opportunity to register their presence in a world dominated by large powers, as well as some degree of security against external attack.[56] Through the efforts of Meierovics and others, de jure recognition of the new Latvian state by the United States was obtained on July 28, 1922.

Within this framework, the Latvian government developed a neutralist foreign policy, forging bilateral agreements over a wide variety of border, refugee, and economic issues but staying out of the sometimes bitter territorial disputes of even such close neighbors as Lithuania and Poland. Neutrality, however, kept Latvia from creating any effective security links with its immediate neighbors—Estonia and Lithuania—and thus during the interwar period, whereas larger powers tended to view the Baltic states as a virtually interchangeable set of countries, the three tended to practice a "splendid isolation" from one another. Not until 1934 was a document signed by the three states, which, although laying the groundwork for a Baltic entente, was halfheartedly implemented.[57]

During the 1920s, Latvia's relationship with its largest immediate neighbor—the USSR—remained cordial and keyed to the peace treaty signed by the two countries in 1920. Economically, the importance of the USSR to Latvia increased during the 1920s, especially after the signing of a five-year commercial treaty in 1927. Of Latvia's total exports, the proportion going to the Soviet Union increased from a range of 1.7–5.4 percent annually (1923–27) to a range of 9.0–14.7 percent annually (1928–32). But the benefits of this relationship were quickly exhausted—evidently for both sides—and the agreement was not renewed in 1932.

In 1933 exports to the USSR returned to the pretreaty level of 1.5 percent, where they remained throughout the Ulmanis period, when the desirability of economic autarky was stressed. As the low proportions of exports to its eastern big neighbor suggest, the Latvian government, even in the treaty years, was more interested in economic relationships with the West and after 1932 did not pursue the eastern connection with any great vigor. Still, during the remaining years of the 1930s, the cordiality continued, even though the Soviet Union occasionally accused Latvia of unfriendliness and, after Hitler came to power in Germany in 1933, of a pro-German orientation.

After 1934, Kārlis Ulmanis continued the neutrality policy, in part because he distrusted both the Soviet Union and Nazi Germany and in part because his government did not have any other options. Notwithstanding the fact that Latvia was a member of the League of Nations and had on its soil diplomatic representatives from all the major and minor powers, it was, because of its small size and population, isolated and vulnerable militarily and territorially. Historians analyzing Ulmanis's foreign policy conclude that he had convinced himself that maintaining strict neutrality, as well as demonstrations of goodwill and good intentions, would eventually overcome that isolation.[58] Moreover, by reiterating this theme in the late 1930s, he evidently persuaded much of the Latvian population that by minding its own business Latvia would be able to escape the predatory policies of other countries. At the end of his authoritarian rule, after World War II had started, the USSR had defeated Finland in the winter war, and the Soviet army was about to arrive in Latvia, Ulmanis was still "waiting for something and hoping for something" that would allow Latvians to live undisturbed.[59]

8 The Loss of Independence

By the spring of 1939 the authoritarian presidency of Kārlis Ulmanis was concluding its fifth year; by this time he appeared to have settled comfortably into his role as *vadonis* (leader). Despite pleas from some of his oldest political friends that he restore the 1922 constitution and the Saeima, Ulmanis showed little inclination of moving in that direction.[1] Instead, he and his cabinet were redesigning the Latvian economy using a planning system that increased government intervention in all aspects of economic life. Government economic indicators on unemployment and industrial and agricultural productivity suggested that Latvia had recovered from the effects of the depression of the early 1930s, and the neutral course of Ulmanis's foreign policy had kept Latvia from becoming deeply entangled in great-power rivalries.

Because political parties had been dissolved in 1934 and the popular press was censored by the government, it is difficult to discover the public's opinion of the regime. There is a great deal of direct and indirect evidence, however, that Ulmanis's general popularity remained high and perhaps even increased.[2] His support in rural areas was strong, extreme political opinions on both the left and the right could not find public expression, and the democratic left (the Social Democrats) had adopted a stance of resentful waiting. For the generation of Latvians just coming into adulthood, authoritarian rule had brought apparent political and economic stability, an expanding diversity of cultural life, and the idea, constantly reiterated by Ulmanis and his supporters, that Latvians had finally become masters of their own fate. Yet in the late summer of 1939 there began, as a subchapter of the history of World War II, a sequence of events that resulted, by July 1940, in the disappearance of the 1918 Latvian state and, by the end of the 1940s, in the nearly total transformation of the socioeconomic context in which Latvians would live for the foreseeable future.

THE MOLOTOV-RIBBENTROP PACT

The professed neutrality of small countries counted for nothing in the imperial calculations of the leaders of Nazi Germany and the Soviet Union. Adolf Hitler's need for insurance against a two-front war and Joseph Stalin's desire for a free hand in the former borderlands of the Russian Empire overrode all ideological enmity and resulted, on August 23, 1939, in the signing of a nonaggression and friendship pact between the Third Reich and the USSR, the *public* intent of which was to bring lasting peace to eastern Europe.[3] This agreement, however, contained secret clauses that divided Eastern Europe into interest spheres, assigning Estonia and Latvia to the USSR and Lithuania to Germany. In another secret protocol, attached to a border and friendship agreement signed on September 28, Lithuania was added to the USSR's sphere of interest. The August agreement assured Germany that the USSR would not interfere with an invasion of Poland because the USSR would benefit territorially. Hitler's occupation of Poland, which began on September 1, 1939, expanded the borders of the Third Reich to the borders of the USSR as well as to those of Lithuania. The partition of Poland, which on September 3 precipitated declarations of war by England and France against Germany, was concluded by the end of September.

At that time the governments of the three Baltic states wanted to avoid self-defensive measures that could become pretexts for further action by the USSR in its Baltic sphere of interest. The secret protocols of the August and September treaties were known to the Latvian government by early October, but Ulmanis could envisage no course of action save the reiteration of neutrality. Latvian foreign policy at this point consisted of hoping against hope. On his side, Hitler expected the USSR to establish full control of its Baltic sphere of interest; he had issued a call before the August treaty that the Baltic Germans (*Volksdeutsche* in Nazi terminology) settle their affairs in the Baltic and return "home" to the Reich.[4] As a result, over the final months of 1939, the Baltic Germans began a "repatriation" from Latvia that involved some fifty-two thousand persons by its conclusion in 1940 (eighty-four thousand from all three Baltic states). This withdrawal ended the presence in the Latvian territories of a German-speaking subpopulation that, since the twelfth century, had played an important role in the history of the Latvian *tauta*.

The next in this regional sequence of events was the USSR's demand that the three Baltic countries permit Soviet military bases on their soil. Estonia signed such an agreement on September 29, Latvia on October 5, and Lithuania on October 10.[5] The agreement with Latvia called for the stationing of twenty-five thousand Soviet troops, but the actual number by the early months of 1940 was probably larger than that. To create the bases, the Latvian government displaced the occupants of some 1,500 farmsteads. To explain such actions, Ulmanis and his advisers sought to portray the introduction of the bases as the result of normal transactions between friendly neighbors without mentioning the larger context. The Latvian government's strategy of accommodation was evidently meant to persuade the USSR that an independent, though cooperative, Latvia constituted no threat to the strategic interests of the USSR.

In the winter and early spring of 1939–40 the government's portrayal of the situation as normal seemed to be working. The presence of the Soviet bases was received calmly by the Latvian population, the soldiers stationed on them remained segregated from the general public, and high Soviet military officials were invited to government receptions and given tours of eastern Latvia to demonstrate the country's pacific intentions. Despite the public show, however, a worried Ulmanis hinted in some of his speeches of the need for vigilance. Still, the general policy of accommodation remained unchanged, even after Finland rejected the USSR's demands for similar bases and the USSR and Finland entered into the winter war. Reading between the lines in the speeches of Latvia's political leaders during the months of the winter war suggests that they understood that an accommodationist policy provided no safeguards, but this perception was not translated into any kind of action.

THE JUNE 1940 OCCUPATION

As World War II unfolded in Western Europe during the spring of 1940, the Latvian government continued its neutralist-accommodationist policy, waiting to see what would happen. Memoirs of the period suggest that there was in Latvia at that time an atmosphere of unreality, with daily life going on while Ulmanis and his advisers tried desperately to interpret what the effect on Latvia would be as the Germans invaded Denmark and Norway in April and France in May and the British and French fled Dunkerque. On May 18, Ulmanis gave the Latvian ambassador in England,

Kārlis Zariņš (1879–1963), the authority to act on Latvia's behalf internationally in case the Latvian government ceased to be able to issue instructions to its diplomats.[6]

When the decision was made in Moscow to occupy the Baltic states outright is not known, though Soviet military maps from the fall of 1939 and school maps from the spring of 1940 show the three Baltic countries as constituent republics of the Soviet Union. In any event, the collapse of resistance to Hitler in the west in the spring and summer months of 1940 provided an excellent cover. Thus in the first week of June, the ambassadors of Estonia, Latvia, and Lithuania in Moscow were summoned to the Kremlin and presented with a declaration: that the Soviet Union considered the present governments of the three states to be unfriendly and incapable of fulfilling the terms of the October 1939 agreements, that new governments must be chosen that would implement the agreement, and that Soviet armed forces be admitted to all three countries to ensure that friendly governments would come into being and the agreements fulfilled. During a confrontation between Foreign Minister Vyacheslav Molotov and Latvian ambassador Fricis Kociņš (1895–1949) on June 16, Molotov added that the Soviet army had already received orders to cross the Latvian-USSR border regardless of whether the ultimatum was accepted.

The Latvian government protested to no avail, and during the night of June 16–17 Soviet tank convoys entered Latvia on their way to Riga. There were at least ten to twelve Soviet infantry divisions and one tank division, involving as many as 200,000 soldiers.[7] On the morning of June 17, the people of Riga found Soviet tanks at key street crossings and government buildings. Later they listened to a radio speech by Ulmanis in which the president talked of difficult times ahead and urged the citizenry to remain in their places just as he was going to remain in his.[8] The Latvian government had decided not to oppose the occupation of the country, apparently fearing the loss of life such resistance would have brought to the grossly outnumbered Latvian army and to the civilian population.

THE PROCESS OF SOVIETIZATION

Events unfolded rapidly thereafter. During July 1940 Ulmanis signed documents that, among other things, formed a new Latvian cabinet of persons sympathetic to the new order and vetted by the Soviet embassy in Riga, where Andrei Vishinskii was supervising the political side of the occupation. Surprisingly, the new government did not include any Latvian Communists.[9] Augusts Kirchensteins (1872–1963), a microbiologist at the University of Latvia and an active member of the Soviet-Latvian Friendship

Society before 1940, became prime minister. On July 14–15 a quickly called election, controlled by the on-site Soviet officials in the embassy who permitted only one candidates' list, was held to create a "people's Saeima." Not surprisingly, the election returned a Saeima that promptly voted to proclaim Latvia a Soviet republic and to request annexation to the USSR. On July 21, Ulmanis resigned as president, turning that office over to Kirchensteins; Ulmanis himself was deported on July 22 by Soviet authorities to Moscow and then to Voroshilovsk (later Stavropol).

Immediately thereafter, the new Saeima began to pass measures aimed at rapidly transforming the Latvian economy by nationalizing all banks and bank accounts, business enterprises, and the property of professional organizations and churches. An agrarian reform law nationalized all privately owned land exceeding thirty hectares in size and distributed it to smallholders. After a delegation headed by Kirchensteins visited Moscow to request annexation, Latvia was admitted into the USSR on August 5, and on August 8 the Latvian Communist Party formally became a constituent part of the Communist Party of the Soviet Union.[10]

The *Gleichschaltung* (merging and coordination) of Latvian institutions and laws with those of the USSR continued throughout the fall of 1940 and the spring of 1941. The Latvian constitution was replaced by the constitution of the USSR on August 27, and during that month the Latvian national army began to be integrated into the army of the USSR. An estimated ten thousand Latvians now entered Soviet military service. The legal system of the USSR was adopted in Latvia (now the Latvian Soviet Socialist Republic) starting on November 8, and on November 25 the Soviet ruble was introduced as a parallel currency to the Latvian lats (the lats was withdrawn from circulation on March 25, 1941).

Strict control was established over the printed and spoken word, and publications (especially religious publications, including Bibles) of the pre-Soviet period were removed from libraries and stored in special collections or ground into pulp. The personnel of governmental institutions and what now had become state enterprises were vetted for loyalty to the new regime; those judged to be "reactionary" or "potential counterrevolutionaries" were dismissed or moved to peripheral positions. Such actions, however, created serious problems because there were not enough "loyalists" to replace tens of thousands of experienced and knowledgeable employees. The new authorities made repeated pleas to party officials in the USSR for experienced administrators and specialists; this recruitment was partially successful, but totally replacing the older workforce with new "cadres" proved to be impossible. With respect to agriculture, the new authorities repeatedly asserted that collectivization would proceed only on a voluntary basis. Although a few state farms (kolkhozy) were created in this period, resistance in the countryside to collectivized agriculture was deep and persistent.

The new authorities rationalized all these events and actions with appropriate concepts from Marxist-Leninist ideology.[11] The new regime was presented as the culmination of class conflict that had grown increasingly bitter in the Latvian Republic during the interwar years. It was said that in 1919, with material assistance from western imperialist powers, the Latvian "bourgeoisie" had repressed Stučka's embryonic Latvian Soviet Republic and created a state of their own. In that "bourgeois republic" agrarian reform had expanded the kulak class (in Latvian, *budži*), while the bourgeoisie, claiming to represent the Latvian *tauta*, consolidated their monopoly of political and economic institutions, as the churches preached accommodation to the new ruling class. The Saeima had been an instrument of bourgeois power; the Ulmanis regime exemplified the fascistic trend in all western capitalist economies.

In the interwar period, the situation of the "proletariat" had grown increasingly worse, while the vanguard of that class—the Latvian Communists—had worked surreptitiously but assiduously to weaken the bourgeois state. The events of June 1940, which proclaimed the proletarian revolution in Latvia, had been produced by the inner workings of Latvian history. The USSR, responding to the invitation of the Latvian working classes, in August 1940 responded to the expressed desire of the new Latvian proletarian state, the true representative of the Latvian *tauta*, to join the other fraternal republics of the Soviet Union. Henceforth the fate of the Latvian *tauta* would be guided by the working classes. The organization that embodied their will, the Latvian Communist Party, would, in turn, exercise its "leading role" by coordinating its activities with the other components and the leadership of the Communist Party of the Soviet Union.

In reality, the role of indigenous Communists in the 1940 events in Latvia was at the outset a relatively minor one.[12] The disintegration of the 1919 Latvian Soviet Republic, the Bolshevization of many members of the Latvian *strēlnieki* units, and the nationalist victory in the 1919–20 independence wars had caused the Latvian Communist Party to disappear when its leadership (including Pēteris Stučka) emigrated to and took up residence in the USSR. In Latvia, the party was illegal, though its activities continued underground throughout the interwar years, heavily subsidized by Latvian Communists in the USSR.

By contrast, in the USSR the Latvian Communists had helped consolidate Bolshevik power and, until Stalin's liquidation of the Old Bolsheviks in 1936–37, had developed a thriving Latvian subculture involving newspapers and journals, a publishing house, schools, and several theaters.[13]

During the interwar years the congresses of the Latvian Communist Party took place in the USSR.

In early 1940, in Latvia there were only about five hundred party members, many of whom had been or were currently incarcerated for illegal political activity. By July 1940, however, the party was the *only* legal political organization in the country, with Jānis Kalnbērziņš (1893–1986)—a Soviet Latvian Communist who had illegally returned to Latvia in 1936 to work underground—as first secretary. The party's indigenous membership began to grow during 1940 and early 1941, rising to about 2,700. In the summer of 1940, however, the principal actors were the Soviet army, Andrei Vishinskii's team in the Soviet embassy, a handful of Soviet Latvian communist operatives, and noncommunist sympathizers and opportunists in Latvia.

From July 1940 onward the new authorities did not hesitate to use coercion to consolidate their power. Participation in the July elections was mandatory, though the outcome was predetermined. The state security apparatus (the NKVD), which had begun its work after the arrival of the Soviet army and the July elections, arrested and deported unreliable persons, including some Latvians who were instrumental in the June transitional government, at the rate of about two hundred to three hundred a month for the remainder of the year.

Simultaneously, the NKVD was preparing lists of names in a wide variety of categories for more inclusive action. On June 13–14, 1941, these lists were used as the basis for a sweeping deportation, with some 490 boxcars containing about fifteen thousand persons rolling out of Latvia in an easterly direction.[14] Whereas the earlier arrests targeted potentially troublesome *individuals*, the June 1941 deportation was based on *categories* of people. These included not only the predictable category of employees of the pre-Soviet government but also categories of persons who had connections with the outside world (e.g., philatelists and Esperantists), persons expelled from the Communist Party, and members of anticommunist nationalist and leftist political parties of the pre-Ulmanis period. A second deportation was to have been carried out several weeks later but was canceled because of the June 22 German invasion of the Soviet Union. One estimate places the total population loss from executions and deportations during the period from June 1940 to June 1941 at some thirty-five thousand persons.

For the Latvian population these twelve months, especially the summer of 1940, were obviously traumatic.[15] The Ulmanis government, fearing that resistance to the Soviet occupation would only lead to massive, futile bloodshed, had until the last reassured Latvians that things could be much worse. This stance, which lasted into the weeks after the arrival of Soviet troops on June 17, meant that the Kirchensteins cabinet—and the events that followed—appeared to have Ulmanis's imprimatur. Certainly the formal document passing the powers of the presidency to Kirchensteins had Ulmanis's signature on it.

In a matter of weeks, the offices and structures of the Latvian national state disappeared, as did the political leaders whose names and activities had become familiar to the Latvian public during the past seven years. The highest political offices, now bearing such designations as "people's commissar" and "first secretary," were filled by Latvians who before 1940 had never belonged to the indigenous political elite, Latvians from the USSR, some of whom spoke Latvian incorrectly and with heavy Russian accents, and Russians who spoke no Latvian at all. Over all these changes lay the threat of quick arrest and disappearance for employment choices made during the pre-1940 period, for making a wisecrack about the new regime, for having more than someone who could now translate envy and resentment into an anonymous accusation.

There was little overt resistance in Latvia to all these changes; what there was manifested itself in private thoughts and avoiding mandatory meetings. Latvian diplomats still in their posts abroad successfully urged that the governments of such western powers as the United States and England quickly enunciate a policy of nonrecognition of Latvia's annexation to the USSR.[16]

Even though the mass deportations of June 1941 followed from the political philosophy of the new regime, Latvians were still shocked at the brutality. Very quickly, however, the new regime was replaced by a yet newer one, as on June 21, 1941, the German army invaded the USSR, pushed north from Poland, and reached Riga on July 1. On June 28, 1941, an insurrectionary Latvian group in Riga announced it had formed a new Latvian government; the group was suppressed by the Soviet authorities in twenty-four hours. By the time the German military forces arrived, there were two small Latvian groups—the Committee for a Liberated Latvia and the Provisional State Council—that hoped to rebuild what had been lost barely thirteen months ago.

LATVIANS IN THE THIRD REICH

The swift arrival in the Baltic area of the *Wehrmacht* (the German army), together with the civilian planners and the security apparatus of the Third Reich, forced the officials and personnel of the Soviet Latvian regime to flee to the Russian hinterland in great haste. At the same time, hundreds of others—such as Jews—who had good reason to fear the

Third Reich fled as well; one estimate places the total evacuation (officials, government personnel, and civilians) at around forty thousand persons.[17]

Memories of the previous twelve months and the still-reverberating June deportations combined to produce the feeling among many Latvians that the Germans had come as "liberators"; the more cynical believed that, under the circumstances, this "traditional enemy" (Germans) would be an improvement over the "traditional enemy" (Russians), whose brief rule had just concluded. The destructiveness of the year-long Soviet period combined with the assiduous efforts of the newly arrived German propagandists succeeded in labeling 1940–41 as the year of horrors (in Latvian, *baigais gads*), which became a permanent part of the Latvian vocabulary. The German occupation authorities, moreover, worked hard and successfully to direct accumulated Latvian resentments and hatreds into channels useful to the Reich.

Foremost among them was the effort to systematically destroy the Latvian Jewish population. In a matter of days after the German arrival, the work of the German-staffed *Einstazgruppen* (special execution squads) began and proceeded apace after the Latvian-staffed execution squad (headed by Viktors Arājs) was formed. By October 15 the German authorities were able to report to Berlin that 30,025 Jews had been killed and the remainder concentrated in the Riga ghetto.[18] The German authorities and the Latvian participants in, and apologists for, these "actions" portrayed them as the result of the spontaneous and righteous anger of the Latvian population "revenging" itself on the Jews for their "support" of Latvian Sovietization and for "organizing" (in their alleged roles as NKVD operatives) the June 1941 deportations. (Often overlooked or perhaps ignored in all this were the approximately five thousand Jews who in June had been deported along with other Latvian citizens.) The habit of thinking in terms of *categories* of enemies, which had played such an important part in the 1940–41 period of Soviet rule, continued in full force under the German occupation, with different categories now marked for imprisonment, execution, and deportation.

The small political elite that had survived the year of Soviet rule expected that the Third Reich would not only permit Latvians to serve Latvian national aspirations in the short run but would also countenance at least an autonomous if not an independent Latvian state in the long run. In line with German long-term planning, Latvia, together with the other two Baltic states and Byelorussia, was to be part of an administrative unit called *Reichskommissariat Ostland*, which was meant to serve as a component part of Third Reich territories in the east at least until the final German victory. Subsequently, according to German plans, most of the Latvian population was to be deported to conquered Russian territory and the Baltic area was to be resettled with farmers from Germany proper. Although the German authorities gave no sign that these overall plans would change, they were willing at least temporarily to permit (within limits) the use of Latvian national symbols and various kinds of Latvian cultural activity. This suggested to those willing to grasp at straws that the Latvian future could still to some extent be controlled by Latvians.

In line with this thinking, and with the permission of the German authorities, a Latvian self-government (in Latvian, *pašpārvalde*; in German, *Landeseigene Verwaltung*) was organized during July 1941.[19] This structure consisted of ministries (or directorates—the internal organization changed between 1941 and 1944) in charge of such matters as agriculture, social welfare, finances, education, and transportation. The entire structure was headed by a Latvian (for most of the period Oskars Dankers [1883–1965], a former general in the Latvian army), as were each of the subunits. The theory was that these self-governing institutions, in which Latvians dealt with other Latvians rather than with Germans, would maximize Latvian autonomy without challenging ultimate German control. Although the officials and staffs of the *pašpārvalde* did serve as a buffer between the German authorities and the Latvian population over the years of German occupation, their freedom of action was severely restricted and the hoped-for autonomy remained unrealized. All significant policies had to be cleared with the occupation authorities, who made their decisions without referring to the wishes of Latvian officials or the Latvian populace.

The normality some Latvians expected after the Germans expelled the communist government and the Soviet army never had returned. Because the whole Baltic area was adjacent to the fighting on the Russian-German front, everyday life in Latvia was suffused with the German military presence. The military and civilian administration's takeover of *Ostland* territory (including Latvia) had to be accomplished with an eye to the war effort, producing continuous friction between civilian planners and military authorities. Military needs were clear and immediate—to vanquish the Soviet forces—but the long-terms goals of civilian planners much less so. The civilian authorities had to provide a modicum of social and economic order in the short run so as not to be faced with continuous civil disturbances, while disguising their long-term plans for deporting the Latvian population and resettling Latvia with German farmers. The Latvian *pašpārvalde*, as it sought to manage those Latvian affairs over which it had been given (tentative) jurisdiction, had to take care not to offend two sets of masters while reducing the harshest aspects of the occupation and maintaining some control over their own lives. Inevitably, as the German presence in Latvia continued, lines of authority became increasingly confused and jurisdictions less clear.

To keep order, the German civilian authorities kept in force most of the laws and regulations introduced during the Soviet period, while assuming control over all the properties and institutions the Soviet government had nationalized during 1940–41 and making no moves to return them to their pre-Soviet owners. Indeed, the Germans expanded the nationalization process, taking over those institutions—such as cooperative societies—that the Soviets had not had time to reach. The Germans thus forestalled a barrage of private claims for the restoration of private ownership, which they had neither the staff nor the inclination to cope with, and assured that such properties (warehouses, factories, workshops, etc.) could be raided for matériel to help with the war effort. Decrees at the start of the German occupation ordered that continuity with the Soviet period would be maintained in the tax levies paid by the civilian population, in the pension payments to the civilian population, and in the obligatory sale of farm products to the government at low prices. Even though *Ostland* was eventually to be an agricultural zone, in the short run most industrial facilities were kept working, at least in part because of war needs. To administer them, Germans were brought from the Reich, thus adding to the number of German bureaucrats. Many of these were Baltic Germans, returning some eighteen months after their departure in the fall of 1939.

For most Latvians, the German occupation meant reductions in freedom of action and thought, subjection to various kinds of arbitrary decisions, as well as growing shortages. Most of the political elite of the pre-1940 period was gone, having been deported or executed during the Soviet period, and few of those who remained played a role in the *pašpārvalde*. The academic and cultural elites were not eroded as much, and the University of Latvia was able to function, though within strict guidelines laid down by the German authorities. Latvian-language literature continued to be published, but its volume and scope were far smaller and more restricted than they had been during the independence period. In this atmosphere few domains of life remained untouched by uncertainty, which increased as an ever-growing number of young Latvians became involved in the German war effort.

As the German invasion of the USSR ground to a halt in January 1943, the most far-reaching plan that the *pašpārvalde* was to implement surfaced when the German authorities decided to create military units made up of Latvian recruits. Latvian men had been recruited for the police force and various auxiliary units throughout 1941 and 1942, but by the end of 1942, when German failures on the eastern front dictated the need for additional manpower, such volunteers had become scarce. The *pašpārvalde* sought to use this turn of events to obtain the status of a protectorate for Latvia (patterned on Slovakia), arguing that Latvian units would only fight for a

Latvian cause. The Germans ignored these attempts to set conditions; in February Hitler ordered the creation of a Latvian Legion as part of the Waffen SS organization, and the German authorities in Latvia began to mobilize Latvian men born between 1919 and 1929.[20] The *pašpārvalde*'s demand that Latvians be placed under Latvian command was not met, though a former Latvian general, Rudolfs Bangerskis (1878–1958), was made inspector general of the Latvian troops.

Over the next eighteen months, approximately 146,000 Latvian men were mobilized into the legion's battalions and assigned auxiliary and fighting roles throughout the northern part of the eastern front. By May 1945 Latvian and German units, remnants of the *Wehrmacht*'s 19th Division, were still resisting the advance of the Russian army in the northern part of Kurzeme (Courland). By the time Germany surrendered, an estimated fifty thousand to sixty thousand of these Latvian Legionnaires had been wounded and some four thousand had been killed; twenty-five thousand to thirty thousand were in Allied prisoner-of-war camps.

By the summer of 1943, some Latvians, perceiving the Latvian Legion as a sign of German desperation, began preparing for a postwar period they thought would see a defeated Germany, a weakened Soviet Union, and a revived Latvian state. The secret seven-man Latvian Central Council, which was formed in August 1943, led a furtive existence until the fall of 1944, when most of its leaders were arrested and deported to Germany. But a reconstituted and enlarged council proposed a provisional government in the very weeks of German capitulation, by which time the Soviet army had reoccupied virtually all Latvian territory.

Because the return of Soviet power to Latvia had begun to seem inevitable by the summer and fall months of 1944, an estimated 120,000–150,000 persons fled westward.[21] During 1944 most of them went to Germany; in early 1945, when land routes to Germany became difficult, flight by sea to Sweden became more frequent. Most of these refugees were between thirty and fifty years old, with a high proportion of professional people, including 145 of the 241 Lutheran ministers who still had congregations in Latvia in 1944. Those who emigrated to Germany joined approximately 1.2 million other Eastern European refugees who in the immediate postwar years became the responsibility of the U.S., British, and French military authorities as well as of the United Nations. This emigration was the last in a series of wartime population movements that by mid-1945 had reduced the population of Latvia from an estimated prewar (1939) total of 2.0 million to about 1.4 million.

The causes of the population decreases included the Baltic Germans' emigrating during 1939–40; the persons executed, deported, or mobilized into the Soviet army during 1940–41; those who had evacuated to the

Soviet Union when the German forces arrived; the Jews, Gypsies, and Latvians executed or deported during the German occupation; those mobilized into the German army during the German occupation (including the Legionnaires) who did not return to Latvia; the 1944–45 Latvian refugees; and those executed and deported by the Soviet army when it reclaimed Latvia in the fall of 1944 and the spring of 1945. Not all members of these groups were permanently gone, for among those who had fled to the Soviet Union, as well as a relatively small number who had gone west, there were remigrants. Nevertheless, overall the returning Soviet authorities faced the same problem as the new Latvian government did in 1920: restoring normality to a country that had lost upward of a third of its population. Ethnodemographically, the proportion of Latvians in the country's population at the start of the rebuilding process in both periods was also comparable: around 73.0 percent in 1920 and around 80.0 percent in 1945. In absolute terms, however, the *number* of Latvians in Latvia at the end of the war was about 300,000 less than in 1939.[22]

REBUILDING THE SOVIET SOCIALIST REPUBLIC

The power of the party and of Soviet Latvian governmental institutions was now reinforced, both practically and psychologically, by the massive presence of the Soviet army. The Baltic Military Region (Estonia, Latvia, Lithuania, and Kaliningrad), with its headquarters in Riga, was re-created in 1945, raising the number of uniformed persons substantially throughout the country. As elsewhere in the Soviet Union, the new political elite consisted of high officials in the party and the government, with the party playing its constitutionally mandated "leading role."

In the immediate postwar years, though the government faced the problem of recruiting appropriately skilled personnel, recruiting for the party was relatively successful, with its membership leaping from about five thousand in 1945 to almost eleven thousand in 1946 and increasing regularly every year afterward until it reached a total of about forty-five thousand in 1955.[23]

Insofar as party membership was now a necessity for elite positions and high status, the ideologically motivated in the party were joined by the ambitious and the career-minded. Although unreliable, the statistics about the composition of the Latvijas Komunistiskā Partija (LKP) suggest that the proportion of Latvian members, though a small majority (53 percent in 1949) in this period, was less than the proportion of Latvians in the total population. The first secretary of the LKP until 1959 was Jānis Kalnbērziņš, a pre-1940 Soviet Latvian who received his post in 1940. In the governmental hierarchy, Vilis Lācis (1904–66), a Communist from prewar Latvia, occupied the position of chairman of the Council of Ministers from 1940 to 1949; and Augusts Kirchensteins, head of the post-Ulmanis transition government, was chairman of the Presidium of the Latvian Supreme Soviet. From 1944 to 1953, however, the second secretaries of the LKP were all Russians (Ivan Lebedev, Fedor Titov, and V. N. Ershakov) with no ties to the Latvian area.

Throughout the postwar years the LKP appealed to Moscow to send it politically reliable cadres who could speak Latvian.[24] Instead, reliable Communists arrived who did not have the requisite language skills. This continuing problem could have been relieved by the thousands of Latvian Old Bolsheviks who had been liquidated in Stalin's 1936–37 purge. As it was, the Soviet Latvians who did return often spoke no Latvian or used it incorrectly, thus furthering the impression of a party and government imposed by Moscow. From Moscow's point of view, having ethnic Russians and Sovietized Latvians in commanding positions in Latvia was not necessarily undesirable because it diluted the independence period's fearsome "bourgeois nationalism" that the Communists suspected lurked everywhere.

The first five-year plan, which was introduced in Latvia in January 1945, revealed that there were also personnel shortages at all levels in the nonelite population. Because the westward emigration of 1944–45 had carried away large numbers of university-trained specialists, the technical expertise needed to implement planning had been severely impaired; the war had also diminished the ranks of manual laborers. Furthermore, the imperatives of political control tended to override the need for an effective labor force. As the Soviet army moved back into Latvia during the final months of the war, and as the reconsolidation of power continued during 1945, an estimated seventy thousand persons were executed or deported on charges or on suspicion of having collaborated with the Germans.

To replenish the diminished cadres, skilled, semiskilled, and unskilled labor was recruited from other parts of the Soviet Union. In the decade from 1945 to 1955, the population of the Latvian SSR increased by about 650,000 but only about 115,000 were Latvians.[25] The remaining 535,000 were persons of Slavic nationalities: predominantly Russian but also Byelorussian and Ukrainian. As the Latvians recovered from the destruction of the war they learned that their new status as citizens of a Soviet socialist republic included severely diminished control by the Latvian *tauta* over the affairs of the republic, as symbolized by the proportion of non-Latvians (especially Russians) in the LKP and in all domains of socioeconomic life.

Even though the new rules permitted no questioning, there was active opposition to them by persons who stood outside the new system. For instance, during the final months of the war, many soldiers from those units of the Latvian Legion that were still on Latvian soil, as well some civilians, chose to become partisan fighters—the so-called forest brothers (in Latvian, *meža brāļi*). During the decade from 1945 to 1955, there may have been as many as twelve thousand forest brothers organized into some seven hundred bands, but no accurate count is available. The number was in any case large enough to worry the Soviet Latvian authorities because these partisans—in some three thousand raids—inflicted damage on uniformed military personnel, party cadres (especially in the rural areas), buildings, and ammunition depots. The authorities reported 1,562 Soviet personnel killed and 560 wounded over the entire period of partisan activity.[26]

Such partisan activities, however, did not keep Soviet Latvian authorities from consolidating their rule in urban areas. And the number of partisans diminished every year, as the rural civilian population that at first helped the movement became reluctant to do so and as special military and security units were sent to control partisan activity. By the mid-1950s, most partisans had concluded that their activities were pointless, and the last of the partisans surrendered to the authorities in 1956.

If the total population of the Latvian SSR in 1950 was about 1.9 million, and the Latvians among them numbered about 1.2 million, then the proportion of Latvians in the west as refugees was approximately 10 percent (some 120,000) of the total in Latvia. A slightly higher proportion (perhaps 12 percent) are estimated by 1950 to have been scattered throughout the labor camps and prisons of the Soviet Union. In round figures, therefore, some 22 percent of the Latvian *tauta* in 1950 was living outside the borders of the Latvian SSR.[27] Most of the "western" Latvians at the end of the 1940s were designated "displaced persons" and lived in U.N.-sponsored camps in what by 1948 had become the Federal Republic of Germany. During 1949–51, the vast majority of them emigrated to Sweden, North America, or Australia.

AGRICULTURAL COLLECTIVIZATION

One problem faced by the party in 1940–41 as it began to bring the Latvian economy into line with the Soviet Union's was that the agrarian reforms of the interwar years had increased the number of individual farm owners to higher levels than ever before. Although landed property above 30 hectares was nationalized in 1940, the government had added to the rolls of individual owners by redistributing land in parcels of 10 hectares to those who were still landless. Hence, after 1945, Latvian agriculture still retained its individualistic character and was therefore difficult to subject to centralized planning. During 1940–41 the party repeatedly stated that agricultural collectivization would not be introduced forcibly but rather by example and on a voluntary basis. After 1945, however, all reasons for restraint disappeared as Latvian farmers continued to resist voluntarism. The tradition of separate and individual farmsteads (in Latvian, *viensētas*) was deeply ingrained, having continued to exist even during the centuries of serfdom. For many the farm properties obtained during the interwar reform were the first their families had owned, and the rumors of the harshness of life on collective farms were rife.

The pressure from Moscow continued, however, and the Latvian authorities sought to reduce the number of individual farmers— increasingly being designated as kulaks (in Latvian, *kulaki* or *budži*)—by requisitioning their agricultural products for state use and by higher taxes. These measures were only partially successful: by 1948 there had come into being 617 kolkhozes, integrating 13,814 individual farmsteads (or 12.6 percent of all farmsteads).[28] This pace was unacceptably slow to the party, and in March 1949 the authorities moved against approximately ten thousand kulak families and a large number of individuals as well; from March 24 to March 30, 1949, about fifty thousand persons were deported and resettled in various locations throughout the USSR. With this action another important category of undesirables was eliminated.

These deportations effectively sped the pace of collectivization, as a veritable flood of farmers rushed into kolkhozy. By the end of 1950, only 4.5 percent of all farmsteads in Latvia remained outside the collectivized units; approximately 226,900 farmsteads now belonged to collectives, which in turn numbered around 14,700.[29] For the foreseeable future, the Latvian rural population would have to adapt to a way of living and thinking that had played no role in its folkways. Its daily movements would be dictated by plans, decisions, and quotas formulated elsewhere and delivered to them through a hierarchy of nonfarming intermediaries. For the time being, though, most farmstead buildings remained standing, separated from one another by fields; thus in terms of physical appearance the Latvian countryside remained largely unchanged.

THE END OF STALIN'S RULE

Joseph Stalin died on March 5, 1953, and was succeeded as head of the Soviet government by Georgi Malenkov and as first secretary of the Central Committee of the CPSU by Nikita Khrushchev. This changing of the guard also resulted in the execution the same year of Lavrentii Beria, head of the NKVD, and six of his associates, which was the first indication that the new Moscow leadership meant to distance itself from the Stalin era. Signs of change appeared in the Latvian SSR as well, as the relentless push for industrialization relaxed, diminishing the monthly influx of non-Latvians. In September 1955, a general amnesty was proclaimed for some 200,000 Latvian prisoners of the Stalin era, which meant that about 30,000 persons began returning from various exile sites in the Soviet Union.[30] On February 14, 1956, at the opening of the Twentieth CPSU Congress, Khrushchev attacked Stalin and the "cult of personality" and proclaimed that "coexistence" with the "capitalist" world would be the principal goal of Soviet foreign policy.

Also seemingly relaxed was the extreme centralization of the Stalin period, as the union republics were granted some economic rights and a degree of autonomy in agricultural decision making. The thaw was felt as well in the realm of arts and letters, when writers were allowed to refer in print to the "gulag archipelago" and other injustices of the period. That there were limits to how much thawing would be allowed, especially among non-Russian peoples in the Soviet Union, was demonstrated in the Soviet government's response to the Hungarian uprising of October–November 1956. Still, in July 1957, a cluster of Stalinist-era Communists was ousted from the Central Committee of the CPSU, and in March 1958, Khrushchev acquired the position of premier and received the Supreme Soviet's approval for his appointments to high posts in the party and the government.

In the meantime, in Latvia, five-year plans stressing industrialization had increased the proportion of Russian-speaking residents of the republic to some 38 percent by 1955, a growing proportion of monolingual Russian-speakers in the LKP and governmental bureaucracies was peripheralizing the Latvian language in the republic's public life, and Latvians were being recruited to (not mobilized for) various economic developmental ventures in other parts of the Soviet Union. Some prominent members of the LKP thus viewed the thaw period as an opportunity to try to block and perhaps reverse this relentless Russification of Latvian life (see table 3). Spearheading this nonconformism in the party was Eduards Berklāvs (b. 1914), formerly the first secretary of the Riga party organization and since 1957 the deputy premier of the Council of Ministers; opposing him in the heated party discussions over these issues was Arvīds Pelše (1899–1983), the secretary of the Central Committee of the LKP and an uncompromising guardian of Marxist-Leninist ideological purity in the LKP and the Latvian KGB.[31] Pelše had left Latvia in 1918, grown to adulthood in the Soviet Union, survived the Stalinist purges, and then returned to Latvia after 1945 to serve in a series of high party positions.

Berklāvs and his supporters made it known to Moscow that they

TABLE 3:
POPULATION OF LATVIA BY ETHNICITY, 1881–1993
(in percent)

Year	Latian	German	Russian	Jewish	Byelorussian	Ukrainian	Lithuanian	Estonian	Poles	Others[1]
1881[2]	77.0	11.3	4.0	5.5						2.2
1897	68.3	6.2	12.0	7.4			1.4	0.5	3.4	0.7
1920	72.7	3.6	7.8	4.9	4.7		1.6	0.5	3.4	0.7
1925	73.4	3.8	10.5	5.1	2.0		1.2	0.4	2.7	0.9
1930	73.4	3.6	10.6	4.9	1.9		1.3	0.4	3.2	0.7
1935	75.5	3.1	10.5	4.7	1.3		1.1	0.3	2.5	1.0
1959	62.0	0.1	26.6	1.8	2.9	1.4	1.5		2.9	0.8
1970	56.8	0.2	29.8	1.6	4.0	2.3	1.7		2.7	0.9
1979	53.7	0.1	32.8	1.1	4.5	2.7	1.5		2.5	1.1
1989	52.0		33.9	0.8	4.5	3.4	1.3		2.2	1.0
1993	53.5		33.9	0.6	4.2	3.1	1.2		2.2	1.3

[1]Including unknown nationality.
[2]Excluding Illuxt district in southeastern Kurland.
Sources: Skujenieks, *Latvija: zeme un eedzīvotāji*, pp. 256, 259; Jērāns, *Latvijas padomju enciklopēdija*, vol. 2, p. 120; Illmārs Mežs, "Analysis of the Population Geography of Latvia after Independence," paper presented at the Association for the Advancement of Baltic Studies Conference, Chicago, June 1994.

opposed and would oppose policies likely to alter further the nationality composition of the republic, whereas Pelše became notorious in party circles and elsewhere for venerating the "historic" tie between Latvians and Russians and the great benefits that, according to him, Russian "protection" had brought to the Latvian people. Although the authorities in Moscow and those on the Pelše side of the dispute in Latvia were willing to listen to those who questioned extreme centralization, they would not hear criticism of any kind cast in nationality terms.

Thus Khrushchev, on a visit in June 1959 to Riga to meet with East German communist leaders, decided the dispute in favor of Pelše and his supporters, accusing Berklāvs of disfiguring Leninist principles concerning nationality. The consequence of this decision for the LKP was a purge of some two thousand functionaries who had been sympathetic to Berklāvs's brand of "national communism." Berklāvs himself was sent into administrative exile in eastern Russia, and Pelše became first party secretary. The purge did not involve bloodletting but rather demotion and administrative exile; correspondingly, those who had harbored resentments about Russification could continue to do so but no longer in policy-sensitive positions.

Pelše was right to worry about the continued attachment of many Latvians to the memory of national independence. By the late 1950s most Latvians holding responsible positions were of an age to remember the independence period, which meant that those who were ostensibly loyal to the new regime could still make silent comparisons. Moreover, although children did not remember, their parents certainly did—not to mention their grandparents' generation; not enough time had passed, in other words, for memories to have disappeared.

Pelše and the other party leaders were also aware that, in such Western countries as Sweden, West Germany, England, the United States, and Canada, the Latvians who had emigrated in 1944–45 showed little sign of assimilating to the cultures of their host countries.[32] In fact, by the late 1950s they had begun to mobilize to influence public opinion in the West to maintain the policy of nonrecognition of the 1940 incorporation and had succeeded in developing a robust Latvian-language cultural life with newspapers and periodicals, publishing houses, and Saturday schools. Most Latvians in Latvia knew little about this, of course, but LKP leaders, who were permitted to read Western materials kept in special collections (in Latvian, *specfondi*), did. A thriving cultural life among the Latvian émigrés ensured that the *idea* of an independent Latvia continued to lead a life beyond LKP control, and, therefore, in addition to its other tasks, the party had to ensure that political thinking in Latvia be kept uninfected by such information from abroad.

THE TWO WORLDS OF
LATVIAN CULTURE

The Berklāvs phenomenon was a sign that even compliant party members in Latvia felt squeezed by the growing demographic and linguistic weight of the Russian presence, but the resulting purge limited disagreements with official policy. Hence among artists and intellectuals in Latvia—or "cultural workers," as they were known—who since 1945 had been vulnerable to all manner of "deviationist" charges from the Latvian Writers Union that supervised literary expression, the thaw period was less a turning point than it was in Russia proper.[33]

In the 1950s Latvian literature was still recovering from the ravages of the war and the return of Soviet power. A substantial proportion of the generation of writers in ascendancy during the 1930s had fled westward, among them such established figures as Jānis Jaunsudrabiņš (1877–1962), Kārlis Skalbe (1875–1945), Anšlāvs Eglītis (1906–93), Mārtiņš Zīverts (1903–90), and Zenta Mauriņa (1897–1978); those who remained in the Latvian SSR—such as the gifted poet Aleksandrs Čaks (1901–50)—had to shape their work, when they were allowed to publish, to the tenets of socialist realism.

A handful of talented writers, however, made the transition relatively easily and in terms of volume of output and ideological orthodoxy dominated the Latvian literary scene during the two decades after 1945. These authors—Andrejs Upīts (1877–1970), Vilis Lācis (1904–66), Jānis Sudrabkalns (1894–1975), Arvīds Grigulis (1906–89), and Anna Sakse (1905–81)—all received Stalin Prizes for literature in the period 1945–55 and could therefore be relied on by the political authorities not to allow the thaw to go too far.

Some search for new ways was permitted. The poet Ojārs Vācietis (1933–83) offered the thought that "art before everything else should be art" and should not be forced to serve political purposes, but this idea found little resonance among the lions of the literary establishment. Although there were efforts to portray human activities in venues other than the farm field, the factory, and the "war against fascism," perhaps the most significant accomplishment of the thaw was a reevaluation of pre-Soviet Latvian literature and a reprinting of some of the nonsocialist realists of earlier days. At the very least, the thaw period relaxed the draconian prohibitions on access to the Latvian literary past that began in November 1940, when Soviet authorities, armed with the *List of Banned Books and Brochures* containing some four thousand titles published before 1940, sought to suppress all earlier creativity.

Still the cleavages remained. Not all pre-Soviet Latvian literary creations were accessible to all readers in Latvia; the main beneficiaries of controlled access to special collections (in Latvian, *specfondi*) were those politically reliable literary scholars and critics who could be counted on to evaluate the past in the appropriate Marxist-Leninist manner. Control was even more rigorous over the Latvian-language writings being published in Western "capitalist" countries, rendering them virtually inaccessible to all except the most trustworthy.

Despite the difficult conditions in which they were living and working, the authors of the 1944–45 emigration continued to write and to publish in Latvian, even when they were in the displaced persons (DP) camps in postwar Germany. The years between 1946 and 1950 saw the publication outside Latvia of some 1,500 new Latvian titles in all genres, and the decade between 1951 and 1960, some 1,200 new titles.[34] Belles lettres, which formed some 29 percent of these publications, contained the artists' reactions to a range of new experiences: fleeing the homeland, living in the DP camps, leaving Europe, and, as a consequence, adapting (in most cases) to English-language environments.

Providing a measure of unification in the diaspora after 1950, when the outflow from the DP camps began, were Latvian-language newspapers (e.g., *Laiks*, published in New York); the activities of Lutheran, Catholic, and Baptist congregations; and political-cultural organizations such as the American Latvian Association, founded in 1951 with an initial membership of some 3,500 persons. From 1945 onward, then, the writings of the Latvian *tauta* were emerging in two very different settings from two very different experiential bases and subject to two very different sets of constraints.

THE ONSET OF THE BREZHNEV ERA

In 1964, Nikita Khrushchev was deposed as first secretary of the CPSU and as premier; he was replaced in the party position by Leonid Brezhnev and in the premiership by Aleksei N. Kosygin. Soon after, in 1966, in Latvia Arvīds Pelše ended his tenure as first secretary of the LKP, left for Moscow to join the Politburo of the CPSU, and was replaced as first secretary of the LKP by Augusts Voss (1916–94), a Latvian who had grown up in the Soviet Union and returned to Latvia in 1945 as an LKP functionary. Both Brezhnev and Voss had long tenures in their respective secretaryships, Brezhnev until his death in 1982 and Voss until he moved to Moscow in 1984. In Latvia, Voss's eighteen-year leadership of the party was unremarkable except that the proportion of Latvians in it stabilized at around 35 percent—the lowest proportion in the Baltic republics.[35] The absolute size of party membership continued to increase, almost doubling, from 76,642 in 1961 to 131,130 in 1970, but its Latvian membership did not exceed about one-third of that number. Of the Latvians in Latvia, only 5 percent belonged to the party.

By the end of the 1960s everyday life in Latvia by some standards had achieved considerable stability and predictability. In a material sense, by comparison with the 1940s and 1950s, conditions were decidedly better. By 1968 per capita income in Latvia exceeded the Soviet average by 42 percent, and consumption patterns had reached prewar levels.[36] Median incomes during the decade almost doubled, while price inflation was kept to less than 1 percent. By 1970, industrial production was 4.7 times higher than it had been in 1955 and mean rural incomes were approaching mean urban incomes.

By the late 1960s the partisan movement was a memory, a generation of Latvians that had never known the independence period had just reached adulthood and appeared to take Soviet institutions for granted, and the Latvian Soviet Socialist Republic now seemed a permanent state of affairs. "It seemed that problems could eventually be talked out with Moscow on a rational level based on respect for mutual interest."[37]

At the same time there were feelings of uneasiness, particularly with respect to the balance of and relations among Latvians and non-Latvians in the republic, as Latvians felt increasingly hemmed in by Russians in their home republic and dominated by Russians in the larger Soviet Union. This could not help but be an important psychological factor in Latvian attitudes toward the *Soviet* state and *Soviet* culture. By 1970, because of the industrialization policy that recruited a labor force for large-scale state enterprises from outside the Latvian SSR, the proportion of non-Latvians in the republic's total population had increased to 43.2 percent.

The Baltic region generally had become an inextricable part of a state apparatus centered in Moscow, which meant that, in dealing with the institutions of the state—even in the Latvian Republic itself—Latvians more often than not needed to speak Russian. The Baltic region was still the Baltic Military District, manned by some 250,000 Soviet soldiers with Riga as the district's headquarters. The presence of large numbers of uniformed persons served as a constant reminder of the country's dependent status.[38]

Latvian recruits to the Soviet army were sent far from their native region to do their army service. Soviet military personnel in Latvia, in contrast, especially retired military officers, expected and received preferential treatment in the form of housing and consumer goods from the civilian population. The Soviet military tended to view the Baltic populations generally, and Latvians in particular, as a potentially troublesome part of the union, prone to fascist ideas.

Only one-third of the Latvian police force (i.e., *milicija*) consisted of Latvian speakers, which meant that many of the daily contacts between Latvian civilians and the keepers of law and order had to be conducted in Russian. Although the nationality composition of the Committee for State Security (KGB) is not known, it was seen by the Latvian population as the principal organ of state control, responsible entirely to Moscow's wishes and capable of overriding all republic-level decisions. In the early 1970s, the top levels of both the party and the republic government were dominated by Latvians born and raised in the prewar Soviet Union who spoke broken Latvian, if any, and by Russians and other non-Latvians who felt no need to learn Latvian since the people they moved among (as well as some 40 percent of the republic's general population) spoke Russian.

STAGNATION AND RESENTMENT

The term *stagnation* has been used to describe the second half of Leonid Brezhnev's tenure, and economic indicators for the 1970s in Latvia do suggest a slowing of all rates of development and growth as well as per capita income. Reflecting the situation in Moscow and the rest of the Soviet Union, the party and state organs in Latvia were becoming increasingly rife with corruption and preferential treatment, thus increasing the distance between party slogans and socioeconomic reality and giving rise to widespread cynicism in the party itself as well as in the general population. Membership in the party continued to grow (158,000 in 1980), but reasons for joining spanned the range, from ideological conviction to sheer opportunism.[39] Those who were not true believers had to live a double life, reiterating party ideas and slogans in public while holding in abeyance views that might be thought unorthodox. For many, such dissembling seemed a small price to pay for benefits party membership brought in status, employment, housing, and material goods such as automobiles.

Such anomalies, discrepancies, and contradictions pervaded Latvian society during the 1970s, despite official pronouncements that progress was being made. Both party officials and state authorities promised to heed the demands for consumer goods from a population becoming knowledgeable about living standards in the so-called capitalist countries. Indeed, general knowledge about the West was on the increase as a result of several decades of peaceful coexistence, improved mass media, and increased travel. These trends were visible throughout the Soviet Union and by the mid-1970s had produced a new species of Soviet citizen—the dissident.

In Latvia as well, publicly voiced dissatisfaction with the local situation began to appear with increasing regularity.[40] In 1971, for example, a letter signed by "17 Latvian Communists" was sent to the Central Committees of the Communist Parties of Western Europe; in it the seventeen signatories (later revealed to have been Eduards Berklāvs and some of his like-minded colleagues) complained about the "systematic Russification" of the LKP and the republic. But most instances of dissatisfaction or dissent in Latvia were of lesser magnitude and tended to use as ammunition the relics of the independence period. Flowers were laid at night on the Freedom Monument in Riga (built in 1936), words of the former national anthem were scribbled on walls, the graves of statesmen were visited on the national holidays of the interwar republic, and the old crimson and white flag was waved at sports competitions. The authorities were in a bind over such incidents: although they did not hesitate to arrest and sentence the individuals involved, the absence of the total terror of the Stalin period made the arrested martyrs rather than spreading fear throughout the population.

Some long-term policies the party regarded as "progressive" were instead breeding dissatisfaction. For example, agricultural collectivization in Latvia had been completed by the mid-1950s, but twenty years later, the new consciousness that collectivization was supposed to produce seemed woefully incomplete.[41] Although the vast majority of rural dwellers were enrolled in one form or another of collective enterprise—kolkhozy, sovkhozy, rural kombinats—and were responding to production quotas, there was still, from the authorities' point of view, an unseemly attachment to rural individualism, which expressed itself in the high proportion (44 percent) of collective farm income that came from the individually farmed plots (in Latvian, piemājas zeme).

Also, the physical symbols of the old individualized farmsteads— residential quarters, barns, granaries—were still omnipresent in the Latvian countryside, despite efforts to create rural hamlets (in Latvian, ciemati) and to resettle rural people in them. To make the ciemati more attractive, social services such as schools and stores were built only there and permits for new residential dwellings were granted only in the hamlets. The many old separate farms that remained were used either as rural residences or as summer places for urban dwellers; consequently, the Soviets began destroying them in the early 1970s—1,544 in 1971, 1,747 in 1972, 1,969 in 1973, and 2,750 in 1974.[42] Such efforts to extirpate all physical remnants of the old rural regime seemed gratuitous to many.

Industrial progress was also not seen as the authorities intended. By the end of the 1970s Latvia was in fact an urban and industrial republic, with its rural population having decreased to just below 30 percent. But, as part of the larger Soviet planning system, the bulk of its industrial output was exported to other parts of the Soviet Union. Also, by the late 1970s, the Latvian environment was being harmed by giant state enterprises producing goods Latvians did not consume; total production costs were thought to be substantially greater than returns from other republics in either finances or imported goods; and more Russians were employed in these production units than Latvians. Moreover, by the end of the 1970s, output statistics did not report the high quantities of products rendered unusable by hurried or sloppy production techniques. Thus official statements that the Latvian Republic was a smoothly functioning and well-integrated cog in a giant and efficiently planned production machine were sounding increasingly hollow.[43] In the everyday life of the urban population, long queues and shortages ("deficits") appeared unpredictably and frequently even of commonplace products. By the end of the 1970s, then, the inadequacies of the macrolevel planning system were visible not only within the general population but also among the middle-level managers and specialists who worked within the system and its shortcomings on a daily basis. By the early 1980s, the mood in the Baltic area and in Latvia was a somber one.[44]

RIGA IN THE LATE 1970s

The postwar experience of the republic's capital city exemplified the widening rift between official pronouncements and reality. In many ways, since 1945 Riga had reassumed the position it had had before the First World War—a large and important urban center in an "empire" with leaders who made "imperial" plans with little reference to regional or republic sensitivities. Because the Latvian Communist Party—the "guiding structure" of the republic—showed no sign of disagreeing (at least publicly) with Moscow-directed central plans, Latvians had to adjust to the thought that the future of "their" capital would be determined by decisions in which their views counted for little.

In the decades after 1950 Riga in fact expanded by any measure of growth. The city's population rose from about 482,000 in 1950 to about 883,000 in 1985, surpassing its pre–World War I population (the maximum previously recorded) by the end of the 1950s (see table 2, p. 108).[45] Thus in the mid-1980s fully one-third of the republic population lived in Riga and its environs. By the end of the 1970s, 52 percent of all industrial labor in the republic was employed in Riga industries, which accounted for 52.6 percent of Latvia's industrial production.[46] Certain prewar features were evident in this expansion of industrial productivity: electronic technology continued to be an important sector, as did transportation. The new elements in this growth, visible from the late 1950s on, were internal differentiation and the trend toward smaller production units that could be more easily automated. At the same time, units became more specialized as Riga industries were fitted into all-union plans and linked into a vast network with equally specialized production units in other republics.

Industrial expansion required a larger labor force. In the years just after World War II, the birthrate in Riga had shown a strong upward movement, but after the mid-1950s that trend reversed itself and the birthrate decreased. The expansion of the Riga population after the mid-1950s, therefore, was mostly the result of an in-migrating labor force recruited from outside the republic. The most visible signs of that enlarged labor force were the giant residential complexes built on the city's outskirts, in Jugla, Ķengarags, Imanta, Bolderāja, Purvciems, Ilǧuciems, and Vecmīlgravis.[47] The new housing tracts, however, proved insufficient, and therefore the in-migrants received apartments in more established neighborhoods as well, frequently ahead of Latvians who had been waiting for years to move from communal apartments into individual ones. The in-migrant population also had a high turnover rate, with those who remained permanently in Latvia being only a small proportion of those who came and went in a given time period.

Overshadowing those concerns, however, was the fact that virtually all of the migrants were non-Latvians. In Riga, the Latvian proportion of the population steadily decreased, from 44.6 percent in 1959 to 40.9 percent in 1970 to 36.5 percent in 1989.[48] In 1970 the Latvian proportion of the city's population was about what it had been in 1913, when it was more than three times the German proportion (12 percent) and more than twice the Russian proportion (19 percent). Soviet demographic analysts claimed that Riga had always been an multinational city, that current trends were in line with traditional patterns, and that in any event migration was a natural phenomenon that always accompanied industrializing. Other prognoses, however, showed the city to be becoming, not more international but increasingly and visibly Russian, starting with street signs and ending with the language necessary for everyday social interaction. For Latvians even to raise the nationality question in Riga was dangerous, as the 1959 purge of the Latvian Communist Party had shown. If Moscow planners totally disregarded the sensitivities of titular republic nationalities in planning for industrialization, the Latvian Communist Party was careful not to offend Russian sensibilities by treating these developments as anything but inevitable.

9 The Reemergence of an Independent Latvia

Leonid Brezhnev's death in November 1982 at the age of seventy-five initiated a leadership crisis in the USSR that continued until 1985. It began when Brezhnev was succeeded as general secretary of the CPSU by Yuri Andropov, age sixty-eight, who had been head of the KGB. During the rest of 1982 and 1983, Andropov consolidated his position in the Kremlin leadership amid rumors that his health was failing. When Andropov died in February 1984, after only fifteen months as general secretary, he was succeeded by Konstantin U. Chernenko, age seventy-three, who had been chairman of the Presidium of the Supreme Soviet. After only thirteen months in office, Chernenko died in March 1985 and was succeeded by Mikhail S. Gorbachev, age fifty-four, who had been a full member of the Politburo since 1980 and a protégé of Yuri Andropov's. In Gorbachev, the CPSU had found a leader who seemed well-disposed toward much-needed revitalization in the USSR. Gorbachev quickly appointed persons to the Politburo who were favorably inclined toward reform and began to visit various parts of the Soviet Union, an activity Soviet citizens had not seen from their leaders since Khrushchev. Expectations of change were in the air during 1985 and continued to grow during 1986.

In Latvia, a similar turnover in the party's leadership also signaled the beginning of a new period. Efforts to streamline economic planning were evident during the brief Andropov era, as the party under Augusts Voss began responding to critics of stagnation.[1] In 1984, however, Voss left for Moscow, having been appointed chair of the Committee of Nationalities of the USSR's Supreme Soviet, and was replaced as first secretary of the LKP by Boriss Pugo (1937–91), who had been born in Moscow and thus represented the second generation of pre-1940 Soviet Latvian Communists to be prominent in the Latvian party. Pugo had been active in the LKP since the 1950s and had become head of the Latvian KGB in 1980. With Gorbachev's accession to the general secretaryship, Pugo began exercising his powers, replacing a host of high party and government officials with more reform-minded persons.

Among the new men, Anatolijs Gorbunovs (b. 1942) replaced Imants Andersons (b. 1923) as ideology secretary of the bureau of the LKP Central Committee, and Jānis Vagris (b. 1930) replaced Pēteris Strautmanis (b. 1919) as chair of the Presidium of the Supreme Soviet. Although these and other changes were not accompanied by statements about what kinds of reforms would be undertaken, the turnover itself, involving many high officials in a short period of time, strongly suggested that some kind of corner was being turned. The last turnover of this magnitude occurred in connection with Berklāvs and the "national Communists" in 1959, when it was widely perceived to be a purge. Now, however, the departing officials were retired with banquets and toasts about long service and a job well done. At the Twenty-fourth LKP Congress in January 1986, Pugo spoke at length about the absolutely necessary changes the Latvian party would make in the republic's economy.

MOSCOW CALLS FOR REFORMS

Mikhail Gorbachev believed that reinvigorating the Soviet Union required, first, a restructuring (perestroika) of the economy (essentially, less central planning) so as to release the energies of local and regional talent; second, openness (glasnost) so that there would be no hesitation or fear about identifying problems and proposing solutions for them; and, third, democratization (demokratizaatsia) so as to allow more input and participation by those who were not part of the frequently criticized nomenklatura, the privileged ranks in the party and government who had been the beneficiaries of the corruption of the stagnation period. These processes, Gorbachev thought, could be initiated at all levels and allowed to run their course without affecting the leading role of the Communist Party or the distribution of power within the Soviet Union as a whole.[2] Indeed, Gorbachev's visit to Latvia and Estonia in February 1987 and his praise of regional reform initiatives suggested that the Moscow leadership believed strongly in its ability to control events.

In Latvia, these urgings from the Kremlin leadership, combined with the leadership changes in the republic itself, reduced long-standing fears about outspokenness even among those who did not see themselves as dissidents. The dissidents themselves—idiosyncratic and brave individuals whose numbers in Latvia were just barely large enough to be called a movement—had by the mid-1980s established a long record of questioning the basic tenets of Soviet Latvian society and paying the price through arrest, imprisonment, loss of employment, and expulsion.

In the early 1980s, there had been a severe crackdown on dissident activities, ending with the arrests and sentencing of Gunārs Astra, Jānis Barkāns, Ints Cālītis, Lidija Doroņina-Lasmane, Jānis Rožkalns, and Jānis Vēveris.[3] But this did not frighten others. In June 1987 a group called Rebirth and Renewal was founded within the Latvian Lutheran Church whose goal was to challenge the regime's restrictions (with the cooperation of the generally quiescent church) on what these dissidents called "leading the Christian life."

Others responded to Gorbachev's call by protesting against the ecological damage created by industrialization—a kind of moderate opposition the authorities had been willing to permit, though under their watchful eye, since the 1970s. Thus, in October 1986, the journalist Dainis Īvāns (b. 1955) and the writer Arturs Snīps (b. 1949), in the pages of the prominent literary journal *Literatūra un Māksla*, criticized the hydroelectric complex that was to be built at Pļaviņas on the Daugava River, saying it would destroy the environment and damage historical sites. This project had already been approved by the Council of Ministers at the republic and all-union levels. The protest, which became an organized campaign of letter writing, suggested so much grassroots opposition to the complex that in 1987, to the great surprise of its opponents, the USSR Council of Ministers abandoned the project. This eye-opening experience evidently meant that certain kinds of collective opposition to traditionally irreversible decisions could bring results in the new, more tolerant atmosphere.[4]

Seen from above, in Moscow, Gorbachev's reform policies, it was thought, would produce change guided and channeled by the party and governmental institutions, resulting in an improved socialism in a stronger USSR. Seen from below in Latvia, however, the reform policies appeared to sanction challenges to those aspects of life about which resentments had been building for a long time. These new freedoms, then, landed in a population in which articulate elites—party and nonparty alike—felt all manner of frustrations, not just economic ones. To expect that the workings of glasnost would remain within approved guidelines throughout the USSR could have been seriously entertained only by Moscow leaders, who took it for granted that the unique histories of the different parts of the Soviet

Union counted for little and that the local populations, such as those in the Baltic, were well integrated into the Soviet system.

Whereas from Moscow's vantage point, it was a perversion of glasnost and perestroika to cast reform initiatives in *national* terms, to Latvian activists the connection between system reform and the unmet needs of the Latvian *tauta* seemed natural and logical.[5] Thus in the Baltic ecological protests quickly gave way to national ones. In 1987, three large demonstrations in Riga were timed to coincide with three fateful dates of Latvian political-national history: On June 13–14 (the dates of the 1941 deportations), the Latvian human rights group Helsinki-86 placed flowers at the Freedom Monument (in Latvian, Brīvības Piemineklis) in Riga; on August 23 (the date of the 1939 signing of the Molotov-Ribbentrop Pact), a large demonstration at the Freedom Monument denounced the pact and suffered numerous beatings by the *milicija* (police); and on November 18 (the date of the 1918 proclamation of Latvian independence), because the Freedom Monument was surrounded by militia and KGB troops, demonstrators placed flowers and candles at other historical sites and in some places posted the crimson and white flag of the interwar republic.[6] The reforms called for by the Gorbachev government were responded to in many ways, but in Latvia and the other Baltic republics the most publicly visible response in 1987 appeared to be (ominously, to the authorities and to the Communist Parties) nationalistic.

THE PLENUM OF THE CREATIVE SOCIETIES

The practice of marking the dark events of the Soviet period of Latvian history with public gatherings continued into 1988, when on March 25 a meeting organized by the Latvian Writers Union (in Latvian, Rakstnieku Savienība) and permitted by the authorities commemorated the 1949 deportations of the collectivization drive. By this time, the Writers Union, an official organization, was moving into the forefront of activism. Led since 1985 by the respected poet Jānis Peters (b. 1939), the union for years had been attentive to the complaints of its members about censorship, the shrinking role of the Latvian language in Latvian society, prohibitions against contacts with émigré authors, and the despoliation of the Latvian environment by industrialization policies. In the past, the union's leadership had itself been an instrument of censorship and control; more recently it had served as a buffer between the party and hotheaded authors unwilling to take party admonitions seriously.

On June 1 and 2, 1988, the union, seeking to ride a wave, held a general meeting (plenum) that included not only its own members but also those of the other creative unions (in Latvian, *radošās savienības*): architects, designers, cinematographers, painters and sculptors, theater workers, and journalists.[7] The event produced a sharply worded and wide-ranging indictment of the Soviet Latvian status quo, as in speech after speech leading members of the intelligentsia called for transforming Latvia into a distinct entity in the USSR, with laws guaranteeing republic sovereignty and with Latvian as the state language. The transformation was to take place, it was said, in the process of implementing the general policy of perestroika.

In what became perhaps the most notorious speech at the plenum, Mavriks Vulfsons (b. 19180, a noted television journalist and political commentator, declared that, as an eyewitness to and participant in the events of 1940, he could testify that Soviet power in Latvia that year had arrived not as the result of a socialist revolution (the orthodox party interpretation) but as a consequence of the presence of a Soviet occupation army.[8] This interpretation, among other things, challenged the legitimacy of the LKP; moreover, it was the interpretation of the 1940 events that, over the decades, the stalwarts of the Writers Union, as well as all politically reliable Latvian intellectuals, had been condemning as a "falsification" put forward by "bourgeois émigré historians" in the pay of the Central Intelligence Agency. Now, however, the interpretation came from a seemingly unimpeachable source, and, at the very least, the question was now open for historians to examine.[9]

The speeches of the plenum were published in *Literatūra un Māksla* in four successive issues from June 10 to July 8 and thus accessible to a wide reading public. In any event, a substantial portion of the Latvian intelligentsia had declared itself on the side of reform and given more than a suggestion of where in Latvia such reform might lead. Although to many the notion of republic sovereignty still seemed one of the many unrealistic ideas glasnost allowed to be bruited about, to some the notion did seem to follow from the new ideas being approved by Moscow. The Central Committee of the LKP was utterly bewildered; there appeared to be no guidelines from Moscow about how much force, if any, could be used against such heterodoxy.[10]

NEW POLITICAL ORGANIZATIONS

The Writers Union plenum was but the first challenge to the LKP in the summer of 1988. On June 14 another commemorative meeting of the 1941 deportations took place, organized by the environmentalist

VAK (Vides Aizsardzības Klubs—Environmental Protection Club), which turned into a demonstration for Latvian independence, complete with many crimson and white flags. On July 16, at the folklore festival Baltica-88 at the Mežaparks amphitheater, there were demands that the interwar colors in the national flag be restored. On August 11 a demonstration at the Freedom Monument celebrated the 1920 peace treaty between Latvia and Soviet Russia in which Russia renounced for all times any claim on Latvian territory. In early October another mass meeting in the Mežaparks amphitheater called for the creation of a law-based state in Latvia.[11]

There was also coming into being a network of interrelated informal organizations. Some, such as the VAK, had been formed earlier; others began to experiment with the new freedoms perestroika appeared to allow. The Writers Union plenum had provided the impetus for the creation of a Popular Front (in Latvian, Latvijas Tautas Fronte, or LTF) ostensibly to support perestroika and similar to organizations that had already formed in Estonia (April) and in Lithuania (early June). A more intransigent viewpoint on the question of national sovereignty/independence was coalescing in the Latvian National Independence Movement (in Latvian, Latvijas Nacionālās Neatkarības Kustība, or LNNK), with Eduārds Berklāvs— the erstwhile "national Communist" purged in 1959—emerging as its leading figure.[12] In the non-Latvian population, defenders of a *Soviet* Latvia began an organization of their own, calling it the International Front (or Interfront). Public opinion during the summer of 1988 remained in turmoil, as these organizations tested the limits of the permissible. Although Latvian disillusionment with membership in the USSR was increasing, not all were prepared to say that their lot would be improved by totally separating from the larger system. Perhaps the deepest uncertainty was among members of the LKP, who reflected the bewilderment of the party's leadership.

The fall of 1988 began with change at the top: Boriss Pugo, the first secretary of the LKP, resigned to become head of the Party Control Commission in Moscow and was replaced by Jānis Vagris (b. 1930), the first native Latvian to hold that position since 1959. Anatolijs Gorbunovs (b. 1942) became chairman of the Presidium of the Latvian Supreme Soviet. But such changes were not as unprecedented as the first congresses of the new organizations for which the groundwork had been laid during the summer.

During October 8–9 the First Congress of the Latvian Popular Front took place, with some one thousand delegates representing, it was said, about 110,000 dues-paying members (perhaps 90 percent of them Latvians) in 2,300 local chapters.[13] The congress, which elected the journalist-turned–political organizer Dainis Īvāns as president (in Latvian, *priek-*

ssēdis), used the demands of the June Writers Union plenum as the basis for its platform, expanding and elaborating them to spell out what it meant by the concept of national sovereignty. The composition of the congress delegates suggested that the term *popular* in the organization's name was appropriate: some one-third were Communist Party members; represented as well were environmentalists, dissidents, radical, independence-minded religious groups, and the creative intelligentsia. Because of its umbrella-like nature, the LTF could not satisfy the more radical Latvians, for whom mere sovereignty within the USSR was a compromise.

The Latvian National Independence Movement (LNNK), which from the beginning had espoused separation from the USSR, held its first congress February 18–19, 1989, in the city of Ogre and chose Eduards Berklāvs to be its leader. The LNNK was considerably smaller than the LTF, but its presence in the Latvian political spectrum signaled the existence of a not insubstantial component of public opinion that, while cooperating with the LTF, insisted that the idea of complete independence be kept at the center of political discussion.

Both the LTF and the LNNK, as well as most other Latvian organizations, understood that seizing the moment was important because they could not be certain how long the permissive atmosphere generated by Gorbachev's reforms would last. It was necessary to demonstrate growing, or at least unflagging, popular support for the idea of republic sovereignty if not outright independence. Thus organized meetings and demonstrations followed one upon the other.[14] On October 23, 1988, a large meeting in the Daugava sports stadium in Riga protested the policy of recruiting Russian-language "migrants" to Latvian industrial enterprises. On November 11 the crimson and white flag was raised in the main tower of Riga Castle (the presidential residence of the interwar republic). On November 18 the seventieth anniversary of Latvian Independence Day was formally celebrated in the National Theater in Riga and at the Freedom Monument.

The pace of action continued throughout the first half of 1989, with a demonstration, organized by the LTF, of some 200,000 participants on March 12, another on March 25 commemorated the 1949 deportations, and yet another on May 18 expressed sympathy for the civilians killed by the Soviet army in Tbilisi, Georgia, on April 8 and 9. This last demonstration revealed the Latvian organizers' readiness to express solidarity with similar national movements in other Soviet republics.

This solidarity was most evident in the cooperation the three Baltic Popular Fronts had engaged in ever since the "front" idea emerged in 1988. There had been frequent meetings among individual leaders as well as among the "foot soldiers" of the movement, culminating in the May 12–13, 1989, conference of the Popular Front leadership in Tallinn, Estonia, where it became clear that the similar interests of the three movements could serve as grounds for an ongoing coordination of effort. The strength of this cooperative impulse manifested itself in the Moscow meetings of the USSR Congress of People's Deputies, elections to which had been held in March and in which the Baltic republics were now represented by strong delegations of reformers. Throughout the summer of 1989 the Baltic delegations, spurred on by the three Popular Fronts, pushed the congress to create a special commission to investigate the secret protocols of the 1939 Molotov-Ribbentrop Pact. The commission's deliberations led it to conclude that the secret protocols had existed, but the next step—admitting that they were connected to the 1940 Soviet occupation of Latvia and thus might have something to do with current Baltic efforts to achieve independence—was too sensitive to be taken. By the time the congress did adopt the commission's report (December 1989), the independence momentum in the Baltic republics had increased to the point of making such "official" admissions of past wrongdoing nearly irrelevant.

Latvian activists, then, perceived themselves as involved in a common Baltic effort, a notion that found its most vivid expression in the Baltic Way demonstration on August 23, 1989, when perhaps two million people, organized by the Latvian, Lithuanian, and Estonian Popular Fronts, linked hands in a human chain stretching from Tallinn to Vilnius. This joint action substantially increased the international reputation of the Baltic Popular Fronts and gave the international media the image of a Baltic nonviolent "singing revolution."[15] Throughout the rest of 1989 nonviolent demonstrations continued in Latvia, the rhetoric surrounding "republic sovereignty" inflated to suggest complete separation, and the Popular Front leaders claimed that the LTF, not the Latvian Communist Party, spoke for the Latvian population. The LKP was losing members just as the LTF was claiming a membership of about 250,000 by midyear 1989. By November 18, 1989, the anniversary of the 1918 independence declaration, the LTF was able to mobilize some 300,000 participants under the slogan of an Independent Latvia.

Although it was the Popular Front that now attracted the support and energies of the activist Latvians, informal organizations of all kinds proliferated, as did the number of periodicals, newspapers, and other publications, many of a transitory sort. Political groups appeared claiming to be continuations of such pre-1940 political parties as the Social Democrats and the Agrarian Union. Local chapters of international organizations such as the Boy Scouts and the Red Cross were founded. The Latvian immigrant communities in Western Europe and North America, where many of these organizations had retained a corporate existence over the past four decades, played a significant role in this organizational effort.

The policy of economic decentralization and the tendency of Latvians to act as if republic sovereignty was a reality led to a search for joint business ventures of various kinds. The increased number of visitors to Latvia, especially from the émigré communities, led the local Latvian press to debate the question of who belonged to the Latvian *tauta*: whether, for example, Latvian-speaking citizens of the United States were Americans of Latvian ancestry or Latvians residing in the United States.

Soviet authorities were losing legitimacy as definers of nationality, and, equally ominous from Moscow's point of view, in 1989 mothers of draft-age boys founded the League of Women, which aimed to protect young soldiers who reported being abused in the Soviet army and to promote the idea of alternative military service. This remarkably successful organization was thus challenging the authority of a heretofore sacrosanct all-union institution.[16] During the next two years, the army periodically threatened to enforce the draft in the Baltic with massive force. But these threats were not acted on, and the proportion of inductees in the Baltic continued to dwindle.

The startling transformation of the "people's democracies" in Eastern Europe, starting with the September 11, 1989, opening of the Hungarian border with Austria and the flight across it of some twenty-four thousand East Germans, created a new context for the Latvian events in the final months of that year. On October 18, the Hungarian National Assembly proclaimed the country a multiparty democracy, and East German communist leader Erich Honecker resigned. On November 9 the Berlin Wall was opened; on November 10 Todor Zhivkov, the Bulgarian communist leader, resigned, as did, on November 24, the secretary general of the Czechoslovak Communist Party, Milos Jakeš. By the end of December, Romanians had ousted Nicolae Ceauşecu, and Vaclav Havel had been elected president of Czechoslovakia. In the borderland republics of the Soviet Union, including Latvia, Moscow's noninterference in these events was an encouraging sign, as was the idea, which was becoming widespread, that Soviet power in Latvia and the other Baltic states, just as in Eastern Europe, was the result of USSR empire building, not some internal "socialist revolution."

By the spring of 1990 there was no sign that the USSR would try to reestablish its power in Eastern Europe, and Baltic and Latvian political activists began to think in terms of independence. In Latvia the Popular Front was now confronted by adamant demands from a strong indepen-dence-minded segment within its membership that promised to accept no compromise on the issue. Over the next few months this segment evolved into a Citizens' Congress that had its first meeting on April 30, 1990.[17]

THE SUPREME SOVIET
ELECTION OF 1990

Although political questions dominated public debate in the early months of 1990, economic decentralization was also much talked about but with little effect. Shortages of consumer goods continued, and there were few signs that they would disappear in the near future. Moreover, glasnost, having informed Latvians about life in other European countries, gave them a basis for comparison, making many feel that Latvia would have been "like Finland" (for example) had it been allowed to develop instead of being made part of a centrally directed economy. Latvians were also conscious that events unfolding in the republic were part of larger developments around them, particularly in Lithuania and Estonia. The relationship between the Popular Fronts of the three Baltic countries had been formalized in 1989 (as mentioned earlier), and there was an effort, at least among the leadership of these organizations, toward common policy, with Lithuania leading the way toward independence.

In the elections to the Lithuanian Supreme Soviet in early March—the first multiparty elections in the Soviet Union—candidates supported by the Popular Front (Sajudis) won 98 of 141 seats, and on March 11 the new Supreme Soviet formally voted to restore the Republic of Lithuania. On March 18, Supreme Soviet elections were held in Estonia and in Latvia. In Estonia, supporters of the Popular Front won only 43 percent of the seats but improved their position by striking deals with reform Communists. In Latvia the March vote (and subsequent runoffs) produced a substantial majority for the Popular Front platform (134 of 170 seats).[18] On March 30 the Estonian Supreme Soviet proclaimed the de jure existence of the Republic of Estonia and its current political institutions "in a transition phase toward independence."

By mid-April Moscow had begun an economic blockade of Lithuania, curtailing deliveries of such essential products as oil. In the same weeks, there was a split within the Latvian Communist Party. On April 8, at the LKP Congress in Riga, some one-third of the 250 delegates walked out of the meeting to protest the congress's delay in discussing independence.[19] The remaining delegates replaced Jānis Vagris with Alfrēds Rubiks (b. 1935) as first secretary; a week later, on April 14, the "independent Communists" elected as their leader Ivars Ķezbers (b. 1944), the ideological secretary of the LKP since 1988. As the communist split materialized,

Lenin's statue was removed from the Riga Museum of Revolution, and other Soviet statuary began disappearing from public places.

In an effort to stay the hand of the Estonian and Latvian Supreme Soviets, Mikhail Gorbachev offered the two republics special status within the Soviet Union but threatened economic sanctions if the two joined Lithuania on the independence question. But these efforts came to naught, and on May 4, 1990, the Latvian Supreme Council voted to renew the Republic of Latvia, setting an indeterminate transition period to accomplish the withdrawal from the USSR and asking Moscow to form a negotiating committee to discuss the process.[20] The Supreme Council, the declaration said further, would be the highest authority in the Latvian Republic until the final withdrawal. The council elected Anatolijs Gorbunovs (b. 1942) as its chairman and Ivars Godmanis (b. 1951), a senior lecturer in physics at the University of Latvia, as premier of its Cabinet of Ministers. According to an April public opinion poll of 24,600 respondents, 92 percent of the Latvians and 45 percent of the non-Latvians in Latvia supported such a move. On May 14, Gorbachev issued two statements declaring the moves toward independence by Estonia and Latvia to be illegal because they violated the secession clause in the USSR constitution. Although meetings among Gorbachev, other Moscow leaders, and the new Baltic political elite continued to take place, the three Baltic republics and the central government of the USSR were at an impasse.[21]

THE IMPASSE OF 1990

The dispute over Baltic independence lasted for the rest of 1990, amid growing turmoil throughout the Soviet Union. Representatives of the new Latvian government met with Gorbachev again in June and found him implacable; for its part, the Latvian government was being pressured by the Citizens' Congress to hold fast on independence. Also in June, the quadrennial national Song Festival (a tradition begun in 1873) was held in Riga; this time the main choir was composed of regional choirs not only from Latvia but also from émigré Latvian colonies in Western Europe, North America, and Australia. Symbolizing the unity of the Latvian *tauta* regardless of place of residence, the festival, with its thirty-seven thousand participants, was seen as part of a healing process that would eventually normalize Latvian cultural life and correct the deformations brought on by a half-century of domination by Moscow.

At the end of July the three Baltic governments refused to participate in drafting a new union treaty and in mid-August declared themselves in favor of a common market of republics in which Moscow economic planners would play no role. Also, the Supreme Council in Latvia decided to renew its 1940 borders with Belorus, Russia, Estonia, and Lithuania and set up customs posts on the eastern border. By early fall, the new Latvian government, which had been in existence for four months, was acting on Latvian domestic affairs and external relations with increasingly less deference to Moscow's wishes. Meanwhile Moscow was too preoccupied with other serious problems to focus on the situation in the Baltic area.

The fall of 1990 placed the future under a question mark, as Gorbachev began pulling back from the consequences of his reforms to placate his opponents. Correspondingly, the processes of change in Latvia, which in the spring and summer seemed nearly irreversible, began to look less permanent, and rumors of an impending coup—resulting in Gorbachev's introduction of direct presidential rule in the Baltic republics—began to hover around the fringes of public discussion. Reform measures once discussed as the groundwork for independence now seemed imperiled, even though the Supreme Council continued its work.

In September, separate treaties on economic cooperation were signed between Latvia and Belorus and between Latvia and the Russian FSR. Commentaries in the Latvian press suggested that a successful crackdown by Moscow would kill the reforming spirit, not only by removing the reformers but by crushing hope and leaving the population exhausted. Yet in its October congress, the Popular Front reiterated the desirability of independence, called for the complete withdrawal of all Soviet armed forces from Latvia and for Soviet state institutions to cease their activities in Latvia. A November poll in Riga suggested that more than 90 percent of the Latvian population of Latvia opposed the new Gorbachev-proposed union treaty.[22] Also in November, the Supreme Council instructed municipalities to stop providing supplies and social services to the Soviet army stationed in Latvia; in early December the council voted to prohibit soldiers of the Soviet army from voting in elections in the country. From his headquarters in Riga the commander of the Baltic Military District warned that the council was pushing the army to "extreme measures." Prime Minister Ivars Godmanis opined that Gorbachev might use the Soviet army to depose the parliaments of the Baltic republics. By Christmas 1990, army representatives were appealing to the USSR Congress of People's Deputies to introduce presidential rule in the Baltic area.

THE CRACKDOWN THAT NEVER CAME: JANUARY 1991

In the early weeks of 1991, with the attention of the United States and other Western countries focused on the war in the Persian Gulf, the press in Latvia noted that the 1940 Soviet occupation of Latvia had happened precisely when the Western democracies were otherwise occupied. But the crackdown in the Baltic and in Latvia never materialized as a single act.[23] Rather, there was a series of relatively small-scale but violent actions against institutions and civilians, with the authorities in Moscow either apologizing or denying responsibility. The end result was to further discredit Moscow's position on the Baltic republics.

Thus, in Latvia, on January 2, the special forces (the so-called OMON troops, or Black Berets) of the USSR Ministry of the Interior seized the press building in Riga and halted the publication of most newspapers and magazines. On the seventh, the commander of the Baltic Military District advised Prime Minister Godmanis that several thousand airborne troops would be sent to Latvia to enforce the military draft. On January 10, the Interfront organization held a mass rally calling for the resignation of the Latvian government. The most violent of these incidents, however, took place on the thirteenth in Vilnius, Lithuania, where Soviet troops attacked the main Lithuanian radio and television center, killing 14 people in the crowd and injuring some 150 others. In Riga, where a similar attack appeared imminent, some 700,000 persons poured into the streets, forming hastily constructed barricades around the most important public buildings. Continuous civilian patrols lasted for the next three weeks, as skirmishes with the Black Berets continued sporadically throughout the city. The biggest loss of life in Riga took place on January 20, when the Black Berets invaded the Ministry of Internal Affairs buildings and in the ensuing gunfire killed four people and injured ten. Latvians knew that their barricades and patrols offered no realistic obstacle if the Soviet army chose to act with all the means at its disposal. Rather, they symbolized the will to resist, an element, some said, that had been missing in 1940 when the Soviet armed forces moved into Latvia without any noticeable resistance from the Ulmanis government or the general population.

The events of January reverberated throughout the spring and early summer. The Black Beret units in Riga did not receive any punishment for their actions and, though small in number, continued to manifest a threatening presence. Neither the Moscow government nor the Baltic military authorities took responsibility for them, but their unpredictable and threatening activities were widely interpreted as a Moscow policy of continuous, low-level harassment (some said terrorism) to remind the Latvian government where the real power lay. In March there were three unexplained explosions in Riga around Soviet facilities; investigators termed them efforts to destabilize the situation. In June the Black Berets were involved in a series of attacks on the Latvian-Lithuanian border control posts. It was widely suspected that the republic KGB and the Moscow-oriented rump of the Latvian Communist Party were colluding with the Black Berets or at least supplying them with arms and transportation.

If these incidents were indeed the result of a Moscow policy of harassment, that policy was counterproductive. The January events had demonstrated that large numbers of Riga residents—Latvians and non-Latvians alike—would rally around the republic's political leaders, who also took comfort from the rapidity with which the Vilnius and Riga attacks had become known to the Western world and condemned by it. This reassured the Latvian government that a serious crackdown would not go unnoticed. The willingness of the Moscow authorities to permit military and police actions in which civilians were killed, wounded, or maimed had caused widespread revulsion among the non-Latvian populations in the Baltic and in other republics as well; leading Russian intellectuals, as well as Boris Yeltsin, who was now president of the Russian Federation, had condemned them as a blow against emerging democracy. All this strengthened the independence sentiment.

In a poll in Latvia on March 3 in which 87.5 percent of the people participated, some 73.6 percent were in favor of independence and 24.8 percent against; most encouraging for independence supporters was that a high proportion of non-Latvians supported independence.[24] On the seventeenth, the Latvian government announced that Latvia would not officially participate in the all-union referendum that Moscow hoped would demonstrate support for preserving the Soviet Union but would not oppose informal efforts to carry it out. As a result, in Latvia participation (mostly by Russians living there) was meager and the results inconclusive. But in April, Moscow agreed to change Latvia's name from the Latvian Soviet Socialist Republic to the Republic of Latvia.

Still, the sentiment in favor of independence in Latvia was not by any means unanimous, as the March voting results indicated. Opponents of independence, who included some Latvians, argued that the March voting showed the population of Latvia polarized along national lines and that independence would bring civil war. Alfrēds Rubiks, leader of the pro-Moscow and anti-independence Latvian Communist Party, called repeatedly for the introduction of presidential rule in Latvia to avert what he called "nationalist excesses" and civil strife. In May, the party reportedly organized forty-two anti-independence work collectives in Riga to strike if the government did not sign the new union treaty and reverse its decision to return property to those individuals from whom it had been taken by the nationalization decrees of 1940. The planned strike, however, came to naught.

By June 1991, a degree of normality had returned to Latvia, despite the impasse on the union treaty. Confrontations had become a series of claims and counterclaims by the Riga and Moscow governments against each other, with no third parties available to resolve them. Capitalizing on the popularity the Baltic republics had achieved in the West, Latvian political leaders made frequent trips to Western Europe and North America to argue for Latvian independence. The Supreme Council acted with greater self-assurance every month, as if it were already the government of a successor state. The formal process of separation from the USSR, however, was bogged down because the Moscow committee formed to handle the matter met with Latvian representatives only sporadically and frequently canceled meetings.

In March, Prime Minister Godmanis alerted the government to the economic consequences of Latvia's not meeting Moscow's demands for funds to stabilize the Soviet economy and compensate individuals for price increases. At the end of May, however, the Supreme Council, in discussing Latvia's contribution to the Soviet budget, concluded that it was the USSR that was in debt to Latvia. In June, Moscow warned the Latvian government that it would take measures to see that the army draft quota for the spring was fulfilled, and Mikhail Gorbachev, in Oslo to receive the Nobel Peace Prize, blamed Latvia and Lithuania for separatist nationalism. Later that month the foreign minister of Latvia, Jānis Jurkāns (b. 1946) announced that if Moscow exerted economic pressures on Latvia by charging world market prices for oil and gas, Latvia would charge world prices for the food supplies it was exporting to the Soviet Union. In July Black Berets attacked customs posts at the Riga airport and main railway station; a similar attack on the railway customs office was reported in mid-August.

During June and July, the Latvian Supreme Council had to deal with domestic issues as well because many if not most of the laws it had passed since the election of 1990 were waiting for the questions of Latvia's status vis-à-vis the Soviet Union to be resolved. Laws dealing with privatization of both rural and urban properties, with the elimination of price and wage controls, with the meaning of citizenship, with the creation of a postal service and a new monetary system, and with the return of property nationalized in 1940 were only partially implemented; some were not implemented at all. The Latvian press voiced the public's dissatisfaction at the pace of reform but pointed out that elsewhere in the Soviet Union there was only deterioration. The declarations of independence issued by other republics, especially by the Russian Federation and its president, Boris Yeltsin, were hailed by Latvians because Yeltsin was perceived as a friend of Baltic independence. At the same time, the public in Latvia felt that a conservative coup in Moscow was likely. Several of Gorbachev's closest advisers, including Foreign Minister Edvard Shevardnadze, had recently resigned, warning of precisely that eventuality.

THE COUP OF AUGUST 19, 1991

The August 19 coup broke the impasse in a way that neither side of the constitutional dispute had expected.[25] When it was announced in Latvia that Soviet vice president Gennadii Yanaev was assuming the position of acting president immediately, some, such as the leaders of the Supreme Council, took it to mean that the forces of reaction had finally begun the counterrevolution, and others, such as Alfrēds Rubiks and the hard-line Communists, that the chaos of nationalism and separatism would finally end.

The Latvian Supreme Council president, Anatolijs Gorbunovs, delivered a radio address in which he stated that the coup attempt was illegal, that the Moscow Emergency Committee had no jurisdiction in Latvia, and that Latvian citizens should not cooperate with unlawful groups and, if need be, should engage in peaceful protest. The proindependence Communists (now called the Latvian Democratic Labor Party) supported Gorbunovs's announcement. The anti-independence Communists, however, were pleased by the Moscow events, and Alfrēds Rubiks, the first secretary, announced that a new government would be formed in Latvia and that all parties except his own would be banned.

By the evening of August 19, Soviet tanks and armored vehicles had taken up positions in and around Riga and Soviet troops were in control of the Latvian Ministry of Internal Affairs. The Black Berets, in turn, had seized the Latvian radio and television building, as well as the Latvian Ministry of Internal Affairs. The deputy chairman of the Supreme Council, Dainis Ivāns, in Stockholm for a meeting, evidently received instructions to begin forming a government in exile. By August 21, as the coup began to unravel, three persons in Riga had been killed, two by gunfire.

Despite Riga's beleaguered situation, the Latvian Supreme Council was able to respond to the situation. The council amended the May 4, 1990, declaration of independence, announcing that Latvia was an independent sovereign republic whose internal affairs were to be guided by the February 1922 constitution. Thus by August 22, when Gorbachev returned to Moscow and his position as president, the Latvian government considered the country's formal relationship with the USSR at an end. On the twenty-fourth, Boris Yeltsin, on behalf of the Russian Federation, recognized Latvia's independence. By that date the Latvian government had declared the Communist Party unconstitutional and begun to confiscate the party's offices and properties throughout Latvia. Alfrēds Rubiks was arrested on August 27 and charged with conspiracy to seize power from the democratically elected government. On the twenty-ninth, the Latvian government and the USSR KGB signed a protocol liquidating the Latvian branch of the KGB and spelling out the steps for transferring its property.

Over the next week, the independence of the Baltic states was recognized by Ukraine, Belarus, Georgia and the twelve nations of the European Community; by August 29, thirty countries had extended recognition. Gorbachev, in contrast, declared these acts of recognition hasty and complained that the three Baltic countries had not observed the secession provisions of the USSR constitution. By this time, however, Gorbachev's cavils were irrelevant because his own power in a quickly changing Moscow had virtually disappeared. On August 31, the Black Berets withdrew from Latvia, and on September 3, the Latvian government announced its full control over the banking system. On September 2, the United States extended diplomatic recognition to all three Baltic countries, and on the fourth, the State Council, which was now the new government of the USSR, followed suit. At the end of September, when the United Nations General Assembly opened its new session, Latvia was seated as an independent sovereign state.

10 Continuities and Discontinuities

The independent Republic of Latvia, which took its seat in the United Nations on September 17, 1991, had by no means buried the past. Its basic law was the constitution of 1922, which now had to be amended to fit the new circumstances. Its highest political authority was the Supreme Council, an institution of the Soviet period; the council's presiding officer, a former ideological secretary of the Communist Party, was the new nation's head of state. Its currency was the Soviet ruble, and most of its labor force, despite some decentralization and a few privatization laws, was employed in state-owned and state-managed enterprises. The majority of seats in the Supreme Council were held by supporters of a political movement—the Popular Front—rather than by a political party, and the movement was finding it increasingly difficult to sustain discipline within its ranks.

The country's population of 2.68 million (1989) was of mixed nationality—52 percent Latvians, 34 percent Russians, 14 percent others—so that only slightly more than half the population would feel unalloyed joy about the reemergence of what was likely to be a *Latvian* state (see table 3, p. 158).[1] The new state had an estimated forty-five thousand Soviet soldiers within its borders, and the leaders of the Soviet Union were still struggling to preserve the union as a single, undivided entity.

A TRANSITION GOVERNMENT

In the spring of 1990, the elections to the Supreme Soviet had returned a majority of deputies whose political sympathies were with the Latvian Popular Front and the Latvian National Independence Movement. In the period from May 1990 to September 1991 this coalition—the council, sixteen standing committees of the council, the Cabinet of Ministers, nineteen ministries, and thirteen state boards and commissions—had produced a body of laws and regulations predicated on the idea of eventual independence. This government understood itself to be a de facto transitional government, to be changed at some time in the future when total separation from the USSR had been achieved. But independence arrived overnight, and, by virtue of the August 21, 1991, declaration that the constitution of 1922 was the basic law of the land, the government had become a de jure transition government as well.

This status was double-edged. On the one hand, the Latvian government no longer had to coordinate its actions with a local "guiding institution" (the Communist Party was now illegal), nor did it have to keep an eye on Moscow as it legislated. In fact, in this respect the Latvian government's independence of action had been growing with every month in the pre-August 1991 period. On the other hand, the government was faced with maintaining the reform momentum of the pre-August months and adapting political and social institutions to the new circumstances. The new political context in which these tasks had to be carried out included the stresses and strains—already manifested in the Popular Front coalition—caused by the myriad problems independence was creating throughout the general population and that could now be voiced in the popular press.[2] The question at the end of 1991 and beginning of 1992 was how long the Supreme Council could retain its 1990 mandate. Most of the citizenry showed no signs of challenging the council's legitimacy; there was, after all, no other "government" to be had at the moment. But political opinions were now unfettered, as was the possibility of differing opinions becoming embodied in new movements, groups, coalitions, and parties.[3]

From March 1990 until June 1993 (when the council was replaced by a newly elected parliament), the leadership of two individuals—Anatolijs Gorbunovs (b. 1942), the president of the council and the transition head of state, and Ivars Godmanis (b. 1951), the prime minister—bridged the late Soviet and full independence periods. Gorbunovs had been a longtime member of the Latvian Communist Party and ideological secretary of its Central Committee from 1985 to 1988, when he became active in the

Popular Front. Chosen in March 1990 as the presiding officer of the council, he demonstrated considerable political savvy in the precoup period and after September 1991 and maintained high popularity ratings among both the Latvian and the minority nationality populations. He seemed to stand above the fray of everyday politics and became a useful symbol of institutional continuity.

Godmanis, by contrast, was an academic—a physics professor at the University of Latvia and a relative newcomer to political life, becoming active in the Popular Front in 1988 and then the presiding officer of a cabinet of ministers. Since 1990 he had been the lightning rod for all the dissatisfactions that governmental action and inaction generated. Although Godmanis survived repeated no-confidence votes in the council, his public popularity diminished among both the Latvian and the minority nationality populations, in large part because his name was associated with every measure that became law or was proposed as law. Godmanis became a symbol of unnecessary foot-dragging, and his ministers were under constant attack because reforms did not bring the rapid positive results many had expected once independence had been achieved.

The council had to work on numerous reform fronts while revising the pre-1940 basic documents (principally the constitution of 1922 but also the civil law of 1937) that had now become the fundamental laws of the land. Beyond this assignment, there was pressure to revoke or change Soviet-era laws, regulations, and practices to conform with the models promised by the Popular Front since 1990: a free-market economy with a social safety net, a secure new monetary system, economic links with both Western and Eastern markets, a wage and salary structure reflecting performance, a free press and freedom to organize, a less specialized and less coercive educational system, and a civil society that would be autonomous from, and if need be provide countervailing power to, the central government.[4]

In addition, the government had to create a diplomatic service and a civil service, ensure that foreign diplomats had access to Riga properties to establish embassies, and develop recruiting mechanisms for an army, border guards, and customs officials. All these changes had to be brought about by a relatively small number of knowledgeable persons who were themselves going through intellectual transformations of various kinds. The Latvian state of 1991 had not been created by revolutionaries sweeping aside an easily identifiable old politico-economic elite, such as the Baltic Germans after 1918. This time, the only part of the old elite that had been decisively extruded from power were the members of the pro-Moscow Latvian Communist Party. The new elite was a patchwork of former Communists, erstwhile members of the Latvian *nomenklatura*, early anti-Communists such as Eduards Berklāvs and recent ones, and many energetic and ambitious persons who had remained outside the party and the government but had developed considerable administrative and political talents in other state structures such as the university system, collective farms, the Academy of Sciences, or the media.[5]

During the seventeen months after August 1991, the basic structure of the Latvian government remained what it had been before independence: a Supreme Council, now more frequently called the parliament; a cabinet of ministers headed by a prime minister; and ministries and departments that were being slowly reduced in number. What was changing more rapidly than this structure was the international and domestic context in which this government continued to work. By the end of 1991, the Soviet Union had dissolved and been replaced by the Commonwealth of Independent States (CIS), in which Latvia and the other two Baltic countries repeatedly refused membership. Latvia's foreign policy, which during these months was decidedly oriented toward Western Europe, had as its goal the fastest possible integration with existing European international organizations such as the Nordic Council, the European Community, and the Council of Europe.[6] With respect to most new states of the former Soviet Union, Latvia's policy instruments were bilateral treaties and agreements, but with regard to the other two Baltic states, Latvians sought to build on the cooperative traditions that had come into being during the heyday of Popular Front activity. Latvia's professed neutrality in international dealings was at bottom an effort to link itself with Western organizations, to practice a guarded regionalism in the Baltic area, and to remain circumspect in relations with CIS and non-CIS states, especially the Russian Federation.

The domestic context of the government's activities was changing more rapidly than the international scene, demonstrating the efficacy of public debate and public pressure. Politics was no longer simply a matter of official institutions. Moreover, the government had been legislating for some eighteen months before independence, creating many policies that were heartily disliked by different segments of the population, and the outcome of the August 1991 coup left large numbers of persons—especially the Slavic-speaking part of the Latvian population—uneasy about their future in a Latvian state. As time passed and the Supreme Council took up the question of the next parliamentary elections, extrainstitutional political discussion reached a high pitch. The spectrum of attitudes tended to be protean, but some hard-line positions did become identifiable. On the right, critics complained about the large numbers of *nomenklatura* persons in high places in the new regime and the correspondingly low number of persons who had refused to compromise with the old system. The right argued that the main purpose of the new state was to ensure the preservation of the Latvian *tauta* and its unique culture and that the former *nomenklatura* could not be entrusted with such a serious task. Now that the basic nation (in Latvian, *pamattauta*) had regained control of the country that bore its name, the government had to ensure that that control would remain in its hands.[7]

On the left, the most pressing issue was the political and economic future of the Slavic minorities, primarily the Russians. Although the left could no longer realistically question the fait accompli of an independent Latvia (though fringe groups continued to do so), it did argue that the government's primary responsibilities were to ensure legal equality (including citizenship) for all residents of the country and continued employment of the labor force. By and large, the opinions on the fringes of the political spectrum were voiced most loudly outside the Supreme Council, although on occasion they were articulated by individuals within the council. The fringes of the spectrum also had a distinct national coloration, with the activists on the right being Latvians and those on the left having their base of support in the Russian population. The arguments of both groups, however, presupposed a dominant role for the central government in the economy and in many domains of social and cultural life. In this respect, the fringes were in line with the political philosophy of the interwar Latvian Republic, which remained unapologetically statist during the parliamentary period (1918–34), and especially during Kārlis Ulmanis's authoritarian rule (1934–40).

Expressing numerous and varied positions in the middle of the political spectrum were the pragmatically inclined, in and out of government. Their policies (in government) and arguments (outside government) were grounded in the need to address and solve the many problems pressing in from all sides. Their guidelines were preserving independence and implementing reforms that would result in a Westernized Latvia. Those problems ranged from simple and easily solvable (for example, using Latvian in parliamentary discussions) to the complex (such as privatizing state industrial enterprises), and most were dictated by the situation obtaining at the moment independence was renewed in August 1991. There was, in other words, little room for new directions and specifically Latvian innovations. The Supreme Council had been a transitional government from 1990 to 1991 when the Soviet Union still existed; it continued to be transitional once independence had been achieved.

MINORITY NATIONALITIES AND THE QUESTION OF CITIZENSHIP

Latvians worried that the nationality structure and demographic patterns of the republic's population again threatened the survival of their national culture. Under Alexander III and Nicholas II, Russification had been undisguised and unapologetic; in the Soviet period, Russification was more surreptitious, taking a form of industrial policy that brought hundreds of thousands of Russians and other Slavic peoples into Latvia. When that in-migration was combined with the unchallenged weight of Russians in the Latvian Communist Party and the Moscow-dictated policy of enlarging the role of the Russian language at all levels in the educational process, it amounted to cultural genocide.[8] As a result of such policies, by 1989 only 52 percent of Latvia's population declared itself to be Latvian; only 36.5 percent of the inhabitants of Riga, the nation's capital, were Latvian; and, though some 66 percent of Latvians in Latvia were relatively fluent in Russian, only 21 percent of the ethnic Russians and 18 percent of other non-Latvian nationalities were able to converse in Latvian.[9] Much of the energy that produced the Popular Front movement had to do precisely with this issue, and one of the first successes of the Popular Front—even before the 1990 independence declaration—was the 1989 decree by the Supreme Council making Latvian the official language of the state. The new language law envisioned a transition period of three years during which, among other things, the non-Latvian-speaking employees of state institutions would be required to learn Latvian. But because of precoup uncertainties, the law was weakly enforced.

After the August coup the demographic situation began to change. Monthly statistics concerning migration showed that emigration of non-Latvians was exceeding immigration, resulting in the incremental expansion of the proportion of Latvians in the total population (53.5 percent by fall 1993). Also, in early 1992, the language law was strengthened, testing commissions were created, and implementation was begun in earnest.[10] Although these events defused the issue somewhat on the Latvian side, a rigorously enforced language law created charges from political organizations among the non-Latvian population that human rights were being violated. Notwithstanding the fact that ethnic Russians made up only about 34 percent of the country's population (with Belarussians constituting 4.5 percent, Ukrainians 3.5 percent, Poles 2.3 percent, and Lithuanians 1.3 percent), the public disputes over this and related issues tended to be cast in terms of Latvians and Russians.[11]

Uncertainties were further compounded by the hesitant manner in which the Supreme Council dealt with the questions of citizenship in the new state. Temporary regulations on citizenship before August 1991 declared that, because Latvia was a "renewed" state, those who had been citizens before June 17, 1940, and their descendants were ipso facto citizens but that those who arrived in the republic after that date had to be screened before citizenship rights would be granted. Although this and all laws passed by the Supreme Council scrupulously avoided targeting any ethnic subpopulation for special treatment—positive or negative—the migration patterns of the Soviet period ensured that, in absolute numbers, statelessness would be the lot of more ethnic Russians than of any other subpopulation.[12]

As a transition government, the Supreme Council during 1992 became increasingly uncertain about such fundamental issues as citizenship, and by the end of 1992 had decided to bequeath the question to the new parliament that was to be elected in 1993. Further extensions of the temporary regulation were passed, however, because the pending parliamentary election required a clear definition of the "political community" (i.e., who would have the right to vote). Citizenship continued to be granted on the basis of the temporary regulations, and thus the process of reducing the numbers of the stateless went on, albeit slowly. By mid-1993, 98.4 percent of all Latvians, 39.0 percent of Russians, 20.0 percent of Belarussians, 6.3 percent of Ukrainians, 21.5 percent of Lithuanians, 61.6 percent of Poles, and 45.5 percent of Jews had received citizenship. Even so, the process left an uncomfortably large number of Russians—some 550,000—without citizenship, holding only internal passports issued by the Soviet Union, which by that time no longer existed.[13]

In the council debates over the citizenship question, two positions emerged. The so-called zero-option—granting all current residents of Latvia citizenship immediately—had more support in the general population, especially among the political activists of the minority nationalities, than in the council, where it had virtually none. The other position was based on the fear of a two-community state (in Latvian, *divu kopienu valsts*), which was difficult to translate into specific legislation. There was general consensus that, to be naturalized, one should know Latvian and swear loyalty to the Latvian state, but no agreement could be reached on how advanced the language skills should be, on whether or not naturalization should proceed by means of annual quotas linked to total population growth, on the minimum residency requirement, on whether dual citizenship should be permitted, on how to deal with offspring of mixed marriages, or on how to classify the estimated forty thousand–plus pensioned former Soviet military personnel (and their offspring) who were residents of Latvia.

Predictably, those who perceived the Latvian state as an instrument for preserving the Latvian *tauta*, its language, and its unique culture pulled for a citizenship law that would increase the proportional weight of the Latvian population; those who wanted their status certain and those who feared ethnic polarization pulled for the zero option.[14] By the end of 1992, the debate on the citizenship question had been joined by two sets of outsiders: (1) political leaders, including President Boris Yeltsin of the Russian Federa-

tion, who initiated a campaign charging the Latvian state with discrimina-
tory practices and violations of human rights and (2) visiting teams of
human rights experts from such international bodies as the Council of
Europe and the United Nations, who repeatedly concluded that human
rights were not being violated. At the same time, Latvian becoming the
language of governmental affairs did reduce the proportion of non-Latvians
in positions of political authority. All those who could not use the language
fluently were disadvantaged, regardless of what other skills or knowledge
they possessed.

ECONOMIC REFORM AND
THE PRIVATE SECTOR

The most successful of all the economic changes initiated by the
Supreme Council was the currency reform that moved the Latvian economy
away from the Russian ruble zone.[15] The Bank of Latvia, confirmed as the
central financial institution after the August 1991 coup, introduced the
Latvian ruble as a parallel currency to the Russian ruble, while enunciating
and maintaining a conservative stance on the Latvian rubles' being put into
circulation. Because the value of the Russian ruble was diminishing rapidly
throughout 1992 because of a liberal printing of money in the Russian
Federation, the Latvian ruble appreciated in value in relation to it. Thus by
the second half of 1992, the government was confident enough to start
preparing to replace the Latvian ruble with the Latvian lats, the currency of
the interwar republic. The currency reform, while earning plaudits from
such international bodies as the World Bank and the International Monetary Fund, heightened uncertainty in the Latvian population because it took
almost two years to complete.[16]

Adding to the feeling of insecurity was the Supreme Council's determination gradually to withdraw subsidies from all state enterprises and
organizations and then privatize them. Desubsidizing had begun before
August 1991 but continued in full force after that date, bringing with it the
expected drop in industrial production (20–30 percent annually starting
with 1990). Enterprises that had been able to count on distributing their
products throughout the Soviet Union on the basis of central planning were
now limited to the consumers in a Latvian market and such customers
outside Latvia as could be recruited through bilateral agreements. Enlarging
the market economy, which required entrepreneurship, management skills,
and the ability to raise venture capital quickly, favored those who had
become skilled at using the old system. By early 1993 it was rumored that
most of the new consumer-oriented enterprises in Latvia were in the hands

of non-Latvians, suggesting that many in the Latvian population were exhibiting considerable standoffishness toward a fundamental sector (small business) of the free-market system.

After August 1991 ownership reform continued on the basis of laws passed in 1990 and 1991. Although in 1940 nationalization had been accomplished overnight with a governmental decree, returning property rights to private persons (or corporations) turned out to be far more complicated. A bundle of privatization laws required that assets national- ized in 1940 first be turned over by the national government to municipali- ties; the municipalities would then return them to their original (i.e., pre- 1940) owners or, more likely, to their descendants. Then state and munici- pal property that had never had private owners would be sold.[17] The entire process was slowed considerably by a lack of clarity about the original owners. Titles had to be researched in the national archive and certified as being true in court, and disputes between serial owners of the same property had to be resolved. Many 1940 owners (or their descendants) were now living in other countries, so dealings with them had to be conducted by mail.

With respect to state-owned industrial enterprises and retail establish- ments, the process had barely begun in August 1991 and continued at a relatively slow pace during 1992. By the summer of 1993, privatization plans had been approved for only thirty-five of the several hundred state- run enterprises, although a much larger proportion of the smaller units already had private owners. The process of transforming state farms into private holdings proceeded much more quickly: by early 1992, the number of private farms had climbed to 17,538; by the beginning of 1993 that number was approaching 40,000. Ownership changes in the industrial, service, and agricultural sectors brought with them reductions in the labor force, compounding the problems of under- and unemployed created by the withdrawal of subsidies to state industry.

Particularly disillusioning to the Latvian intelligentsia was the diminu- tion of central government support for education and research and for all organizations and institutions that dealt with the printed word. The process of dismantling the Latvian Academy of Sciences and its numerous research institutes began before August 1991 and continued thereafter, so that by 1992 the academy had become largely an institution of individuals elected by their peers for outstanding accomplishment. Some research institutes of the academy were dissolved, others became private research centers, and still others became autonomous units within the University of Latvia. These changes entailed such severe reductions in staff for the academy and the institutes that the government was charged with the "systematic elimination of scientific work."[18] The main universities—the University of Latvia and Riga Technical University—had to continue their work with flat or reduced budgets, which meant an increase in student-faculty ratios as well as a considerable amount of "moonlighting" on the part of staff and faculty. The autonomy the universities had sought and obtained even before August 1991 had weakened their influence on the government, which was trying, through flat or reduced budgets, to instill an entrepreneurial spirit in its educational institutions. In the near-total absence of a wealthy private sector, private foundations, or well-to-do alumni that would build endowments, the universities entered hard times. Similarly, organizations that in the Soviet system had been able to count on state funding—publishing houses, museums, orchestras, theaters, journals, and libraries—were also adrift, with their budgets eliminated or severely reduced and their managers and directors having to raise support from business "sponsors." In this respect, the government's cultural and educational policies were reversing the practices not only of the Soviet period but also of the interwar Latvian republic, which provided substantial endowments and prizes for cultural and educational activities.

THE CONTINUING RUSSIAN MILITARY PRESENCE

The existence since 1945 of the Baltic Military District, with Riga as its headquarters, meant that when independence arrived in August 1991, there were some forty-five thousand Soviet troops on Latvian soil. When the Soviet Union collapsed and the Russian Federation assumed authority of the Soviet army, the three Baltic states found themselves negotiating this question with a government whose leader—Boris Yeltsin—had supported Baltic independence. By early 1992, it was evident, however, that the withdrawal of Russian troops would not be immediate. In September 1991 the commander of the Baltic Military District announced that troop withdrawals would not be concluded until 1994, and the Russian side seemed not to want to change this target date. The continued presence of a foreign army offended the Baltic states' sense of sovereignty, as did the fact that the Latvian territory was dotted with Soviet bases, practice bombing ranges, firing ranges, storage depots, housing complexes, radar sites, and naval installations. Another problem was the large number of high-ranking retired military personnel who had decided to stay in Latvia but behaved as though they were living in the Soviet Union or the Russian Federation. The postcoup Latvian government negotiated first with the Soviet authorities and then with the Russian Federation over all these problems throughout 1992 and 1993. The long-term nature of the negotiations meant that they would be affected by the changing political climate.

Occasionally, Russian political leaders linked the pace of withdrawal to the alleged mistreatment of the Russian population of Latvia in the matters of language and citizenship; such linkages were rejected by the Latvian government. The Russian government's position continued to harden, especially after December 1993, when Vladimir Zhirinovski, a Russian nationalist ideologue, showed surprising popularity in the Russian parliamentary election of that month. The total number of Russian military personnel continued to drop throughout 1992 and 1993, however, and military property continued to be turned over to the Latvian government on a regular basis, after being stripped by everything of value that could be transported out of the country.[19]

THE PARLIAMENTARY ELECTIONS OF 1993

By declaring in August 1991 that the 1922 constitution was the country's basic law, the Supreme Council had bound itself to a parliamentary election in the near future. Throughout 1992 the election date continued to be postponed in expectation of the passage of a citizenship law that would also define the "political community." This hope was abandoned in the fall of 1992, and the council accepted a temporary solution, defining the *political community* as those who would be citizens at the time of the election, which was then set for the late spring of 1993. In the discussions surrounding the electoral procedures, the new parliament-to-be was designated as the *fifth* Saeima, the fourth having been elected in 1931 and dismissed by Kārlis Ulmanis in 1934. Just as the laws of the renewed republic were to be infused with legitimacy by the 1922 constitution, so the principal lawmaking body would receive its legitimization by being connected with the interwar parliamentary tradition. The absence of a citizenship law, however, meant that a substantial number of adult residents (most of them ethnic Russians) would not be able to vote in the parliamentary election and would have to depend on other citizens to represent their interests. The constitution called for a Saeima of one hundred deputies, and the electoral procedures specified that a candidate's list receiving less than 4 percent of the total vote would not receive any seats.

Campaigning for the election began in earnest in mid-spring of 1993 and became intense after the election date was set as June 5–6. The array of groupings and parties that eventually submitted candidate lists numbered twenty-three and contained virtually every identifiable viewpoint on the Latvian political spectrum. Public opinion polls during April and May consistently gave the highest ratings to an electoral coalition called Latvia's

Way (in Latvian, Latvijas Ceļš), which merged in its candidate's list such popular figures of the Supreme Council as Anatolijs Gorbunovs, the council's president, and Georgs Andrējevs (b. 1932), the current foreign minister, and political leaders of the Latvian émigré community such as Gunārs Meierovics (b. 1920), the chairman of the World Federation of Free Latvians. Meierovics had the additional appeal of being the son of Zigfrīds Meierovics, the first foreign minister of the interwar republic who had obtained Western de jure recognition of the new state after 1918. Other electoral groups receiving good ratings in the preelection polls included the Agrarian Union (in Latvian, Zemnieku Savienība), which announced itself as the continuation of the interwar party of the same name that, as the party of Kārlis Ulmanis, had played a major political role in the parliamentary period; the Latvian National Independence Movement (in Latvian, Lātvijas Nacionālās Neatkarības Kustība), which was founded in 1988 and had been the mainstay of the political right during the ensuing changes; the Popular Front (in Latvian, Tautas Fronte), which had as one of its candidates Ivars Godmanis, the unpopular prime minister; the Democratic Center Party (in Latvian, Demokratiskā Centra Partija), which also declared itself to be a version of the successful interwar moderate party of the same name; the Social Democratic Workers Party (in Latvian, Socialdemokratiskā Strādnieku Partija), which described itself as the heir of the powerful interwar Social Democrats; and the somewhat clumsily named Harmony for Latvia—Revival for the Economy Party (in Latvian, Saskaņa Latvijai—Ekonomiskā Atdzimšana), which was led by Jānis Jurkāns, a former foreign minister in the Godmanis government who had formed the Harmony Party to voice the interests of non-Latvian minorities.

The campaign was sprightly, with relatively little extremism in evidence, but its short duration as well as the large number of parties did not allow any one of them to develop a clear identity, at least not with respect to a platform. All the contestants, save the Popular Front, were critical of the Godmanis government, and all stated, in different variations and with different emphases, unobjectionable goals: economic development, continued privatization, vigilance with respect to sovereignty, and integration with the rest of Europe. But public interest in the campaign remained acute, and 89 percent of the eligible voters participated in the election.

Of the twenty-three competing parties, eight obtained a sufficiently high proportion of the vote to be represented in the Saeima: Latvia's Way (32.4 percent), National Independence Movement (13.4 percent), Harmony for Latvia (12.0 percent), the Agrarian Union (10.6 percent), For Fatherland and Freedom (5.4 percent), Democratic Center (4.7 percent), Christian Democratic Party (5.0 percent), and the Equal Rights Movement (5.7 percent).[20] The two surprises were the poor showing of the Latvian Popular

Front, which received only 2.6 percent of the vote and was therefore excluded from the Saeima, and the relatively strong showing of the so-designated Russian parties—Harmony for Latvia and the Equal Rights Movement, both of which stressed the interests of the non-Latvian population.[21] Latvia's Way, though having by far the largest plurality, did not receive a majority and had to depend on a coalition to form a government.

The new Saeima met for the first time on July 6 and, following the 1922 constitution, elected from among its deputies both a Saeima president, Anatolijs Gorbunovs, and a president of the country, Guntis Ulmanis (b. 1939), a deputy from the Agrarian Union. Between them Gorbunovs and Ulmanis bridged the period of the Supreme Council, which Gorbunovs had headed since 1990, with the interwar republic (Ulmanis was the grandnephew of Kārlis Ulmanis, the interwar republic's last president). Later in July, Latvia's Way and the Agrarian Union agreed to form a coalition cabinet, which could command forty-eight votes if party discipline were maintained and a majority by recruiting additional votes from smaller groupings. The cabinet was headed by Valdis Birkavs (b. 1942) of Latvia's Way and included among its thirteen ministers three persons from the Latvian diaspora: the minister of defense, Valdis Pavlovskis (b. 1934, United States), the minister of welfare, Jānis Ritenis (b. 1925, Australia), and the minister of justice, Egīls Levits (b. 1955, Germany). The Saeima and the cabinet immediately began to work on the tasks inherited from the Supreme Council, the most important of which were the citizenship law and the continuing presence of the Russian army.

The Latvians elected a government that differed sharply from those elected by Lithuanians and Estonians in their first post–August 1991 parliamentary elections (fall of 1992).[22] In Lithuania, the Lithuanian Popular Front (Sajudis) suffered an embarrassing defeat that gave an absolute majority in the Sejmas to the Lithuanian Democratic Labor Party (the former independent Communist Party) and its leader Algirdas Brazauskas, who in February 1993 also became Lithuania's first popularly elected president. In Estonia, the September 1992 *Riigikogu* elections resulted in a right-of-center three-party majority and led to the formation of a cabinet (by Prime Minister Mart Laar, b. 1960), most members of which were a new political generation and, with a few exceptions, had virtually no connections with the communist past.

The leaders of the new Latvian government, through their personal histories, reflected virtually every aspect of the political experiences of the Latvian *tauta*. Latvia had a center-right coalition majority in the Saeima, but the center, Latvia's Way, was far larger than its right-wing partner, the Agrarian Union; moreover, the center had a substantial infusion of persons who in the past had been orthodox Communists, then reform Communists,

and then former Communists. The country's new president, Guntis Ulmanis, had been deported and had had to take another surname for a while
to hide his relationship to the interwar president. Moreover, the cabinet had
three ministers from the Latvian émigré communities of the Western world.

The transfer of power from the old Supreme Council and the new
Saeima was uneventful, with Latvia's Way immediately entering discussions
about possible cabinet coalitions with the less numerous parties. Deputies
from all the smaller parties quickly became integrated into the ongoing
work of the Saeima committees, and their public statements on issues
before the Saeima were from the beginning responsible and constructive in
tone. The Saeima parties remaining in opposition predicted a short life for
the new cabinet, but the Birkavs government survived until July 1994, when
the president called upon the Latvian National Independence Movement to
initiate discussions for a new cabinet.

During the second half of its year in office, the Birkavs government
managed to bring to fruition a citizenship law, which was passed by the
Saeima in an extraordinary summer session on July 28, and struck an
agreement with the Russian government that all Russian troops, save a
handful guarding the Skrunda radar facility, would be withdrawn from
Latvia by August 31. In both issues, compromise was necessary: the
citizenship law finally excluded quotas, and the troop agreement included a
promise by the Latvian government to safeguard the social welfare of the
retired Russian military officers in Latvia. Although Western observers were
pleased that these difficult controversies had been resolved, no such pleasure
was exhibited by large segments of the Latvian population. Substantial
resentment remained over having to extend citizenship to persons thought
to be "colonists" and of being forced to pay social benefits to the remnants
of a "colonial army."

Despite these continuing dissatisfactions, by the fall of 1994 most
evidence suggested that Latvians had accepted the basic political rules of
the new state. In September, after President Ulmanis gave the right-of-
center parties an opportunity to form a new government, the Saeima
rejected the cabinet proposed by them, and the president turned once again
to Latvia's Way, which formed a cabinet that was acceptable to the Saeima.
Valdis Birkavs assumed the post of foreign minister. The transition was
uneventful, and the losers—the right-wing parties—rather than taking to
the streets, initiated talks with one another about how to form an effective
parliamentary opposition. During the fall months, the Russian Duma and
the Latvian Saeima ratified the troop withdrawal treaty, thus reducing to
relative insignificance an issue that, at least from the Latvian side, had been
dominant in Latvian-Russian relations since 1991. The quiet effectiveness
of President Ulmanis continued to place him at the top of all public

opinion polls among Latvians and non-Latvians alike. On the November anniversary of the Bolshevik Revolution, few people in Riga brought flowers to the former site of Lenin's statue. As 1994 drew to a close, Latvia looked forward to being admitted to the Council of Europe, from which it had been excluded due to its delays in passing a citizenship law.

Appendix: Latvian State Structures and Political Leaders—1918 to 1994

I. 1918–1922

  A. Provisional "national government" created by the Latvian National Council pursuant to November 18, 1918, independence declaration; its work continued in three distinct phases (November 18, 1918–July 12, 1919; July 14, 1919–December 8, 1919; December 9, 1919–June 11, 1920). Prime minister in all three phases, Kārlis Ulmanis (Agrarian Union).

  B. Seeking unsuccessfully to replace the provisional national government during 1919 were

    The government of the Latvian Soviet Socialist Republic (January–May 1919). Chair of executive committee, Pēteris Stučka (Bolshevik).

    The German-oriented Niedra government (April–June, 1919). Prime minister and interior minister, Andrievs Niedra (nonparty).

  C. Constitutional convention, elected April 1920, created two governments (cabinets):

    June 11, 1920–June 18, 1921, government. Prime minister, Kārlis Ulmanis (Agrarian Union).

    June 15, 1921–January 26, 1923, government. Prime minister and foreign minister Zigfrīds Meierovics (Agrarian Union).

II. 1922–1934

Political structures of this period operated under the constitution of 1922, which provided for the election of a parliament (Saeima), which in turn elected its own and a national president and formed governments (cabinets).

A. Parliaments (Saeimas):

First, elected 1922 (president, F. Vesmanis [Social Democrat])
Second, elected 1925 (president, P. Kalniņš [Social Democrat])
Third, elected 1928 (president, P. Kalniņš [Social Democrat])
Fourth, elected 1931 (president, P. Kalniņš [Social Democrat])

B. Presidents of the Republic of Latvia (1922–1936):

Jānis Čakste (Democratic Center) 1922–1927
Gustavs Zemgals (Agrarian Union) 1927–1930
Alberts Kviesis (Agrarian Union) 1930–1936

C. Prime Ministers:

J. Pauļuks (also transportation minister) (nonparty), January 27, 1923–June 26, 1923

Z. Meierovics (also foreign minister) (Agrarian Union), June 28, 1923–January 26, 1924

V. Zāmuēls (also foreign minister and justice minister) (nonparty), January 27, 1924–December 18, 1924

H. Celmiņš (also agriculture minister) (Agrarian Union), December 19, 1924–December 23, 1925

K. Ulmanis (Agrarian Union), December 24, 1925–May 6, 1926

A. Alberings (Agrarian Union), May 7, 1926–December 18, 1926

M. Skujenieks (also interior minister) (Progressives), December 19, 1926–January 23, 1928

P. Juraševskis (Democratic Center), January 24, 1928–November 30, 1928

H. Celmiņš (Agrarian Union), December 1, 1928–March 26, 1931

K. Ulmanis (also foreign minister) (Agrarian Union), March 27, 1931–December 12, 1931

M. Skujenieks (also finance minister) (Progressives), December 6, 1931–March 23, 1933

A. Bļodnieks (New Farmers), March 24, 1933–March 16, 1934

K. Ulmanis (also foreign minister) (Agrarian Union), March 17, 1934–May 15, 1934

III. 1934–1940

Coup by Kārlis Ulmanis (Agrarian Union) on May 15, 1934, suspended constitution of 1922 and the Saeima. Ulmanis governed as prime minister from May 16, 1934, to June 19, 1940, with a cabinet of his own choosing and as president from April 11, 1936, to July 21, 1940.

IV 1940–1941

A. Invasion of Latvia by the Soviet Union on June 16, 1940, left Kārlis Ulmanis as president until July 21; he was replaced as prime minister on June 20 by Augusts Kirchensteins, who, together with a new elite of pro-Soviet leaders, was acting on behalf of Andrei Vyshinskii, the Moscow emissary in Riga from June 17 to August 5. Latvia was incorporated into the USSR on August 5, becoming the Latvian Soviet Socialist Republic.

B. Thereafter, new governmental institutions modeled on the Soviet system were introduced, including

Council of People's Commissars, chairman, Vilis Lācis (August 25, 1940–June 1941)
Supreme Soviet, chairman of Presidium, Augusts Kirchensteins (August 25, 1940–June 1941)

C. Outside the structure of government but possessing decisive political power was the Latvian Communist Party, with its principal leaders

First secretary, Jānis Kalnbērziņš (June 1940–June 1941)
Second secretary, Žanis Spure (August–December 1940)

V. 1941–1945

The political restructuring of Soviet Latvia was interrupted by the successful German invasion and subsequent occupation, with

General commissioner, Otto Drechsler (September 1941–May 1945)
First director of Latvian "Self-Government," Oskars Dankers (August 1941–September 1944)

VI. 1945–1990

The Soviet governmental system returned in 1944/1945 and put in place the following

A. Council of Ministers
   Chairmen:
   Vilis Lācis (1940–1959)
   Jānis Peive (1959–1962)
   Vitālijs Rubenis (1962–1970)
   Juris Rubenis (1970–1988)
   Vilnis Bresis (1988–1990)

B. Supreme Soviet
   Chairmen of Presidium:
   Augusts Kirchensteins (1940–1952)
   Kārlis Ozoliņš (1952–1959)
   Jānis Kalnbērziņš (1959–1970)
   Vitālijs Rubenis (1970–1974)
   Pēteris Strautmanis (1974–1985)
   Jānis Vagris (1985–1988)
   Anatolijs Gorbunovs (1988–)

C. Latvian Communist Party
   First secretary:
   Jānis Kalbērziņš (1940–1959)
   Second secretary:
   Ivan Lebedev (1944–1949)
   Fedor Titov (1949–1952?)
   Valentin Ershov (1952–1953)
   Vilis Krumiņš (1953–1956)
   Filip Kashnikov (1956–1958)
   Arvīds Pelše (1958)
   First secretary:
   Arvīds Pelše (1959–1966)
   Second secretary:
   Vilis Krūmiņš (1958–1960)
   Mikhail Gribkov (1960–1963)
   Nikolai Belukha (1963–1978)
   First secretary:
   Augusts Voss (1966–1984)
   Second secretary:
   Nikolai Belukha (1963–1978)
   Igor Strelkov (1978–1980)
   Valentin Dimitriev (1980–1986)
   First secretary:
   Boriss Pugo (1984–1988)

Second secretary:
Vitali Sobolev (1986–1990)
First secretary:
Jānis Vagris (1988–1990)
Second secretary:
Vitali Sobolev (1988–1990)
Party divided in 1990
First secretary of Moscow-oriented wing: Alfrēds Rubiks
Leader of "independent Communists": Ivars Ķezbers

VII. 1990–1993

A. The Latvian Supreme Soviet elected in March 1990 became a transition government. The dominant majority in the Supreme Soviet was the Latvian Popular Front.

B. Supreme Soviet in May 1990 declares its intention to extract Latvia from the USSR.

C. The chairman of the Presidium of the Supreme Soviet, Anatolijs Gorbunovs, serving from 1988 on but now member of the Latvian Popular Front movement, was the titular head of state.

D. Chosen as chairman of the Council of Ministers was Ivars Godmanis, also of the Latvian Popular Front.

E. During these years the old institutional names were phased out, as the Supreme Soviet was becoming known as the parliament and the Council of Ministers as the cabinet.

F. After August 1991 and the reestablishment of Latvian independence, the country again became the Republic of Latvia and its basic document was, again, the constitution of 1922.

VIII. 1993–

A. Fifth Saeima (parliament) elected in June 1993, as provided by the constitution. Anatolijs Gorbunovs (Latvia's Way) elected as president of Saeima.

B. President of the Republic of Latvia: Guntis Ulmanis (Agrarian Union), 1993–

C. Prime Minister: Valdis Birkavs (Latvia's Way) July 1993–July 1994

SOURCES: Arvēds Švābe, *Latvju enciklopēdija* (Stockholm: Trīs Zvaigznes, 1950–51) vol. 2, pp. 1707–9; Adolfs Šilde, *Latvijas vēsture 1914–1940* (Stockholm: Daugava, 1976), pp. 386–419; Romuald Misiunas and Rein Taagepera, *The Baltic States: The Years of Dependence 1940–1990* (Berkeley: University of California Press, 1993) pp. 350–52; Edgars Andersons, *Latvijas vēsture 1914–1920* (Stockholm: Daugava, 1967), pp. 352–56.

Notes

PREFACE

1. In Latvian, Garlības Merķelis, *Latweeschi, sewischki widsemneeki, filozofiskā gadu simteņa beigās* (Saint Petersburg: A. Gulbis, 1905).

2. Alfreds Bīlmanis, *A History of Latvia* (Princeton: Princeton University Press, 1951); Arnolds Spekke, *History of Latvia: An Outline* (Stockholm: M. Goppers, 1957).

3. The series, published by Daugava Publishers in Stockholm, Sweden, consists of the following titles: A. Spekke and E. Dunsdorfs, *Latvijas vēsture 1500–1600* (1964); E. Dunsdorfs, *Latvijas vēsture 1600–1710* (1972); E. Dunsdorfs, *Latvijas vēsture 1710–1800* (1973); A. Johansons, *Latvijas kultūras vēsture 1710–1800* (1975); A. Švābe, *Latvijas vēsture 1800–1914* (1958); E. Andersons, *Latvijas vēsture 1914–1920* (1967); E. Andersons, *Latvijas vēsture 1920–1940. Ārpolitika*, vol. 1 (1982) vol. 2 (1984); A. Šilde, *Latvijas vēsture 1914–1940* (1976); A. Aizsilnieks, *Latvijas saimniecības vēsture 1914–1945* (1968).

4. A. Drīzulis, ed., *Latvijas PSR vēsture* (Riga: Zinātne, 1986).

CHAPTER 1

1. See, for example, Uldis Ģērmanis, *Latviešu tautas piedzīvojumi* (Riga: Jāņa Sēta, 1990), pp. 13–24.

2. The most complete account of these early millennia is Marijas Gimbutas, *The Balts* (London: Thames and Hudson, 1963). See also Arvēds Švābe, *Latvijas vēsture*, vol. 1 (Riga: Avots, 1990), pp. 20–35; Indulis Ķēniņš, *Latvijas vēs-*

ture (Riga: Zvaigzne, 1992), pp. 5–20; A. Drīzulis, ed., *Latvijas PSR vēsture no vissenākajiem laikiem līdz mūsu dienām*, vol. 1 (Riga: Zinātne, 1986), pp. 7–23; Agnis Balodis, *Latvijas un latviešu tautas vēsture* (Riga: Kabata, 1991), pp. 13–26; Alfrēds Bīlmanis, *A History of Latvia* (Princeton, N.J.: Princeton University Press, 1951), pp. 3–49; Arnolds Spekke, *History of Latvia: An Outline* (Stockholm: M. Goppers, 1957), pp. 13–28.

3. Gimbutas, *Balts*, pp. 37–73. A. Spekke, "Baltu tautas kristīgas ēras pirmajā gadu tūkstotī," in B. Ābers, T. Zeids, and T. Zemzaris, eds., *Tautas vēsturei: Veltijums Profesoram Arvēdam Švābem* (Riga: A. Gulbis, 1938), pp. 61–76.

4. For the origins of the tribal societies, see Gimbutas, *Balts*, pp. 155–78; Balodis, *Latvijas un latviešu tautas vēsture*, pp. 17–18; Ģērmanis, *Latviešu tautas piedzīvojumi*, pp. 28–40; J. Plāķis, "Baltu tautas un ciltis," in F. Balodis and P. Šmits, eds., *Latvieši: rakstu krājums*, vol. 1 (Riga: Valters and Rapal, 1930), pp. 45–49; Arvēds Švābe, *Straumes un avoti*, vol. 2 (1938; reprint, Lincoln, Neb.: Pilskalns, 1962), pp. 45–114.

5. Spekke, *History of Latvia*, pp. 100–119; Gimbutas, *Balts*, pp. 141–54.

6. Spekke, *History of Latvia*, pp. 52–75; Gimbutas, *Balts*, pp. 109–50; Bīlmanis, *History of Latvia*, pp. 38–49.

7. Gimbutas, *Balts*, p. 155.

8. Odisejs Kostanda, ed., *Latvijas vēsture* (Riga: Zvaigzne, 1992), pp. 19–23; Švābe, *Latvijas vēsture*, 1: 90–95.

9. Gimbutas, *Balts*, p. 171.

10. Ibid.; Jakob Ozols, "Die vor- und frühgeschichtliched Burgen Semgallns," *Commentationes Balticae* 14/15 (1968/70): 105–213. One such kingdom is described by Švābe on the basis of post-1200 sources; see Arvēds Švābe, "Jersikas karaļvalsts," in *Straumes un avoti*, vol. 3 (1938; reprint, Lincoln, Neb.: Pilskalns, 1962), pp. 5–33.

11. Drīzulis, *Latvijas PSR vēsture*, pp. 32–37; Kostanda, *Latvijas vēsture*, pp. 19–22.

12. Drīzulis, *Latvijas PSR vēsture*, pp. 24–32; Gimbutas, *Balts*, pp. 158–66.

13. Arnolds Spekke, *Senie dzintara ceļi un austrum-Baltijas ģeogrāfiskā atklāšana*, 3d expanded ed. (Stockholm: Zelta Ābele, 1962); F. Balodis, "Latviešu starptautiskie sakari ap 1000.g. pēc Kristus," *Latvijas Vēsture Institūta Žurnāls* 3, no. 1 (1939): 5–20; Spekke, *History of Latvia*, pp. 76–99; Ģērmanis, *Latviešu tautas piedzīvojumi*, pp. 33–37; E. Šturms, "Der ostbaltische Bernsteinhandel in der vorchristlichen Zeit," *Commentationes Balticae* 1 (1953): 167–205.

14. Švābe, *Straumes un avoti*, 2: 312–402; Arnolds Spekke, *Balts and Slavs: Their Early Relations* (Washington, D.C.: Alpha Printing Co., 1968).

15. Gimbutas, *Balts*, p. 179.

16. P. Šmits, "Latviešu mitoloģija," in Balodis and Šmits, *Latvieši: rakstu krājums*, 1:161–77; V. Sinaiskis, "Latviešu senā sabiedriskā iekārta tautas dziesmu

spoguli," in B. Ābers, T. Zeids, and T. Zemzaris, eds., *Tautas vēsturei: Veltijums Profesoram Arvēdam Švābem* (Riga: A. Gulbis, 1938), pp. 115–31.

17. The following information is from Šmits, "Latviešu mitoloģija," pp. 163–70.

18. Drīzulis, *Latvijas PSR vēsture*, pp. 37.

19. Ibid.; Spekke, *History of Latvia*, pp. 113–19; Nikolajs Vīksniņš, *Latvijas vēsture jaunā gaismā* (Chicago: Draugas, 1968), pp. 26–27. The developmental model, of course, can be used with considerable sophistication; see R. Abelnieks, "Gaujas lībiešu sabiedrības attīstības pakāpe XII un XIII gs. mijā," in *Latvijas Universitātes Zinātniskie Raksti. 555. Vēsture. Feodālisma problēmas Baltijā* (Riga: Latvijas Universitāte, 1990), pp. 6–17.

CHAPTER 2

1. Leonid Arbusow, *Grundriss der Geschichte Liv-, Es-, un Kurlands* (Riga: von Jonck und Polieweski, 1908), pp. 8–13; Ernst Seraphim, *Grundriss der baltischen Geschichte* (Reval: Franz Kluge, 1908), pp. 7–23; Alfreds Bīlmanis, *A History of Latvia* (Princeton, N.J.: Princeton University Press, 1951), pp. 55–59.

2. Bīlmanis, *History of Latvia*, pp. 57–60; Arnolds Spekke, *History of Latvia: An Outline* (Stockholm: M. Goppers, 1957), pp. 120–31; A. Drīzulis, *Latvijas PSR vēsture* (Riga: Zinātne, 1986), pp. 38–44; Nikolajs Vīksniņš, *Latvijas vēsture jaunā gaismā* (Chicago: Draugas, 1968), pp. 61–70; Odisejs Kostanda, *Latvijas vēsture* (Riga: Zvaigzne, 1992), pp. 24–44; Agnis Balodis, *Latvijas un latviešu tautas vēsture* (Riga: Kabata, 1991), pp. 29–41; Uldis Ģērmanis, *Latviešu tautas piedzīvojumi* (Riga: Jāṇa Sēta, 1990), pp. 51–92.

3. Bīlmanis, *History of Latvia*, pp. 61–69.

4. Ibid., pp. 71–79; Juozas Jakstas, "Das Baltikum in der Kreuzzugsbewegung des 14. Jahrhunderts," *Commentationes Balticae* 6/7 (1958/59): 139–83; William Urban, *The Baltic Crusade* (Dekalb: Northern Illinois University Press, 1975); William Urban, *The Samogitian Crusade* (Chicago: Lithuanian Research Center, 1989).

5. Seraphim, *Grundriss der Baltischen Geschichte*, pp. 37–40; Bīlmanis, *History of Latvia*, pp. 80–85.

6. V. Klišāns, *Livonija 12.-16.gs.pirmajā pusē* (Riga: Latvijas Universitāte, 1992), pp. 23–30; Bīlmanis, *History of Latvia*, pp. 86–91; Balodis, *Latvijas un latviešu tautas vēsture*, pp. 42–43.

7. Arbusow, *Grundriss der Geschichte Liv-, Est- un Kurlands*, pp. 59–65; Bīlmanis, *History of Latvia*, pp. 92–98.

8. Balodis, *Latvijas un latviešu tautas vēsture*, pp. 45–56; Bīlmanis, *History of Latvia*, pp. 88–90.

9. Balodis, *Latvijas un latviešu tautas vēsture*, pp. 56–59; Bīlmanis, *History of Latvia*, pp. 84–85.

208 Notes to pages 21–30

10. L. Adamovičš, "Latvieši un katoļu baznīca," in F. Balodis and P. Šmits, eds., *Latvieši* (Riga: Valters un Rapa, 1930), p. 182.

11. Jānis Straubergs, *Rīgas vēsture* (Riga: Grāmatu Draugs, n.d.), pp. 9–136; Teodors Zeids, ed., *Feodālā Rīga* (Riga: Zinātne, 1987), pp. 12–115; T. Līventāls and V. Sadoskis, eds., *Rīga kā Latvijas galvas pilsēta* (Riga: Rīgas pilsētas valde, 1932), pp. 5–18.

12. Zeids, *Feodālā Rīga*, pp. 70–74.

13. Straubergs, *Rīgas vēsture*, pp. 112–69.

14. Bīlmanis, *History of Latvia*, pp. 98–103.

15. Teodors Zeids, *Senākie rakstītie Latvijas vēstures avoti līdz 1800. gadam* (Riga: Zvaigzne, 1990), pp. 20–43; A. Feldhuns, trans., *Indriķa hronika* (Riga: Zinātne, 1993); James A. Brundage, trans., *The Chronicle of Henry of Livonia* (Madison: University of Wisconsin Press, 1961); Arvēds Švābe, "Latviešu Indriķis un viņa chronika," in *Straumes un avoti*, 2: 121–220.

16. Arvēds Švābe, ed., *Latvju enciklopēdija*, vol. 1 (Stockholm: Trīs Zvaigznes, 1950–1951), p. 768.

17. Drīzulis, *Latvijas PSR vēsture*, p. 49; Zeids, *Feodālā Rīga*, pp. 56–70.

18. Bīlmanis, *History of Latvia*, pp. 91–93; Spekke, *History of Latvia*, pp. 173–74. A full discussion of manorial dues and responsibilities of Livonian peasants can be found in Arvēds Švābe, *Pagasta vēsture*, vol. 1 (Riga: J. Roze, 1926), pp. 39–188.

19. The most credible research on the origins of the manor is contained in Edgars Dunsdorfs and Arnolds Spekke, *Latvijas vēsture 1500–1600* (Stockholm: Daugava, 1964), pp. 282–384. See also Edgars Dunsdorfs, *Muižas* (Melbourne: Kārļa Zariņa Fonds, 1983); for comparisons, see Drīzulis, *Latvijas PSR vēsture*, pp. 52–56, and V. Klišāns, *Livonija 12.-16.gs.pirmajā pusē* (Riga: Latvijas Universitāte, 1992), pp. 40–54.

20. A. Schwabe, *Grundriss der Agrargeschichte Lettlands* (Riga: Berhard Lamey, 1928), pp. 50–58.

21. Accounts of the Livonian period written by Latvian researchers of the interwar period suggest that the non-German peoples of Livonia, though assigned different names by the chroniclers, were all subpopulations of one "Latvian nation." See Augustus Tentelis, "Latvieši Ordena laikmetā," in Balodis and Šmits, *Latvieši*, 1: 121–37.

22. Spekke, *History of Latvia*, p. 148, puts it in the following terms: "The national aristocracy, its leading circles, were either annihilated or had degenerated to become assimilated, part of them being absorbed by the conquerors."

23. A systematic analysis of the question itself and some possible answers can be found in Dunsdorfs and Spekke, *Latvijas vēsture 1500–1600*, pp. 695–706.

CHAPTER 3

1. Edgars Dunsdorfs and Arnolds Spekke, *Latvijas vēsture 1500–1600* (Stockholm: Daugava, 1964), pp. 209–44.

2. The Lutheran Reformation in the Latvian territories is discussed in Arvēds Švābe, *Latvijas vēsture,* vol. 1 (Riga: n.p, n.d.), pp. 148–53; Leonid Arbusow, *Grundriss der Geschichte Liv-, Est-, und Kurlands* (Riga: von Jonck and Poliewski, 1908), pp. 121–30; Edgars Dunsdorfs and Arnolds Spekke, *Latvijas vēsture 1500–1600* (Stockholm: Daugava, 1964), pp. 76–108; A. Drīzulis, ed., *Latvijas PSR vēsture* (Riga: Zinātne, 1986), pp. 61–64; and Ludvigs Adamovičs, *Dzimtenes baznīcas vēsture* (n.p.: P. Mantnieks, 1947), pp. 17–22. The Reformation plays a relatively small part in the description of the sixteenth century by Arnolds Spekke, *History of Latvia: An Outline* (Stockholm: M. Goppers, 1957), pp. 178–80, and Alfrēds Bilmanis, *A History of Latvia* (Princeton, N.J.: Princeton University Press, 1951), mentions it only in passing in connection with political events. But see L. Adamovics, "Latvieši un evaņģēliskā baznīca," in F. Balodis and P. Šmits, *Latviesi,* vol. 1 (Riga: Valters and Rapa, 1930), pp. 198–230.

3. Spekke, *History of Latvia,* p. 178, suggests that "amidst the rural populations [the Reformation's] results were manifest in the fulfilling of administrative regulations, which, rather than affecting the people's conscience, increased hopes of certain social reforms, as was also the case in other countries during political revolutions."

4. Dunsdorfs and Spekke, *Latvijas vēsture 1500–1600,* p. 104, observe that "in view of what is known about Latvian religious life in the 17th century, Lutheranism did not have an echo among the Latvian peasantry. . . . Formally, as Lutherans were counted those peasants who were added to the new faith by their lords according to the principle *cujus regio, ejus religio.* In fact these 'Lutheran' peasants either remained Catholic, or retained the [pagan] faith of their ancestors."

5. Some examples of these are in Ludvigs Adamovičs, *Dzimtenes baznīcas vēsture* (N.p.: P. Mantnieks, 1947), p. 21.

6. Dunsdorfs and Spekke, *Latvijas vēsture 1500–1600,* pp. 88–94; L. Adamovičs, "Latvieši un evaņģēliskā baznīca," in F. Balodis and P. Šmits, *Latvieši,* 1: 198–230.

7. V. Dorošenko, "Lauksaimniecības preču eksports no Rīgas 1620–1630," in T. Zeids, ed., *Latvijas agrāra vēsture XVI–XIX gs.* (Riga: Zinātne, 1966), pp. 3–30; V. Pāvuāns, *Satiksmes ceļi Latvijā XIII–XVII gs.* (Riga: Zinātne, 1971); Dunsdorfs and Spekke, *Latvijas vēsture 1500–1600,* pp. 444–501.

8. Drīzulis, *Latvijas PSR Vēsture,* pp. 52–56.

9. Heinrihs Strods, *Latvijas lauksaimniecības vēsture* (Riga: Zvaigzne, 1991), pp. 51–58.

10. These so-called Couronian kings (in Latvian *kuršu ķoniņi*) are described at length in Arveds Švābe, *Straumes un avoti,* vol. 1 (1938; reprint, Lincoln, Neb.: Pilskalns, 1962), pp. 115–348.

11. Voldemārs Kalniņš, *Latvijas PSR valsts un tiesību vēsture,* vol. 1 (Riga: Zinātne, 1972).

12. The Livonian war is described in detail in Dunsdorfs and Spekke, *Latvijas vēsture 1500–1600,* pp. 109–47; Bilmanis, *History of Latvia,* pp. 117–33; and Spekke, *History of Latvia,* pp. 184–99.

13. The policies of Sigismund II Augustus in Livonia are discussed at length by Arveds Švābe in "Sigismunda Augusta Livonijas politika," in *Straumes un avoti*, 3: 66–147.

14. Juris Juškēvičs, *Kurzemes hercogi un viņu laikmets* (1935; reprint, Riga: Zvaigzne, 1993), pp. 5–7; Alexander Berķis, *The History of the Duchy of Courland 1561–1795* (Towson, Md.: Paul M. Harrod, 1969), pp. 1–17.

15. The general coverage of the Polish period (in Latvian, *poļu laiki*) of Latvian history can be found in Bīlmanis, *History of Latvia*, pp. 137–59; Spekke, *History of Latvia*, pp. 200–220; and Dunsdorfs and Spekke, *Latvijas vēsture 1500–1600*, pp. 148–204.

16. L. Adamovičs, *Dzimtenes baznīcas vēsture*, pp. 22–28; L. Adamovičs, "Latvieši un evaņģēliskā baznīca," in F. Balodis and P. Šmits, *Latvieši*, 1: 178–97.

17. Ernst Seraphim, *Grundriss der baltischen Geschichte* (Reval: Franz Kluge, 1904), pp. 218–34.

18. Aleksejs Apinis, *Grāmata un latviešu sabiedrība līdz 19. gadsimta vidum* (Riga: Liesma, 1991), p. 25.

19. Jānis Andrups and Vitauts Kalve, *Latvian Literature: Essays* (Stockholm: Zelta Ābele, 1954), pp. 50–53; O. Čakars, A. Grigulis, and M. Losberga, *Latviešu literatūras vēsture no pirmsākumiem līdz gadsimta 80. gadiem* (Riga: Zvaigzne, 1990), pp. 28–30.

20. The question is discussed at some length in Dunsdorfs and Spekke, *Latvijas vēsture 1500–1600*, pp. 695–712. Their conclusion is that "all in all, we have to admit that sixteenth-century Latvia was inhabited not by tribal societies [*ciltis*] . . . but rather by a united Latvian nation [*tauta*] . . . which possessed the main attribute of a nation—a common language" (p. 702).

21. Dunsdorfs and Spekke, *Latvijas vēsture 1500–1600*, p. 700–701.

22. Arveds Švābe, "Latviešu zemnieks 16. gs. historiogrāfijā," in *Straumes un avoti*, 3: 53–64, esp. 61–62.

23. Ernests Blese, "Latviešu valodas attīstības posmi," in Balodis and Šmits, *Latvieši*, 1: 54–60.

24. The use of this material as evidence for the existence of a timeless "national" Latvian culture can be seen in Andrups and Kalve, *Latvian Literature: Essays*, pp. 11–46 .

CHAPTER 4

1. Edgars Dunsdorfs, *Latvijas vēsture 1600–1710* (Stockholm: Daugava, 1962), pp. 127–68; A. Drīzulis, ed., *Latvijas PSR vēsture* (Riga: Zinātne, 1986), pp. 98–100; Julius Eckardt, "Polnisch Livland," in *Die baltischen Provinzen Russlands* (Leipzig: Duncker und Humboldt, 1869), pp. 83–98. Valuable historical materials about Lettgallia in the seventeenth century can also be found in

Edgars Dunsdorfs, *Skaistā Latgale* (Melbourne: Kārļa Zarina Fonds, 1991), a work dealing with cartography; and in Miķelis Bukšs, *Latgaļu literatūras vēsture* (n. p.: Latgaļu izdevniecība, 1957).

2. Dunsdorfs, *Latvijas vēsture 1600–1710*, pp. 180–81.

3. Ibid., pp. 216–17.

4. Ibid., pp. 132–33.

5. L. Adamovičs, "Latvieši un katoļu baznīca," in F. Balodis and P. Šmits, *Latvieši*, vol. 1 (Riga: Valters and Rapa, 1930), pp. 178–97.

6. Some of the problems in establishing Lettgallian history as a subspecialty in Latvian history are described in H. Strods, ed., *Profesors Boļeslavs Brežgo* (Rēzekne: Latvijas Kultūras Centrs, 1990), pp. 3–4. Brežgo (1887–1957) was the leading historian of Lettgallia (Latgale) in the interwar and post–World War II period.

7. Dunsdorfs, *Latvijas vēsture 1600–1710*, pp. 176–78.

8. Alfrēds Bīlmanis, *A History of Latvia* (Princeton, N.J.: Princeton University Press, 1951), pp. 160–81; Arnolds Spekke, *History of Latvia*, pp. 229–34; Arvēds Schwabe, *Grundriss der Agrargeschichte Lettlands* (Riga: Bernnard Lamey, 1928), pp. 181–254; Leonid Arbusow, *Grundriss der Geschichte Liv-, Est- und Kurlands* (Riga: von Jonck und Poliewski, 1908), pp. 176–84.

9. Dunsdorfs, *Latvijas vēsture 1600–1710*, pp. 105–26.

10. Drīzulis, *Latvijas PSR vēsture*, pp. 80–87.

11. For general descriptions, see August Seraphim, *Die Geschichte des Herzogtums Kurland* (Reval: Franz Kluge, 1904), pp. 43–140; Alexander Berkis, *History of the Duchy of Courland* (Towson, Md.: Paul M. Harrod, 1969), pp. 18–166; Juris Juškēvičs, *Kurzemes hercogi un viņu laikmets* (1935; reprint, Riga: Zvaigzne, 1993), pp. 11–39.

12. Bīlmanis, *History of Latvia*, p. 182.

13. Seraphim, *Die Geschichte des Herzogtum Kurlands,* pp. 76–79; Spekke, *History of Latvia*, pp. 245–46.

14. The most authoritative work on Jacob is Juris Juškēvičs, *Hercoga Jēkaba laikmets Kurzemē* (Riga: Valstspapīra Spiestuve, 1931). On Jacob's colonial policy, see Edgars Andersons, *Senie kurzemnieki Amerikā un Tobago kolonizācija* (Stockholm: Daugava, 1970), and Dunsdorfs, *Latvijas vēsture 1600–1710*, pp. 60–64.

15. Teodors Zeids, ed., *Feodālā Rīga* (Riga: Zinātne, 1987), pp. 174–221; Jānis Straubergs, *Rīgas vēsture* (Riga: Grāmatu Draugs, n.d.), pp. 321–60.

16. Dunsdorfs, *Latvijas vēsture 1600–1710*, pp. 317–24.

17. G. Catlaks, *Rīgas priekšpilsētas gadsimtu gaitā* (Riga: Ministry of Education, 1991), pp. 21–31; Dzidra Liepiņa, *Agrārās attiecības Rīgas lauku novadā* (Riga: Latvijas PSR Zinātņu Akadēmija, 1962), pp. 116–28.

18. This theme in Latvian popular culture is explored by Andrejs Johansons, *Rīgas svārki mugurā* (Brooklyn, N.Y.: Gramatu Draugs, 1966).

19. Berkis, *History of the Duchy of Courland*, pp. 29–31.

20. For examples of the ways the Latvian peasantry sought to take advantage of the relatively liberal agrarian policies of the Swedes, see Edgars Dunsdorfs, *Divas gudras latviešu galvas: Muižu dibināšana zviedru Vidzemē* (Stockholm: Daugava, 1986), and Edgars Dunsdorfs, *Turība un brīvība septiņpadsimtā gadsimteņa Latvijā* (Lincoln, Neb.: Pilskalns, 1961), pp. 2–126.

21. Dunsdorfs, *Latvijas vēsture 1600–1710*, pp. 257–59.

22. Jānis Andrups and Vitauts Kalve, *Latvian Literature: Essays* (Stockholm: Zelta Ābele, 1954), pp. 57–62; O. Čakars, A. Grigulis, and M. Losberga, *Latviešu literatūras vēsture no pirmsākumiem līdz XIX gadsimta 80. gadiem* (Riga: Zvaigzne, 1990), pp. 44–49.

23. Andrups and Kalve, *Latvian Literature: Essays*, pp. 62–65; Čakars, Grigulis, and Losberga, *Latviešu literatūras vēsture no pirmsākumiem līdz XIX gadsimta 80. gadiem*, pp. 50–54.

24. Edgars Dunsdorfs, *Pirmās latviešu Bībeles vēsture* (New York: Latv, ev. lut. baznīca Amerikā, 1979); Čakars, Grigulis, and Losberga, *Latviešu literatūras vēsture no pirmsākumiem līdz XIX gadsimta 80. gadiem*, pp. 67–75.

25. L. Bērziņš, "Latviešu rakstniecība svešu tautu aizbildniecībā," in F. Balodis and P. Šmits, *Latvieši*, 1: 277–301.

26. Arveds Švābe, "Tautas dziesmu likteņi," in A. Švābe, K. Straubergs, and E. Hauzenberga-Šturma, *Latviešu tautas dziesmas*, vol. 1 (Copenhagen: Imanta, 1952), pp. v–xxv.

27. Apinis, *Grāmata un latviešu sabiedrība līdz 19. gadsimta vidum*, p. 46.

28. Ibid., pp. 70–71.

CHAPTER 5

1. This and the following population estimates are from Edgars Dunsdorfs, *Latvijas vēsture 1710–1800* (Stockholm: Daugava, 1973), pp. 275–314.

2. These are described at length in J. Straubergs, *Rīgas latviešu pirmās nacionālās cīņas 18.g.s.* (Riga: A. Gulbis, 1936); for a reassessment of the "national" motivation in these disputes, see Dunsdorfs, *Latvijas vēsture 1710–1800*, pp. 120–28.

3. For the course of the war, see Arnolds Spekke, *History of Latvia: An Outline* (Stockholm: M. Goppers, 1957), pp. 264–81; and Alfrēds Bīlmanis, *A History of Latvia* (Princeton, N.J.: Princeton University Press, 1951), pp. 197–213.

4. Edgars Dunsdorfs, *Latvijas vēsture 1600–1710* (Stockholm: Daugava, 1962), pp. 190–96.

5. Dz. Liepiņa, *Vidzemes zemnieki un muiža 18. gs. pirmajā pusē* (Riga: Zinātne, 1983); the controversies surrounding the Rosen declarations are discussed in Spekke, *History of Latvia*, pp. 272–76.

6. H. Strods, *Zemnieku un muižu saimniecību skaita un struktūras izmaiņas Latvijā* (Riga: P. Stučkas Latvijas Valsts Universitāte, 1984), pp. 4–17.

7. This and the following statistics concerning estates are from Dunsdorfs, *Latvijas vēsture 1710–1800*, pp. 315–85.

8. L. Adamovičs, *Vidzemes baznīca un latviešu zemnieks 1710–1740*, 2d ed. (Lincoln, Neb.: Vaidava, 1963), pp. 505–76.

9. A. Vičs, *Iz latviešu skolu vēstures* (1923; reprint, Riga: Zvaigzne, 1992), pp. 67–71.

10. Matīss Kaudzīte, *Brāļu draudze Vidzemē* (Riga: n. p., 1878).

11. Aleksejs Apinis, *Grāmata un latviešu sabiedrība līdz 19. gadsimta vidum* (Riga: Liesma, 1991), p. 72. For a general survey of book production in the eighteenth century, see Andrejs Johansons, *Latvijas kultūras vēsture 1710–1800* (Stockholm: Daugava, 1975), pp. 90–125.

12. Apinis, *Grāmata un latviešu sabiedrība līdz 19. gadsimta vidum*, p. 117.

13. O. Čakars, A. Grigulis, and M. Losberga, *Latviešu literatūras vēsture no pirmsākumiem līdz XIX gadsimta 80. gadiem* (Riga: Zvaigzne, 1990), pp. 84–99; Johansons, *Latvijas kultūras vēsture 1710–1800*, pp. 463–82; Jānis Andrups and Vitauts Kalve, *Latvian Literature: Essays* (Stockholm: Zelta Ābele, 1954), pp. 76–82.

14. Johansons, *Latvijas kultūras vēsture 1710–1800*, p. 447. Other historians of Latvian culture argue, however, that his influence on German-reading contemporaries ensures Merkel a role in Latvian history as well. See P. Zeile, "Garlībs Merķelis kā kultūrfilozofs un kultūrpublicists," in P. Zeile, ed., *Garlībs Merķelis: kulturvēsturiski raksti* (Riga: Zvaigzne, 1992), pp. 5–30.

15. Apinis, *Grāmata un latviešu sabiedrība līdz 19.gadsimta vidum*, p. 117.

16. E. Blese, "Latviešu literāriskā valoda," in F. Balodis and P. Šmits, vol. 2, *Latvieši* (Riga: Valters and Rapa, 1930), pp. 375–98.

17. Johansons, *Latvijas kultūras vēsture 1710–1800*, p. 147.

18. Dunsdorfs, *Latvijas vēsture 1710–1800*, pp. 206–43.

19. A. Drīzulis, ed., *Latvijas LPS vēsture*, vol. 1 (Riga: Zinātne, 1986), p. 111.

20. Miķelis Bukšs, *Latgaļu literatūras vēsture* (n.p.: Latgaļu izdevniecība, 1957), pp. 109–17, 158–63; N. Rudko and P. Tretjuks, *Ieskats Latgales skolu vēsturē* (Viļāni: Izglītības Ministrija, 1990), pp. 15–31.

21. August Seraphim, *Die Geschichte des Herzogtums Kurland 1561–1795* (Reval: Franz Kluge, 1904), pp. 304–51; Alexander Berkis, *The History of the Duchy of Courland 1561–1795* (Towson, Md.: Paul M. Harrod, 1969), pp. 220–300; H. Strods, *Kurlyandskii vopros v. XVIII veke*, 2 vols. (Riga: University of Latvia, 1993).

22. Dunsdorfs, *Latvijas vēsture 1710–1800*, pp. 244–70.

23. Dunsdorfs, *Latvijas vēsture 1710–1800*, pp. 103–28; Teodors Zeids, ed., *Feodālā Rīga* (Riga: Zinātne, 1987), pp. 310–37; Rita Brambe, *Rīgas iedzīvotāji feodālisma perioda beigās* (Riga: Zinātne, 1982), pp. 75–114.

214   Notes to pages 73–81

24. Zeids, *Feodālā Rīga*, pp. 327–28.

25. Ibid., p. 331; Brambe, *Rīgas iedzīvotāji*, pp. 128–32.

26. For this discussion, see J. Straubergs, *Rīgas latviešu pirmās nacionālās cīņas* (Riga: A. Gulbis, 1936), and Dunsdorfs, *Latvijas vēsture 1710–1800*, pp. 126–28.

27. See the two essay collections on Riga by Andrejs Johansons, *Rīgas svārki mugurā* (New York: Grāmatu Draugs, 1966) and *Visi Rīgas nami skan* (New York: Grāmatu Draugs, 1970).

28. Heinrihs Strods, *Lauksaimniecība Latvijā pārejas periodā no feodālisma uz kapitālismu* (Riga: Zinātne, 1972), pp. 271–324.

29. Dunsdorfs, *Latvijas vēsture 1710–1800*, pp. 419–34.

30. Juhan Kahk, *Peasant and Lord in the Process of Transition from Feudalism to Capitalism in the Baltics: An Attempt of Interdisciplinary History* (Tallinn: Eesti Raamat, 1982).

31. Mārģeris Stepermanis, *Zemnieku nemieri Vidzemē* (Riga: Zinātne, 1956), and Stepermanis, *Lielās liesmas atblāzma* (Riga: Zinātne, 1971).

32. See the two studies by Mārģeris Stepermanis, "J. G. Eizens un viņa darbi par dzimtbūšanas atcelšanu," in *Latvijas vēstures pirmavoti*, vol. 1 (Riga: N.p., 1934) and "Aizkraukles v. Šulcs un viņa sabiedriskā darbība," in *Latvijas Universitātes Raksti. Filoloģijas un Filozofijas sērija*, vol. 3 (Riga: Latvijas Universitāte, 1936); and N. Vīksniņš, *Apgaismotāji un agrārais jautājums Vidzemē*, vol. 1 (Riga: n. p., 1937).

33. E. Meļķis and V. Millers, *Garlība Merķeļa politiskie uzskati* (Riga: Liesma, 1972); Heinrihs Strods, *Antifeodālā sabiedriskā doma Latvijā XVIII gs. II puse—XIX gs I puse* (Riga: P. Stučkas Latvijas Valsts Universitāte, 1988), pp. 17–39; Johansons, *Latvijas kultūras vēsture 1710–1800*, pp. 35–44, 444–47.

34. Arveds Švābe, *Latvijas vēsture 1800–1914* (Stockholm: Daugava, 1959), pp. 64–77.

35. A. von Tobien, *Die Agrargesetzgebung Livlands im XIX. Jahrhundert*, vol. 1 (Berlin: n. p., 1899), vol. 2 (Berlin: n. p., 1911); A. Schwabe, *Grundriss der Agrargschichte Lettlands* (Riga: Bernhard Namey, 1928), pp. 293–347.

CHAPTER 6

1. Arvēds Švābe, *Latvijas vēsture 1800–1914* (Stockholm: Daugava, 1958), pp. 134–49; Arvēds Schwabe, *Grundriss der Agrargeschichte Lettlands* (Riga: Bernhard Namey, 1928), pp. 341–47; A. Drīzulis, ed., *Latvijas LPSR vēsture*, vol. 1 (Riga: Zinātne, 1986), pp. 126–29.

2. Arvēds Švābe, ed., *Latvju encikopēdija*, vol. 1 (Stockholm: Trīs Zvaigznes, 1950–51), pp. 768–79; Heinrihs Strods, *Kurzemes kroņa zemes un zemnieki 1795–1861* (Riga: Zinātne, 1987).

3. V. Kalniņš, *Latvijas PSR valsts un tiesību vēsture*, vol. 1 (Riga: Zvaigzne, 1979).

4. Heinrihs Strods, *Latvijas lauksaimniecības vēsture* (Riga: Zvaigzne, 1991), pp. 101–8.

5. Švābe, *Latvijas vēsture 1800–1914*, p. 129; J. Zutis, *Vidzemes un Kurzemes zemnieku brīvlaišana 19.gs.20os gados* (Riga: Zinātne, 1936).

6. K. Upelnieks, *Uzvārdu došana Vidzemes un Kurzemes zemniekiem* (Riga: n. p., 1938).

7. Heinrihs Strods, *Antifeodoālā sabiedriskā doma Latvijā XVIII gs. II pusē– XIX gs I pusē* (Riga: Latvijas Universitāte, 1992), pp. 4–17.

8. Jānis Andrups and Vitauts Kalve, *Latvian Literature: Essays* (Stockholm: Zelta Ābele, 1954), pp. 11–46.

9. Švābe, *Latvijas vēsture 1800–1914*, pp. 176–77.

10. M. Arons, *Latviešu Literariskā (Latviešu Draugu) Biedrība savā simts gadu darbā* (Riga: A. Gulbis, 1929); Jurgen von Hehn, *Die lettisch-literarische Gessellschaft und das Lettentum* (Konigsberg: n. p., 1938).

11. *Pedagoğiskā doma Latvijā līdz 1890. gadam: Antoloğija* (Riga: Zvaigzne, 1991), pp. 76–80.

12. G. Čakars, A. Grigulis, and M. Losberga, *Latviešu literatūras vēsture no pirmsākumiem līdz XIX gadsimta 80. gadiem* (Riga: Zvaigzne, 1990), pp. 143–72.

13. Švābe, *Latvijas vēsture 1800–1914*, pp. 191–216.

14. M. Svarāne, *Saimnieks un kalps Kurzemē un Vidzemē XIX gs. vidū* (Riga: Zinātne, 1971), pp. 167–94; Švābe, *Latvijas vēsture 1800–1914*, pp. 217–33.

15. Boļeslavs Brežgo, "Latgales zemnieku attiecības pret 1861. gada agrārreformu," *Latvijas vēstures institūta žurnāls*, no. 1 (1940).

16. L. Balēvica, "Privātkapitāla loma Vidzemes zemnieku māju iepirkšanā (19.gs. otrā pusē - 20.gs. sākums)," *Latvijas vēstures institūta žurnāls*, no. 1 (1992): 49–73; Švābe, *Latvijas vēsture 1800–1914*, pp. 302–29.

17. J. Krastiņš, ed., *Rīga 1860–1917* (Riga: Zinātne, 1978), pp. 15–29.

18. Mārğeris Skujeneeks, *Latvija: zeme un iedzīvotāji*, 3d ed. (Riga: A. Gulbis, 1927), p. 208.

19. Andrejs Plakans and Charles Wetherell, "The Kinship Domain in an Eastern European Peasant Community," *American Historical Review* 93 (1988): 163–75; Plakans and Wetherell, "Family and Economy in an Early-Nineteenth-Century Baltic Serf Estate," *Continuity and Change* 7 (1992): 119–33. See also P. Zvidriņš and I. Vanovska, *Latvieši: statistiski demogrāfisks portretējums* (Riga: Zinātne, 1992), pp. 5–23.

20. Ansley Coale, Barbara Anderson, and Erna Härm, *Human Fertility in Russia since the Nineteenth Century* (Princeton, N.J.: Princeton University Press, 1979).

21. Švābe, *Latvijas vēsture 1800–1914*, p. 177.

22. A. Tentelis, ed., *Dokumenti par "Pēterburgas Avīzēm"* (Riga: Latvijas Vēstures Institūts, 1937).

23. E. Blanks, *Latvju nacionālā doma sadzīves cīņu ugunīs* (Riga: Latvijas Nacionālais Klubs, 1923); Ģints Apals, "Jaunlatviešu kustības politiskā orientācija 19.gs. 60.os gados," *Latvijas vēstures institūta žurnāls*, no. 1 (1992): 69–80; Ģints Apals, *Jaunlatviešu kustība* (Riga: Izglītības Ministrija, 1990); Andrejs Plakans, "The Latvians," in Edward C. Thaden, ed., *Russification in the Baltic Provinces and Finland 1855–1914* (Princeton, N.J.: Princeton University Press, 1981), pp. 207–84.

24. Anders Henrikkson, *The Tsar's Loyal Germans: The Riga German Community: Social Change and the Nationality Question, 1855–1905* (Boulder, Colo.: East European Monographs, 1983).

25. Ernests Blanks, *Latvju tautas atmoda* (Riga: A. Raņķis, 1927), pp. 178–86.

26. J. Rudzītis, ed., *Atis Kronvalds: Tagādnei* (Riga: Liesma, 1987), pp. 3–23. For a biographical account of Kronvalds, see Arturs Baumanis, *Pa Kronvalda Ata pēdām* (n.p.: K. Goppera Fonds, 1975).

27. For excerpts, see Rudzītis, *Atis Kronvalds: Tagādnei*, pp. 110–26.

28. For the Riga population in the first half of the nineteenth century, see R. Brambe, *Rīgas iedzivotāji feodālisma perioda beigās* (Riga: Zinātne, 1982); for the second half, see J. Krastiņš, ed., *Rīga 1860–1917* (Riga: Zinātne, 1978), pp. 15–20.

29. Švābe, *Latvijas vēsture 1800–1914*, pp. 470–71.

30. K. Lūsis and G. Sīmanis, eds., *Krišjānis Valdemārs: Tēvzemei* (Riga: Avots, 1991), pp. 5–20.

31. Arvēds Švābe, *Latvju enciklopēdija*, vol. 1 (Stockholm: Tris Zvaigznes, 1950–51), p. 869.

32. Ernests Blanks, *Latvju tautas atmoda* (Riga: A. Rankis, 1927), pp. 35–39.

33. Švābe, *Latvju enciklopēdija*, 1: 263–65.

34. A full description of this pathbreaking novel is in Čakars, Grigulis, and Losberga, *Latviešu literatūras vēsture*, pp. 359–74.

35. A. Bīlmanis, "Latviešu avīžniecība," in F. Balodis, P. Šmits, and A. Tentelis, eds., *Latviešu*, vol. 2 (Riga: Valters un Rapa, 1930), pp. 345–74.

36. Ž. Unams, *Krievu laiki Latvijā* (Riga: Valters un Rapa, 1936), pp. 80–106; Paulis Lazda, "The Phenomenon of Russophilism in the Development of Latvian Nationalism in the 19th Century," in Aleksaner Loit, ed., *National Movements in the Baltic Countries during the 19th Century* (Stockholm: Centre for Baltic Studies, 1985), pp. 129–35; Plakans, "Latvians," in Thaden, *Russification*, pp. 227–47.

37. Plakans, "Latvians," in Thaden, *Russification*, pp. 229–30.

38. For Baltic German reactions to Russification, see Michael Haltzel, *Der*

Abbau der deutschen ständischen Selbstverwaltung in den Ostseeprovinzen Russlands 1855–1905: Ein Beitrag zur Geschichte der russischen Unifizierungspolitik (Marburg: Herderinstitut, 1977), and M. Duhanovs, *Baltijas muižniecība laikmetu maiņā* (Riga: Zinātne, 1986).

39. Blanks, *Latvju nacionālā doma sadzīves cīņu ugunīs,* pp. 27–31.

40. Plakans, "Latvians," in Thaden, *Russification,* pp. 248–67.

41. On this subject, see A. Mieriņa, *Agrārās attiecības un zemnieku stāvoklis Kurzemē 19.gs. II puse* (Riga: Zinātne, 1936).

42. For a detailed account of the economic circumstances of the Lettgallian "awakening," see L. S. Jefremova, *Latyshskaya krestyanskaya semiya v Latgale 1860–1939* (Riga: Zinātne, 1982); for the "awakening" itself, see Švābe, *Latvijas vēsture 1800–1914,* pp. 703–21.

43. Miķelis Bukšs, *Latgaļu literatūras vēsture* (n.p.: Latgaļu izdevniecība, 1957), pp. 346–57.

44. Ibid., pp. 378–95.

45. An excellent study of the growth of Latvian influence in Liepāja, the main seaport of Courland, is Dz. Ozoliņa, *Liepājas pilsētas pašvaldība 1877–1913* (Riga: Zinātne, 1990).

46. Švābe, *Latvju enciklopēdija,* 3: 2329–31.

47. Švābe, *Latvijas vēsture 1800–1914,* pp. 591–636; A. Bīrons, ed., *Latvijas strādnieki un zemnieki 1905.–1907.g. revolucijā* (Riga: Zinātne, 1986); Toivo Raun, "The Revolution of 1905 in the Baltic Provinces and Finland," *Slavic Review* 43 (1984): 453–67.

48. Švābe, *Latvju enciklopēdija,* 2: 1248–50.

49. Švābe, *Latvijas vēsture 1800–1914,* pp. 703–19.

50. On the 1901–17 period, see Andrew Ezergailis and Gert von Pistohlkors, eds., *Die baltischen Provinzes Russlands zwischen den Revolutionen von 1905 und 1917* (Köln: Böhlau Verlag, 1982); L. Lapa, "Arodorganizāciju pirmsākumi Latvijā 1905,g.," *Latvijas vēstures institūta žurnāls,* no. 2 (1992): 89–106; J. Bērziņš, "Latvijas valstiskuma ideja 1905.g. revolucijā," *Latvijas vēstures institūta žurnāls,* no. 3 (1992): 84–116.

51. Jānis Rainis, *Kopoti raksti,* vol. 9 (Riga: Zinātne, 1980), pp. 157–248, 542–60.

52. Čakars, Grigulis, and Losberga, *Latviešu literatūras vēsture,* pp. 305–62.

53. Viktors Hausmanis, ed., *Latviešu rakstniecība biogrāfijās* (Riga: Latvijas enciklopēdija, 1992), p. 360.

54. Zeids, *Feodālā Rīga,* p. 328; J. Krastiņš, ed., *Riga 1860–1917* (Riga: Zinātne, 1978), pp. 16–17.

55. Krastiņš, *Riga 1860–1917,* pp. 22–23.

56. Anders Henriksson, *The Tsar's Loyal Germans: The Riga German Community—Social Change and the Nationality Question, 1855–1905* (Boulder, Colo.: East European Monographs, 1983), pp. 83–105.

57. A. Švābe, ed., *Latvju enciklopēdija*, 3: 2127.

58. Emigration statistics from Skujeneeks, *Latvija: zeme un iedzīvotāji*, pp. 367–79.

59. Švābe, *Latvijas vēsture 1800–1914*, pp. 703–6.

60. Ludvigs L. Adamovičs, "Latvieši un evanǧēliskā baznīca," in F. Balodis and P. Šmits, *Latvieši*, vol. 1 (Riga: Valters and Rapa, 1930), p. 224.

61. A. Švābe, ed., *Latvju enciklopēdija*, 3: 2580–81.

CHAPTER 7

1. For the general population see Arvēds Švābe, ed., *Latvju enciklopēdija*, vol. 1 (Stockholm: Trīs Zvaigznes, 1950–51), pp. 768–74; For Riga see J. Krastiņš, ed., *Riga 1860–1917* (Riga: Zinātne, 1978), pp. 15–30.

2. Low birthrates among Latvians began in the nineteenth century; see Edgars Dunsdorfs, "Dažas Latvijas 19. g.s.otrās puses iedzīvotāju skaita attīstības problēmas," *Latvijas vēstures institūta žurnāls* 3 (1939): 241–70.

3. Mārǧers Skujenieks, *Latvieši svešumā un citas tautas Latvijā: Vēsturiski statistisks apcerējums par emigrāciju un imigrāciju Latvijā* (Riga: Valters and Rapa, 1930); Švābe, *Latvijas vēsture 1800–1914*, pp. 540–41.

4. Arnolds Aizsilnieks, *Latvijas saimniecības vēsture 1914–1945* (Stockholm: Daugava, 1968), pp. 23–26.

5. Edgars Andersons, *Latvijas vēsture 1914–1920* (Stockholm: Daugava, 1967), pp. 18–19.

6. Kostanda, *Latvijas vēsture*, p. 168.

7. Adolfs Šilde, *Latvijas Vēsture 1914–1940* (Stockholm: Daugava, 1976), pp. 42–47; Švābe, *Latvju enciklopēdija*, 1: 230–35.

8. The formation and early battles of the Latvian *strēlnieki* are described in Andersons, *Latvijas vēsture 1914–1920*, pp. 78–112. The later activities of those units that went to Soviet Russia to support the fledgling Bolshevik government are described in Andrew Ezergailis, *The Latvian Impact on the Bolshevik Revolution* (Boulder, Colo.: East European Monographs, 1983).

9. The most thorough history of the Latvian *strēlnieki* in the period 1914–16 is M. Penikis, *Pasaules karš 1914., 1915., un 1916. gadā un latviešu strēlnieku bataljonu-pulku cīņas*, 2 vols. (Riga: Militārās literatūras apgādes fonds, 1935). See also Uildis Ģērmanis, *Latviešu tautas piedzīvojumi* (Riga: Jāna Sēta, 1990), pp. 242–45.

10. Ādolfs Šilde, *Latvijas vēsture 1914–1940* (Stockholm: Daugava, 1976), pp. 45–47.

11. A. Ezergailis, *Esejas par 1917. gadu* (Riga: Zinātne, 1991), pp. 58–116; R. Greitjāne, *Vidzemes bezzemnieku padomju darbība: 1917.marts, 1918. aprīlis* (Riga: Zinātne, 1986).

12. Andrew Ezergailis, *The 1917 Revolution in Latvia* (Boulder: Colo.: East European Monographs, 1974), pp. 59–67.

13. Šilde, *Latvijas vēsture 1914–1940*, pp. 207–28.

14. Uldis Ģērmanis, *Pa aizputinātām pēdām* (Stockholm: Daugava, 1956); Jukums Vācietis, *Latviešu strēlnieku vēsturiska nozīme* (Riga: Avots, 1989).

15. Šilde, *Latvijas vēsture 1914–1940*, pp. 255–67; Adolfs Klīve, *Brīvā Latvija* (New York: Grāmatu Draugs, 1969), pp. 217–312.

16. A. Drīzulis, ed., *Latvijas PSR vēsture*, vol. 2 (Riga: Zinātne, 1986), pp. 49–62.

17. Šilde, *Latvijas vēsture 1914–1940*, pp. 308–12; Spricis Paegle, *Kā Latvijas valsts tapa* (Riga: n.p., 1923), pp. 187–203. After the independence wars in 1924, Niedra was tried by the Latvian government for treason and exiled from Latvia for life, but he returned briefly during the German occupation of Latvia, 1941–44.

18. The most detailed military history of the wars of independence is M. Peniķis, *Latvijas atbrīvošanas kara vēsture*, 2 vols. (Riga: Literatura, 1938). See also Pēteris Radziņš, *Latvijas atbrīvošanas karš* (1921; reprint, Riga: Avots, 1991); P. Bērziņš, *Latvijas brīvības cīņas 1918–1920* (1928; reprint, Riga: Junda, 1992).

19. The most informative short statistical survey of the Soviet Latvians is Edgars Andersons, *Latvijas vēsture 1920–1940. Ārpolitika*, 2 vols. (Stockholm: Daugava, 1982); the cited figures are from volume 1, pp. 223–24. See also Drīzulis, *Latvijas PSR vēsture*, pp. 145–48.

20. See Ezergailis, *The Latvian Impact on the Bolshevik Revolution*.

21. Andersons, *Latvijas Vēsture 1914–1920. Ārpolitika* 1: 126.

22. Ibid., p. 122.

23. Ibid., p. 134.

24. Šilde, *Latvijas vēsture 1914–1940*, pp. 343–56.

25. Arnolds Aizsilnieks, *Latvijas saimniecības vēsture 1914–1945* (Stockholm: Daugava, 1968), pp. 164–81.

26. Švābe, *Latvju enciklopēdija*, 1: 220–21; Šilde, *Latvijas vēsture 1914–1940*, pp. 462–73.

27. For statistics on the "reruralization" of Latvia, see Švābe, *Latvju enciklopēdija*, 1: 771. The 1920 agrarian reform law and its implementation are dealt with in detail by V. Markaus, ed., *Agrārās reformas gaita Latvijā 1919–1922* (Riga: A. Gulbis, 1922), and Aleksandrs Mednis, *Agrārais jautājums un zemes reforma Latvijā* (Riga: Latvju Kultura, 1924). The results of the reform by the end of the 1930s are described in the government's assessment *Latvijas agrārā reforma: agrārās reformas izvešanas darbu noslēgums* (Riga: Ministry of Agriculture, 1938). The views of the leader of the 1919 Latvian Bolshevik government are described in P. Bondarevs, *P. Stučka par agrāro jautājumu Latvijā* (Riga: Avots, 1980).

28. *Latvijas agrārā reforma*, pp. 55–65.

29. Ibid., pp. 65–97.

30. Aizsilnieks, *Latvijas saimniecības vēsture 1914–1945*, p. 736.

31. Šilde, *Latvijas vēsture 1914–1940*, pp. pp. 352–64.

32. Ibid., p. 349.

33. Švābe, *Latvju enciklopēdija*, 3: 2219–21; Šilde, *Latvijas vēsture 1914–1940*, pp. 386–413; Alfrēds Bīlmanis, *A History of Latvia* (Princeton, N.J.: Princeton University Press, 1951), pp. 342–56.

34. The founding and growth of the Agrarian Union are described in Adolfs Klīve, *Latvijas neatkarības gadi* (New York: Gramatu Draugs, 1976), pp. 72–91. Klive was one of the Union's cofounders.

35. Šilde, *Latvijas vēsture 1914–1940*, pp. 396–400.

36. Aizsilnieks, *Latvijas saimniecības vēsture 1914–1945*, p. 270.

37. Švābe, *Latvju enciklopēdija*, 1: 769.

38. Andersons, *Latvijas vēsture 1914–1920*, p. 582.

39. Marģeris Skujeneeks, *Latvija: zeme un eedzīvotāji* (Riga: A. Gulbis, 1927), p. 252.

40. Švābe, *Latvju enciklopēdija*, 1: 770–71.

41. Ibid., p. 773. The most exhaustive analysis of the ethnic (nationality) dimension of the population of interwar Latvia is Skujeneeks, *Latvija: zeme un eedzīvotāji*, pp. 253–319.

42. Georg von Rauch, *The Baltic States: The Years of Independence 1917–1940* (Berkeley: University of California Press, 1974), pp. 154–61; Jürgen von Hehn, *Lettland zwischen Demokratie und Diktatur: Zur Geschichte des lettländischen Staatsstreich vom 15. Mai 1934* (1957; reprint München: Isaar Verlag, 1966).

43. The best assessment of Ulmanis's authoritarian tendencies is by Edgars Dunsdorfs, *Kārļa Ulmaņa dzīve* (Stockholm: Daugava, 1978). On the subject of censorship in the Ulmanis regime, see Jānis Rudzītis, *Raksti* (Västeras, Sweden: Ziemeļblāzma, 1977), pp. 153–73. Rudzītis, a literary critic during the Ulmanis era and later in exile in Sweden, opined in this reprinted 1960 essay that censorship during Ulmanis's rule was not particularly harsh.

44. See the following collections of Ulmanis's speeches and writings: *Kārļa Ulmaņa runas un raksti 1899–1918* (Riga: Zemnieka domas, 1939) and Sigizmunds Timšāns, ed., *Kārlis Ulmanis: Atziņas un runu fragmenti* (Riga: Avīze, 1990).

45. Bīlmanis, *A History of Latvia*, pp. 362–71.

46. Šilde, *Latvijas vēsture 1914–1940*, pp. 596–600; Aizsilnieks, *Latvijas saimniecības vēsture 1914–1945*, pp. 609–11.

47. H. Asaris, *Latvijas pilsētas valsts 20 gados* (Riga: Latvijas pilsētu savienība, 1938), p. 5.

48. Asaris, *Latvijas pilsētas valsts 20 gados*, p. 51.

49. Ibid.

50. T. Liventāls and V. Sadovskis, eds., *Rīga kā Latvijas galvas pilsēta* (Riga: Rīgas pilsētas valde, 1932), pp. 178–86.

51. Asaris, *Latvijas pilsētas valsts 20 gados*, pp. 91–99; Švābe, *Latvju enciklopēdija*, 1: 711.

52. See Šilde, *Latvijas vēsture 1914–1940*, pp. 474–507, 638–65; Drīzulis, *Latvijas PSR vēsture*, pp. 130–48; and Heinrihs Strods, ed., *Latviešu etnogrāfija* (Riga: Zinātne, 1969), pp. 384–424.

53. Švābe, *Latvju enciklopēdija*, 1: 827–32.

54. Šilde, *Latvijas vēsture 1914–1940*, pp. 439–43.

55. J. Seskis, *Latvijas valsts izcelšanās* (1937; reprint, Riga: Balta, n.d.), pp. 203–57.

56. John Hiden and Patrick Salmon, *The Baltic Nations and Europe: Estonia, Latvia, and Lithuania in the Twentieth Century* (London and New York: Longman, 1991), pp. 59–75, describe this strategy as the "diplomacy of survival."

57. Edgar Anderson, "The Baltic Entente 1914–1940—Its Strength and Weakness," in John Hiden and Aleksander Loit, eds., *The Baltic in International Relations between the Two World Wars* (Stockholm: Almkvist and Wiksell, 1988), pp. 79–99.

58. Edgars Dunsdorfs, *Kārļa Ulmaņa dzīve* (Stockholm: Daugava, 1978), pp. 449–55. See also M. Duhanovs, I. Feldmanis, and A. Stranga, *1939: Latvia and the Year of Fateful Decisions* (Riga: University of Latvia Press, 1994).

59. E. Andersons, *Latvijas vēsture 1920–1940: Ārpolitika*, vol. 2 (Stockholm: Daugava, 1982), p. 392.

CHAPTER 8

1. Miķelis Valters, *Mana sarakste ar Kārli Ulmani un Vilhelmu Munteru* (Västeras, Sweden: Jauna Latvija, 1957).

2. Adolfs Šilde, *Latvijas vēsture 1914–1940* (Stockholm: Daugava, 1976), pp. 666–74.

3. Raymond Sontag and James Beddie, eds., *Nazi-Soviet Relations 1939–1941* (Washington D.C.: U.S. Department of State, 1948), pp. 76–78.

4. Dietrich André Loeber, ed., *Diktierte Option: Die Umsiedlung der Deutschbalten aus Estland und Lettland 1939–1941: Dokumentation* (Neumunster, Germany: Karl Wachholz, 1972).

5. David M. Crowe, *The Baltic States and the Great Powers: Foreign Relations 1938–1940* (Boulder, Colo.: Westview Press, 1993), pp. 84–117.

6. Edgars Andersons, *Latvijas vēsture 1920–1940: Ārpolitika*, vol. 2 (Stockholm: Daugava, 1984), pp. 412–14.

7. Odisejs Kostanda, *Latvijas vēsture* (Riga: Zvaigzne, 1992), p. 286.

8. See Edgars Dunsdorfs, *Kārļa Ulmaņa dzīve* (Stockholm: Daugava, 1978),

pp. 483–84, for full text of the address. A recent study of Ulmanis's leadership during the months preceding and following the Soviet occupation is Indulis Ronris, ed., *Kārļis Ulmanis Trimdā un Cietumā* (Kārlis Ulmanis in exile and prison) (Riga: Latvijas Vēstures Instituits, 1994).

9. Ilga Gore and Aivars Stranga, *Latvija: neatkarības mijkrēslis. Okupācija* (Riga: Izglītība, 1992), pp. 167–87. For a general account of the diplomacy of the period, see I. Feldmanis, A. Strauga, and M. Virsis, *Latvijas ārpolitika un starptautiskais stāvoklis 30. gadu otrā pusē* (Riga: Latvijas Ārpolitikas Institūts, 1993).

10. Andersons, *Latvijas vēsture 1940–1940. Ārpolitika*, 2: 494–96.

11. A good example of this interpretation, which became the required orthodoxy for all subsequent historical accounts of the period, is E. Žagars, *Socialist Transformations in Latvian 1940–41* (Riga: Zinātne, 1978).

12. Romuald Misiunas and Rein Taagepera, *The Baltic States: Years of Dependence 1940–1990*, expanded and updated edition (Berkeley: University of California Press, 1993), pp. 23–24.

13. A. Drīzulis, ed., *Latvijas PSR vēsture*, vol. 2 (Riga: Zinātne, 1968), pp. 145–48.

14. *These Names Accuse: Nominal List of Latvians Deported to Soviet Russia 1940–1941* (Stockholm: Latvian National Foundation, 1982), pp. xii–lii.

15. A complete account of the Sovietization process, published during the subsequent German occupation of the country, is Alfreds Ceichners, *Was Europa drohte: Die Bolschewisierung Lettlands 1940–41* (Riga: Ceichners Verlag, 1942).

16. Lawrence Juda, "United States' Nonrecognition of the Soviet Union's Annexation of the Baltic States: Politics and Law," *Journal of Baltic Studies* 6 (1975): 272–90.

17. Misiunas and Taagepera, *The Baltic States*, p. 354. The authors ask that citations from this and other statistical tables in their study be accompanied by the warning that these figures are "guesstimates." Drīzulis, *Latvijas PSR vēsture*, 2: 179, estimated the number of evacuated Latvian citizens to have been fifty-three thousand.

18. Andrew Ezergailis's *The Holocaust in Latvia: The Missing Center* (Riga: Historical Institute of Latvia, in press) is now the most thoroughly researched work on the fate of the Jews in Latvia during the 1941–45 period. Aggregate figures for numbers killed in the first three-and-a-half months of the German occupation, as reported by the German authorities, are on p. 222, and are discussed throughout the study. The total number of Jews killed during the entire German occupation is, of course, higher. Ezergailis estimates (p. 203) that of the ninety-four thousand Jews counted in the 1935 Latvian census, about sixty thousand were killed in the first six months of the German occupation. The total number of Jews killed in Latvia (including those brought to the Riga ghetto from other parts of German-occupied Eastern Europe) during the entire World War II period is estimated at eighty-three thousand (Edgars Andersons, ed. *Lat-*

vju enciklopēdija, vol. 3 [Rockville, Md.: American Latvian Association, 1985], p. 305).

19. Seppo Myllyniemi, *Die Neuordnung der baltischen Länder, 1941–1944* (Helsinki: Societas Historica Finlandiae, 1973), is the most thorough recent account of German administration in the Baltic, including the Latvian *pašpārvalde*. A critical evaluation of the work of the *pašpārvalde* is Haralds Biezais, *Latvija kaškrusta varā: sveši kungi, pašu ļaudis* (n.p.: Gauja, 1992); and a pioneering exploration of the *Ostland* plan is contained in Heinrihs Strods, *Zem melnbrūnā zobena: Vācijas politika Latvijā 1939–1945* (Riga: Zvaigzne, 1994).

20. The most detailed history of the legion is Arturs Silgailis, *Latviešu leģions: dibināšana, formēšana, un kauju gaitas Otrā Pasaules Karā* (Copenhagen: Imanta, 1962).

21. Arvēds Švābe, *Latvju Enciklopēdija*, vol. 1 (Stockholm: Trīs Zvaigznes, 1950–51), p. 235, estimates that about 200,000 Latvians were living in occupied postwar Germany. Misunas and Taagepera, *The Baltic States*, table 2, p. 354, contains the "guesstimate" of 100,000 having "evacuated and flown to the West."

22. P. Zvidriņš and I. Vanovska, *Latvieši: statistiski demogrāfisks portretējums* (Riga: Zinātne, 1992), pp. 44–56.

23. Andersons, ed., *Latvju enciklopēdija 1962–1982*, 2: 419–21.

24. Kostanda, *Latvijas vēsture*, pp. 386–87; Drīzulis, *Latvijas PSR vēsture*, p. 212.

25. Misiunas and Taagepera, *The Baltic States*, p. 353.

26. Agnis Balodis, *Latvijas un latviešu vēsture* (Riga: Kabata, 1991), pp. 337–38; Heinrihs Strods, *Latvijas lauksaimniecības vēsture* (Riga: Zvaigzne, 1991), p. 218.

27. This question is discussed at length in Zvidriņš and Vanovska, *Latvieši: statistiski demogrāfisks portretējums*, pp. 137–64.

28. Strods, *Latvijas lauksaimniecības vēsture*, p. 217.

29. Andrīvs Namsons, "Die Entwicklung der Landwirtschaft in Sowjetlettland," *Acta Baltica* 9 (1970): 135–72.

30. Balodis, *Latvijas un latviešu tautas vēsture*, p. 365.

31. Ibid., pp. 355–56; Misiunas and Taagepera, *The Baltic States*, pp. 140–46.

32. Andrīvs Namsons, "Die Letten in der Emigration," *Acta Baltica* 6 (1967): 113–28; Aldis Putniņš, *Latvians in Australia: Alienation and Assimilation* (Canberra: Australian National University Press, 1981); Edgar Anderson, "Latvians," in Stephen Thernstrom, ed., *Harvard Encyclopedia of Ethnic Groups* (Cambridge, Mass.: Harvard University Press, 1980), pp. 638–41.

33. Rolfs Ekmanis, *Latvian Literature under the Soviets 1940–1975* (Belmont, Mass.: Nordland Publishing Company, 1978), pp. 181–234.

34. Andersons, *Latvju enciklopēdija 1962–1982*, 1: 502–9.

35. Misiunas and Taagepera, *The Baltic States*, pp. 356–60.

36. Ibid., p. 178.

37. Ibid., p. 193.

38. Andris Trapāns, "Die Militarbezirk Baltikum und Aspekte sowjetischer Militarpolitik in den baltischen Staaten," *Acta Baltica* 22 (1982): 164–80.

39. Heinrihs Strods, "Die herrschende Klasse (Nomenklatur) der Lettischen SSR," *Acta Baltica* 28 (1990): 189–98. For a description of how this mid-1970s mood expressed itself in literature, see Ekmanis, *Latvian Literature under the Soviets*, pp. 289–354.

40. Misiunas and Taagepera, *The Baltic States*, pp. 260–65; Rainer Herfurth, "Der lettische Widerstand gegen die Sowietisierung und Russifizierung von 1940/44 bis Gegenwart," *Acta Baltica* 27 (1990): 107–74.

41. Strods, *Latvijas lauksaimniecības vēsture*, pp. 270–78.

42. Ibid., pp. 237–45.

43. Andersons, *Latvju enciklopēdija 1940–1990*, pp. 367–71.

44. Misiunas and Taagepera, *The Baltic States*, p. 286.

45. Andersons, *Latvju enciklopēdija 1962–1982*, 4: 87–81.

46. Ibid., 2: 367–75.

47. A. Drīzulis, ed., *Riga sociālisma laikmetā 1917–1975* (Riga: Zinātne, 1980), pp. 347–51.

48. Ibid., p. 351; Zvidriņš and Vanovska, *Latvieši: statistiski demogrāfisks portretējums*, p. 66.

CHAPTER 9

1. Romuald Misiunas and Rein Taagepera, *The Baltic States: Years of Dependence 1940–1990* (Berkeley: University of California Press, 1993), pp. 275–77.

2. Ian Bremmer, "Reassessing Soviet Nationalities Theory," in Ian Bremmer and Ray Taras, eds., *Nations and Politics in the Soviet Successor States* (Cambridge, Eng.: Cambridge University Press, 1993), pp. 3–26.

3. Edgars Andersons, *Latvju enciklopēdija 1962–1982*, vol. 3 (Rockville, Md.: American Latvian Association, 1985), pp. 510–18.

4. Mārīte Sapiets, " 'Rebirth and Renewal' in the Latvian Lutheran Church," *Religion in Communist Lands* 6 (1988): 237–49; Nīls Muižnieks, "Latvia: Origins, Evolution and Triumph," in Bremner and Taras, *Nations and Politics*, pp. 190–91.

5. Walter C. Clemens Jr., *Baltic Independence and Russian Empire* (New York: St. Martin's Press, 1991), pp. 74–97.

6. Juris Dreifelds, "Latvian National Rebirth," *Problems of Communism* 28 (1989): 77–94.

7. Jan Arved Trapāns, "The Sources of Latvia's Popular Movement," in Jan Arved Trapans, ed., *Toward Independence: The Baltic Popular Movements* (Boulder, Colo.: Westview Press, 1991), pp. 32–33.

8. For an eyewitness account of the plenum, see Andris Kolberģis, *Dumpis uz laupītāju kuģa* (Riga: Lauku Apgads, 1993), pp. 47–55. A selection from the resolutions of the plenum is reprinted in Charles F. Furtado and Andrea Chandler, eds., *Perestroika in the Soviet Republics: Documents on the National Question* (Boulder, Colo.: Westview Press, 1992), pp. 111–14.

9. The product of one such reexamination is Ilga Gore and Aivars Stranga, *Latvija: Neatkarības Mijkrēslis. Okupācija* (Riga: Izglītība, 1992).

10. Muižnieks, "Latvia," in Bremner and Taras, *Nations and Politics*, pp. 193–94; Andrejs Plakans, "The Return of the Past: Baltic-Area Nationalism of the Perestroika Period," *Armenian Review* 43 (1990): 109–26.

11. For these meetings see Odisejs Kostanda, *Latvijas vēsture* (Riga: Zvaigzne, 1992), pp. 428–47.

12. Ģints Apals, "Die Nationale Unabhangigigskeitsbewegung Lettlands (1988–1991)," *Acta Baltica* 29/30 (1992): 9–28.

13. Erich von Noltein, "Die 'Volksfront Lettlands': Entstehung, Programm, und Statuten (Dokumentation)," *Acta Baltica* 27 (1990): 191–224.

14. Kostanda, *Latvijas vēsture*, pp. 435–39.

15. Olģerts Eglītis, *Non-Violent Action in the Liberation of Latvia* (Cambridge, Mass.: Albert Einstein Institution, 1992).

16. During the perestroika period, the general view among Latvian activists was that all Latvians, regardless of place of residence, belonged to the same *tauta*; see, for example, the 1989 speech by Jānis Stradiņš, reprinted in his *Treešā Atmoda* (Riga: Zinātne, 1992), pp. 94–98. On the League of Women, see Rasma Kārkliņš, *Ethnopolitics and Transition to Democracy: The Collapse of the USSR and Latvia* (Washington, D.C., and Baltimore, Md.: Woodrow Wilson Center Press/Johns Hopkins University Press, 1994), pp. 71–74.

17. Vera Tolz and Melanie Newton, eds., *The USSR in 1990: A Record of Events* (Boulder, Colo.: Westview Press, 1992), p. 246.

18. Misiunas and Taagepera, *The Baltic States*, p. 331.

19. Tolz and Newton, *The USSR in 1990*, p. 205.

20. Ibid., pp. 256–58.

21. Clemens, *Baltic Independence and Russian Empire*, pp. 242–59.

22. Tolz and Newton, *The USSR in 1990*, p. 738.

23. Kārlis Streips, comp., *Fifteen Months That Shook the World: Latvian Crisis Chronology January, 1991, to March, 1992* (Rockville, Md.: American Latvian Association, n.d.), pp. 1–7.

24. *Presidential Elections and Independence Referendums in the Baltic States, the Soviet Union, and Successor States: A Compendium of Reports 1991–1992* (Washington, D.C.: Commission on Security and Cooperation in Europe, 1992), pp. 8–13.

25. Streips, *Fifteen Months That Shook the World*, pp. 4–7; Tolz and Newton, *The USSR in 1990*, pp. 565–67, 581. See also Andrejs Plakans, "Latvia's Return to Independence," *Journal of Baltic Studies* 22 (1991): 259–65.

CHAPTER 10

1. *Iedzīvotāju dabiskā kustība un migrācija Latvijas Republikā 1989. gadā* (Riga: Valsts Statistikas Komiteja, 1990), p. 15.

2. Dzintra Bungs, "The People's Front of Latvia at the Crossroads," *Report on the USSR*, November 22, 1991, pp. 24–27.

3. Jan Ake Dellenbrandt, "The Reemergence of Multi-Partism in the Baltic States," in Sten Berglund and Dellenbrandt, eds., *The New Democracies in Eastern Europe: Party Systems and Political Cleavages* (London: Edward Elgar, 1992), pp. 75–105.

4. Brian van Arkadie and Mats Karlsson, *Economic Survey of the Baltic States* (New York: New York University Press, 1992), pp. 117–34.

5. See Ulrich-Joachim Schulz-Torge, *Who Was Who in the Soviet Union* (München: K.G. Saur, 1992), for a listing of the governmental political elite in the Supreme Council.

6. Andris Ozoliņš, *Eiropas Kopiena: Latvijas vārti uz Eiropu?* (Riga: Latvijas ārpolitikas institūts, 1992).

7. right and left in this description indicate general orientation rather than absolute positions.

8. For an expression of this argument, see the published papers of a June 1991 conference, *Komunistiskā totalitārisma un ģenocīda prakse Latvijā* (Riga: Zinātne, 1992). The conference was organized jointly by the Latvian Institute of History, the scientific association Latvia and the World's Latvians, and the Riga Club of the Politically Repressed.

9. Ilmārs Mežs, *Latvieši Latvijā: Etnodemogrāfisks apskats* (Kalamazoo, Mich.: Latvian Studies Center, 1992), pp. 21–26. Recent demographic trends point to the gradual enlargement of the Latvian proportion of the population over the next two decades; see Dzintra Bungs, "Recent Demographic Changes in Latvia," *Radio Free Europe/Radio Liberty Reports* (hereafter, *RFE/RL Reports*) 2 (December 17, 1993): 44–50.

10. *Valsts Valoda Latvijā* (Riga: Valsts Valodas Centrs, 1992) describes basic laws, regulations, and their implementation in Latvian, English, and Russian.

11. Elmārs Vēbers, "Demography and Ethnic Politics in Independent Latvia: Some Basic Facts," *Nationalities Papers* 11 (1993): 179–94.

12. Dzintra Bungs, "Latvia Adopts Guidelines for Citizenship," *Report on the USSR*, November 1, 1991, pp. 17–19.

13. Andrejs Plakans, "The Tribulations of Independence: Latvia 1991–1993," *Journal of Baltic Studies* 25 (1994): 63–72.

14. As an example of this viewpoint, see the published papers from a September 28, 1990, conference, *Latviešu nācijas izredzes* (Riga: Zinātne, 1990), in which the conference participants passed a resolution opposing the zero option.

15. See the panel discussion in "The Economic Transformation of the Baltic States," *Journal of Baltic Studies* 23 (1992): 299–306.

16. *Latvia: The Transition to a Market Economy* (Washington, D.C.: World Bank, 1993).

17. Ibid., pp. 73–84.

18. Jānis Stradiņš, "Latvia on the Crossroads of History," *Humanities and Social Sciences. Latvia* 1 (1993): 8.

19. The link between the Russian population in the former Soviet republics and the presence in these same republics of the Russian army is explored in William D. Jackson, "Imperial Temptations: Ethnics Abroad," *Orbis* (Winter 1994): 1–17.

20. Dzintra Bungs, "Latvia: Transition to Independence Completed," *RFE/RL Reports* 3 (January 7, 1994): 96–98.

21. Plakans, "Tribulations of Independence," pp. 65–66.

22. See Toivo Raun, "Post-Soviet Estonia 1991–1993," *Journal of Baltic Studies* 25 (1994): 73–80; Alfred Erich Senn, "Lithuania's First Two Years of Independence," *Journal of Baltic Studies* 25 (1994): 89–98.

SOURCES OF ILLUSTRATIONS

1. F. Balodis and R. Šņore, *Senā Rīga* (Riga: Pilsētas valde, 1937), p. 39.

2. Ž. Unams, *Krievu laiki Latvijā* (Riga: Valters un Rapa, 1936), p. 44.

3. *Senātne un Māksla* (1938), facing p. 128.

4. *Universitas*, no. 55 (1985): 22.

5. *Universitas*, no. 31 (1973): 6.

6. *Universitas*, no. 55 (1985): 17.

7. F. Balodis and F. Šņore, *Senā Rīga* (Riga: Pilsētas valde, 1937), p. 89.

8. Reinis and Matīss Kaudzīte, *Mērnieku laiki* (Riga: K. Rasiņš, 1944), facing p. 376.

9. T. Līventāls and V. Sadovskis, eds., *Rīga kā Latvijas galvas pilsēta* (Riga: Pilsētas valde, 1932), p. 751.

10. *Latvijas agrārā reforma* (Riga: Zemkopības ministrija, 1938), frontispiece.

The author acknowledges with thanks permission from the Latvian academic journal *Universitas* to reprint figures 4, 5, and 6.

Bibliography

Ābelnieks, L. "Gaujas lībiešu sabiedrības attīstības pakāpe XII un XIII gs. mijā" (The phase of social development of the Gauja Livs at the turn of the 13th century). In *Latvijas Universitātes Zinātniskie Raksti. Vēsture. Feodalisma problēmas Baltijā*, edited by A. Rolova, 6–17. Riga: Latvijas Universitātē, 1990.

Adamovičs, Ludvigs. "Latvieši un katoļu baznīca" (The Latvians and the Catholic Church). In *Latvieši*. Vol. 1, edited by F. Balodis and P. Šmits, 178–97. Riga: Valters un Rapa, 1930.

———. "Latvieši un evanģēliskā baznīca" (The Latvians and the Evangelical Church). In *Latvieši*. Vol. 1, ed. Balodis and Šmits, 198–230.

———. *Dzimtenes baznīcas vēsture*. (History of the Homeland Churches) N.p.: P. Mantnieks, 1947.

Aizsilnieks, Arnolds. *Latvijas saimniecības vēsture 1912–1945* (History of the Latvian economy 1914–1945). Stockholm: Daugava, 1968.

Anderson, Edgar. "Latvians." In *Harvard Encyclopedia of American Ethnic Groups*, edited by Stephan Thernstrom, 638–42. Cambridge: Harvard University Press, 1980.

———. "The Baltic Entente 1914–1940—Its Strength and Weakness." In *The Baltic in International Relations between the Two World Wars*, edited by John Hiden and Aleksander Loit. Stockholm: Almqvist and Wiksell, 1988.

———. *Latvia: Past and Present*. Waverly, Iowa: Latvju Gramata, 1968.

Andersons, Edgars. *Latvijas vēsture 1820–1940: Ārpolitika* (History of Latvia: Foreign policy). 2 vols. Stockholm: Daugava, 1982.

———. *Latvijas vēsture 1914–1920* (History of Latvia 1914–1920). Stockholm: Daugava, 1967.

————. *Senie kurzemnieki Amerikā un Tobāgo kolonizācija* (The Old Couronians and the colonization of Tobago). Stockholm: Daugava, 1970.

Andersons, Edgars, ed. *Latvju enciklopēdija 1962–1982* (Latvian encyclopedia 1962–1982). 5 vols. Rockville, Md.: American Latvian Association, 1985.

Andrups, Jānis, and Vitauts Kalve. *Latvian Literature: Essays.* Stockholm: Zelta Abele, 1954.

Angermann, Norbert, ed. *Deutschland-Livland-Russland, ihre Beziehung vom 15. bis 17. Jahrhundert.* Lüneburg: Nordoestdeutsche Kulturwerk, 1988.

————. *Wolter von Plettenberg: Der Grosste Ordensmeister Livlands.* Lüneburg: Nordostdeustches Kulturwerk, 1985.

Apals, Ģints. "Die Nationale Unabhangigskeitsbewegung Lettlands (1988–1991)." *Acta Baltica* 29/30 (1992): 9–28.

————. "Jaunlatviešu kustības politiskā orientācija 19.gs. 6o.os gados" (The political orientation of the Young Latvian Movement in the 1860s). *Latvijas vēstures institūta žurnāls* (Journal of the Latvian Institute of History), no. 1 (1992): 69–80.

————. *Janlatviešu kustība* (The Young Latvian Movement). Riga: Izglītības Ministrija, 1990.

Apinis, Aleksejs. *Grāmata un latviešu sabiedrība līdz 19. gadsimta vidum* (The book and Latvian society to the middle of the 19th century). Riga: Liesma, 1991.

Apkalns, Longins. *Lettische Musik.* Wiesbaden: Breitkopf and Hartel, 1977.

Arbusow, Leonid. *Grundriss der Geschichte Liv-, Est-, un Kurlands.* Riga: von Jonck und Polieweski, 1908.

Arkadie, Brian van, and Mats Karlsson. *Economic Survey of the Baltic States.* New York: New York University Press, 1992.

Arons, Matiss. *Latviešu Literāriskā (Latviešu Draugu) Biedrība savā simts gadu darbā* (The Latvian literary [Latvian Friends] Society in its 100 years of work). Riga: A. Gulbis, 1929.

Balēvica, L. "Privātkapitāla loma Vidzemes zemnieku māju iepirkšanā (19.gs. otra puse - 20.gs. sakums)" (The role of private capital in the purchase of Livland peasant farmsteads from the second half of the 19th century to the first half of the 20th century). *Latvijas vēstures institūta žurnāls,* no. 1 (1992): 49–73.

Balodis, Agnis. *Latvijas un latviešu tautas vēsture* (History of Latvia and of the Latvian nation). Riga: Kabata, 1991.

Balodis, F. "Latviešu starptautiskie sakari ap 1000.g. pēc Kristus" (Latvian international contacts around 1000 A.D.). *Latvijas vēstures institūta žurnāls* 3 (1939): 5–20.

Baumanis, Artūrs. *Pa Kronvalda Ata pēdām* (In the footsteps of Kronvalds). N.p.: K. Goppera Fonds, 1975.

Berķis, Alexander. *The History of the Duchy of Courland 1561–1795.* Towson, Md.: Paul M. Harrod, 1969.

Berklavs, E., et al. "Letter by Seventeen Latvian Communists." In *Samizdat,* edited by G. Saunders, 427–40. New York: Monad Press, 1974.

Bērziņš, J. "Latvijas valstiskuma ideja 1905.g. revolucijā" (The idea of Latvian statehood in the revolution of 1905). *Latvijas vēstures institūta žurnāls,* no. 3 (1992): 84–116.

Bērziņš, Ludis. "Latviešu rakstniecība svešu tautu aizbildniecībā" (Latvian writing in the foster care of other peoples). In *Latviešu,* vol. 1, F. Balodis and P. Šmits, 277–301.

———. "Metrik der lettischen Volkslieder." *Magazin der Lettisch-literärische Gesellschaft* 19 (1896).

Bērziņš, P. *Latvijas brīvības cīņas 1918–1920* (Latvian wars of independence). 1928. Reprint, Riga: Junda, 1992.

Bielenstein, August. *Die Holzbauten und Holzgeräte der Letten: Eine Beitrag zur Ethnographie, Kulturgeschichte, und Archeologie der Völker Russlands im Westgebiet.* 1907–1918. Reprint, Hannover-Dohren, Germany: Harro von Hirschhejdt 1969.

Biezais, Haralds. *Die Gottesgestalt der lettischen Volkreligion.* Stockholm: Almqvist and Wiksell, 1961.

———. *Die Hauptgöttinen der alten Letten.* Uppsala. Almqvist and Wiksell, 1955.

———. *Latvija kāškrusta varā: sveši kungi, pašu ļaudis* (Latvia in the grip of the swastika: Foreign lords, own people). N.p.: Gauja, 1992.

Bīlmanis, Alfrēds. *Baltic Essays.* Washington, D.C.: Latvian Legation, 1945.

———. *A History of Latvia.* Princeton: Princeton University Press, 1951.

———. *Latvia under German Occupation.* Washington, D.C.: Latvian Legation, 1943.

———. "Latviešu avīžniecība" (The Latvian press). In *Latviešu.* Vol. 2, edited by F. Balodis, P. Šmits, and A. Tentelis, 345–74. Riga: Valters un Rapa, 1932.

Bīlmanis, Alfrēds, ed. *Latvian-Russian Relations: Documents.* Washington, D.C.: Latvian Legation, 1978.

Bīrons, A., ed. *Latvijas strādnieki un zemnieki 1905.–1907.g. revolucijā* (The Latvian peasants and workers in the revolution of 1905–1907). Riga: Zinātne, 1986.

Blanks, Ernests. *Latvju nacionālā doma sadzīves cīņu ugunīs* (Latvian national thought in the crossfires of social conflict). Riga: Latvijas Nacionālais Klubs, 1923.

———. *Latvju tautas atmoda* (The Latvian national awakening). Riga: A. Raņkis, 1927.

Blese, Ernests. "Latviešu valodas attīstības posmi" (The phases of development of the Latvian language). In *Latviešiu.* Vol. 1, F. Balodis and P. Šmits, 54–60.

Bobe, Mendel, ed. *Jews in Latvia.* Tel Aviv: Association of Estonian and Latvian Jews in Israel, 1971.

Bohnet, A., and N. Penkaitis. "A Comparison of Living Standards and Consumption Patterns between the RSFSR and the Baltic Republics." *Journal of Baltic Studies* 19 (1988): 22–48.

Bondarevs, P. P. *Stučka par agrāro jautājumu Latvijā* (P. Stucka on the agrarian question in Latvia). Riga: Avots, 1980.

Brambe, R. *Rīgas iedzīvotāji feodālisma perioda beigās* (The inhabitants of Riga at the end of the feudal period). Riga: Zinātne, 1982.

Bremmer, Ian. "Reassessing Soviet Nationalities Theory." In *Nations and Politics in the Soviet Successor States*, edited by Ian Bremmer and Ray Taras, 3–26. Cambridge: Cambridge University Press, 1993.

Brežgo, Boļeslavs. "Latgales zemnieku attiecības pret 1861. gada agrārreformu" (The attitude of the Lettgallian peasant to the 1861 agrarian reform). *Latvijas vēstures institūta žurnāls* 4 (1940): 89–110.

Brockmann, Hartmut. *Der Deutsche Orden: Zwölf Kapitel aus seiner Geschichte.* Munich: Beck, 1981.

Brubaker, W. Rogers. "Citizenship Struggles in Soviet Successor States." *International Migration Review* 26 (1992): 269–91.

Brundage, James A. "Hunting and Fishing in the Law and Economy of Thirteenth Century Livonia." *Journal of Baltic Studies* 13 (1982): 3–11.

Bukšs, Miķelis. *Die Russifizierung in den baltischen Ländern.* Munich: Latgaļu izdevniecība, 1964.

———. *Latgaļu literatūras vēsture* (History of Lettgallian literature). Munich: Latgaļu izdevniecība, 1957.

Bungs, Dzintra. "Latvia Adopts Guidelines for Citizenship." *Report on the USSR.* November 1, 1991, pp. 17–19.

———. "Latvia: Transition to Independence Completed." *Radio Free Europe/Radio Liberty* (hereafter, *RFE/RL Reports*) 3 (January 7, 1994): 96–98.

———. "The People's Front of Latvia at the Crossroads." *Report on the USSR* 1 (November 22, 1991): 24–27.

———. "Recent Demographic Changes in Latvia." *RFE/RL Reports* 2 (December 17, 1993): 44–50.

Čakars, O., A. Grigulis, and M. Losberga. *Latviešu literatūras vēsture no pirmsākumiem līdz XIX gadsimta 80. gadiem* (The history of Latvian literature from the beginning to the 1889s). Riga: Zvaigzne, 1990.

Carson, George B., ed. *Latvia: An Area Study.* New Haven, Conn.: Human Relations Area Files no. 41, 1956.

Catlaks, G. *Rīgas priekšpilsētas gadsimtu gaitā* (The suburbs of Riga in the course of centuries). Riga: Ministry of Education, 1991.

Cedriņš, Inara, ed. *Contemporary Latvian Poetry.* Iowa City: University of Iowa Press, 1984.

Ceichners, Alfreds. *Was Europa drohte: Die Bolschewisierung Lettlands 1940–41.* Riga: Ceichners Verlag, 1942.

Cherney, Alexander. *The Latvian Orthodox Church.* Welshpool, Wales: Stylite Publishing Company, 1985.

Christiansen, Eric. *The Northern Crusades: The Baltic and the Catholic Frontier 1100–1525.* London: Macmillan, 1980.

Clem, Ralph S., ed. *The Soviet West: Interplay between Nationality and Social Organization.* New York: Praeger, 1975.

Clemens, Walter C., Jr. *Baltic Independence and Russian Empire.* New York: St. Martin's Press, 1991.

Constitution of the Republic of Latvia. Stockholm: Latvian National Foundation, 1984.

Corrsin, Stephen B. "The Changing Composition of the City of Riga, 1867–1913." *Journal of Baltic Studies* 13 (1982): 19–39.

Crowe, David M. *The Baltic States and the Great Powers: Foreign Relations 1938–1940.* Boulder, Colo.: Westview Press, 1993.

———. "Germany and the Baltic Question in Latvia, 1939–1940." *East European Quarterly* 26 (1992): 371–89.

Cullen, Robert. *Twilight of Empire: Inside the Crumbling Soviet Bloc.* New York: Atlantic Monthly Press, 1991.

Dellenbrandt, Jan Ake. "The Reemergence of Multi-Partism in the Baltic States." In *The New Democracies in Eastern Europe: Party Systems and Political Cleavages,* edited by Sten Berglund and Jan Ake Dellenbrandt, 75–105. London: Edward Elgar, 1992.

Dorošenko, V. "Lauksaimniecības preču eksports no Rīgas 1620–1630" (The export of agricultural goods from Riga 1620–1630). In *Latvijas agrārā vēsture XVI–XIX gs* (Agrarian history of Latvia, sixteenth–nineteenth centuries), edited by T. Zeids. Riga: Zinātne, 1966.

Dreifelds, Juris. "Belorussia and the Baltics." In *Economics of Soviet Regions,* edited by I. S. Koropeckyj and Gertrude Schroeder, 325–85. New York: Praeger, 1981.

———. "Characteristics and Trends of Two Demographic Variables in the Latvian SSR." *Bulletin of Baltic Studies* 8 (1971): 10–17.

———. "Latvian National Demands and Group Consciousness Since 1959." In *Nationalism in the USSR and Eastern Europe in the Era of Brezhnev and Kosygin,* edited by J. Simmonds, 136–56. Detroit, Mich.: University of Detroit Press, 1977.

———. "Latvian National Rebirth." *Problems of Communism* 28 (1989): 77–94.

Drīzulis, A., ed. *Latvijas PSR vēsture no vissenākajiem laikiem līdz mūsu dienām* (The history of the Latvian SSR from the earliest times to the present). 2 vols. Riga: Zinatne, 1986.

Duhanovs, M. *Baltijas muižniecība laikmetu maiņā* (The Baltic nobility in changing times). Riga: Zinātne, 1986.

Duhanovs, M., I. Feldmanis, and A. Stranga. *1939: Latvia and the Year of Fateful Decisions.* Riga: University of Latvia Press, 1994.

Dunsdorfs, Edgars. "Dažas Latvijas 19. g.s.otrās puses iedzīvotāju skaita attīstības problēmas" (Some problems of the population development of Latvia in the second half of the 19th century). *Latvijas vēstures institūta žurnāls* 3 (1939): 241–70.

———. *Divas gudras latviešu galvas: Muižu dibināšana zviedru Vidzemē* (Two wise Latvian heads: The founding of manors in Swedish Livonia). Stockholm: Daugava, 1986.

———. *Kārļa Ulmaņa dzīve* (The life of Karlis Ulmanis). Stockholm: Daugava, 1978.

———. *Latvijas vēsture 1600–1710* (History of Latvia, 1600–1710). Stockholm: Daugava, 1962.

———. *Latvijas vēsture 1710–1800* (History of Latvia, 1710–1800). Stockholm: Daugava, 1973.

———. *The Livonian Estates of Axel Oxenstierna*. Stockholm: Almqvist and Wiksell, 1981.

———. *Muižas* (Estates). Melbourne: Kārļa Zariņa Fonds, 1983.

———. *Pirmās latviešu Bībeles vēsture* (The history of the first Latvian bible). New York: Latv. ev. lut. baznīca Amerikā, 1979.

———. *Skaistā Latgale* (Beautiful Latgale). Melbourne: Karla Zarina Fonds, 1991.

———. *Turība un brīvība septiņpadsimtā gadsimteņa Latvijā* (Wealth and freedom in seventeenth-century Latvia). Lincoln, Nebr.: Pilskalns, 1961.

Dunsdorfs, Edgars, and Arnolds Spekke. *Latvijas vēsture 1500–1600* (History of Latvia, 1500–1600). Stockholm: Daugava, 1964.

Eckardt, Julius. "Polnisch Livland." In *Die baltischen Provinzen Russlands*, edited by Julius Eckardt. Leipzig: Duncker und Humboldt, 1869.

Economic Legislation of the Republic of Latvia in English. Riga: Department of Foreign Economic Relations, Council of Ministers, 1991–92.

Eģītis, Oļģerts. *Non-Violent Action in the Liberation of Latvia*. Cambridge, Mass.: Albert Einstein Institution, 1992.

Ekmanis, Rolfs. *Latvian Literature under the Soviets, 1940–1975*. Belmont, Mass.: Nordland Publishing Company, 1978.

Ezergailis, Andrievs. "Anti-Semitism and the Killing of Latvia's Jews." In *Anti-Semitism in Times of Crisis*, edited by Sander L. Gilman and Steven T. Katz. New York: New York University Press, 1991.

———. *Esejas par 1917. gadu* (Essays on the year 1917). Riga: Zinatne, 1991.

———. "Holocaust in Latvia, 1940–1945." In *Encyclopedia of the Holocaust*, edited by Israel Gutman. Jerusalem and New York: Macmillan, 1990.

———. *The Holocaust in Latvia: The Missing Center*. Riga: Historical Institute of Latvia, in press.

———. *The Latvian Impact on the Bolshevik Revolution*. Boulder, Colo.: East European Monographs, 1983.

———. *The 1917 Revolution in Latvia*. Boulder, Colo.: East European Monographs, 1974.

Ezergailis, Andrew, and Gert von Pistohlkors. *Die Baltischen Provinzen Russlands zwischen den Revolutionen vom 1905 und 1917.* Cologne: Bohlau Verlag, 1982.

Feldhuns, A., transl. *Indriķa hronika* (Chronicle of Henry of Livonia). Riga: Zinatne, 1993.

Feldmanis, I., A. Stranga, and M. Vinsis. *Latvijas ārpolitika un starptautiskais stavoklis 30 gadra otra puse* (Latvia's foreign policy and international position during the second half of the 1930s). Riga: Latvijas Ārpolitikas Institūts, 1993.

Flint, David. *The Baltic States: Estonia, Latvia, Lithuania.* Brookfield, Conn.: Millbrook Press, 1992.

Furtado, Charles F., and Andrea Chandler, eds. *Perestroika in the Soviet Republics: Documents on the National Question.* Boulder, Colo.: Westview Press, 1992.

Gāters, Alfrēds. *Die lettische Sprache und Ihre Dialekte.* The Hague: Mouton, 1977.

S. Gehtmane, ed. *Pedagoğiskā doma Latvijā līdz 1890. gadam: Antoloğija* (Pedagogical philosophy in Latvia to 1890: An anthology). Riga: Zvaigzne, 1991.

Ğērmanis, Uldis. "Die Agrargesetzgebung auf den herzoglichen Domänen Kurlands zur Zeit Birons." *Acta Baltica* 16 (1976).

———. "The Idea of an Independent Latvia and Its Development in 1917." In *Res Baltica*, edited by A. Sprudžs and A. Rūsis, 27–87. Leyden: A. W. Sijthoof, 1968.

———. *Latviešu tautas piedzīvojumi* (Adventures of the Latvian nation). Riga: Jana Seta, 1990.

———. *Pa aizputinātām pēdām* (Through snow-covered tracks). Stockholm: Daugava, 1956.

Gerner, Kristian. *The Baltic States and the End of the Soviet Empire.* London: Routledge, 1993.

Gimbutas, Marija. *The Balts.* London: Thames and Hudson, 1963.

Gordon, Frank. *Latvians and Jews between Germany and Russia.* Stockholm: Memento, 1990.

Gore, Ilga, and Aivars Stranga. *Latvija: neatkarības mijkrēslis. Okupācija* (Latvia: Twilight of independence). Riga: Izglītība, 1992.

Gotz, Roland. *Die Wirtschaft des Baltikums.* Köln: Bundesinstitut fur Ostwissenschaftliche und Internationale Studien, 1990.

Graham, M. W. *The Diplomatic Recognition of the Border States.* Vol. 3, *Latvia.* Publications of the University of California at Los Angeles in Social Sciences. Berkeley: University of California Press, 1939–1941.

Grava, Sigurd. "The Urban Heritage of the Soviet Region: The Case of Riga, Latvia." *Journal of the American Planning Association* 59 (1993): 9–30.

Greitjāne, G. *Vidzemes bezzemnieku padomju darbība: 1917.marts, 1918. aprīlis* (The work of the Soviets of the landless peasants in Vidzeme: March 1917 to April 1918). Riga: Zinātne, 1986.

Haltzel, Michael. *Der Abbau der deutschen ständischen Selbstvervaltung in den Ostseeprovinzen Russlands 1855–1905: Ein Beitrag zur Geschichte der russischen Unifizierungspolitik.* Marburg: Herderinstitut, 1977.

Hanson, P. "Centre and Periphery: The Baltic States in Search of Economic Independence." *Journal of Interdisciplinary Economics*. 4 (1992): 249–67.

Harned, Frederick. "Latvians." In *Handbook of Major Soviet Nationalities*, edited by Zev Katz. New York: Free Press, 1975.

Hehn, Jürgen von. *Die lettisch-literarische Gessellschaft und das Lettentum*. Königsberg: N.p. 1938.

———. *Lettland zwischen Demokratie und Diktatur: Zur Geschichte des lettlandischen Staatsstreich vom 15. mai 1934*. 1957. Reprint, München: Isaar Verlag, 1966.

Hellmann, Manfred, ed. *Studien über die Anfänge der Mission in Livland*. Sigmaringen: Jan Thordbecke, 1989.

Henrikkson, Anders. *The Tsar's Loyal Germans: The Riga German Community: Social Change and the Nationality Question, 1855–1905*. Boulder, Colo.: East European Monographs, 1983.

Henry of Livonia, the Chronicle of. Translated and annotated by James A. Brundage. Madison: University of Wisconsin Press, 1961.

Herfurth, Rainer. "Der lettische Widerstand gegen die Sowietisierung und Russifizierung von 1940/44 bis Gegenwart." *Acta Baltica* 27 (1990): 107–74.

Hiden, J. W. *The Baltic States and Weimar Ostpolitik*. Cambridge: Cambridge University Press, 1987.

Hiden, John, ed. *The Baltic and the Outbreak of the Second World War*. Cambridge: Cambridge University Press, 1992.

Hiden, John, and Patrick Salmon. *The Baltic Nations and Europe: Estonia, Latvia, and Lithuania in the Twentieth Century*. London and New York: Longman, 1991.

Hough, W. J. "The Annexation of the Baltic States and Its Effect on the Development of Law Prohibiting Forcible Seizure of Territory." *New York Law School Journal of International and Comparative Law* 6 (1985): 300–533.

Hovi, Olavi. *The Baltic Area in British Policy 1918–1921*. Helsinki: Finnish Historical Society, 1980.

Iedzīvotāju dabiskā kustība un migrācija Latvijas Republikā 1989. gada (Natural movements and migration of the population of the Latvian Republic in 1989). Riga: Valsts Statistikas Komiteja, 1990.

Indriķa hronika (Heinrich's chronicle). Translated by A. Feldhūns, with a commentary by E. Mugurēvičs. Riga: Zinātne, 1993.

International Peace Research Institute. *Comprehensive Security for the Baltic: An Environmental Approach*. Oslo, 1989.

Jackson, William D. "Imperial Temptations: Ethnics Abroad." *Orbis* (Winter 1994): 1–17.

Jakstas, Juozas. "Das Baltikum in der Kreuzzugsbewegung des 14. Jahrhunderts." *Commentationes Balticae* 6/7 (1958/59): 139–83.

Jefremova, L. S. *Latyshskaya krestyanskaya semiya v Latgale 1860–1939*. Riga: Zinatne, 1982.

Jēgers, Benjāmiņš, ed. *Latviešu trimdas izdevumu bibliogrāfija* (Bibliography of Latvian publications outside Latvia). 4 vols. Stockholm: Daugava, 1968–1988.

Jērāns, P., ed. *Latvijas Padomju Enciklopēdija* (Latvian Soviet encyclopedia). 10 vols. Riga: Galvenā enciklopēdiju redakcija, 1981–1987.

Johansons, Andrejs. *Der Schirmherr des Hofes im Volksglauben der Letten.* Stockholm: Almqvist and Wiksell, 1964.

———. *Latvijas kultūras vēsture 1710–1800* (History of Latvian culture). Stockholm: Daugava, 1975.

———. *Rīgas svārki mugurā* (Wearing a coat from Riga). Brooklyn, N.Y.: Grāmatu Draugs, 1966.

Juda, Lawrence. "United States' Nonrecognition of the Soviet Union's Annexation of the Baltic States: Politics and Law." *Journal of Baltic Studies* 6 (1975): 272–90.

Juškevičs, Juris. *Hercoga Jēkaba laikmets Kurzemē* (The era of Duke Jacob in Courland). Riga: Valstspapira Spiestuve, 1931.

———. *Kurzemes hercogi un viņu laikmets* (The Courland dukes and their era). 1935. Reprint, Riga: Zvaigzne, 1993.

Kalniņš, Bruno. "How Latvia Is Ruled: The Structure of the Political Apparatus." *Journal of Baltic Studies* 8 (1977): 70–78.

Kalniņš, Voldemārs. *Latvijas PSR valsts un tiesību vesture* (History of the Latvian SSR and Latvian law). Vol. 1. Riga: Zinātne, 1972.

Kārkliņš, Rasma. *Ethnic Relations in the USSR: The Perspective from Below.* Boston, Mass.: Allen and Unwin, 1986.

Kārklis, Maruta, et al., eds. *The Latvians in America, 1640–1973: A Chronology and Fact Book.* Dobbs Ferry, N.Y.: Oceana Publishers, 1974.

Kārļa Ulmaņa runas un raksti 1899–1918 (The speeches and writings of Kārlis Ulmanis). Riga: Zemnieka domas, 1939.

Katzenellenbogen, Uriah. *The Daina: An Anthology of Lithuanian and Latvian Folk Songs.* Chicago: Lithuanian News Publishing Company, 1935.

Kaufmann, Max. *Die Vernichtung der Juden Lettlands.* München: Deutscher Verlag, 1947.

Kavass, Igor I., and Adolph Sprudžs, eds. *Baltic States: A Study of Their Origin and National Development: Their Seizure and Incorporation into the USSR.* New York: William Hein, 1972.

Kenez, Csaba Janos, ed. *Zur gegenwartigen Lage des Bildunswesens in den baltischen Sowjetrepubiken Estland und Lettland.* Marburg: J. G. Herder-Institut, 1986.

Kēniņš, Indulis. *Latvijas vēsture* (History of Latvia). Riga: Zvaigzne, 1992.

King, Gundar. *Economic Policies in Occupied Latvia.* Tacoma, Wash.: Pacific Lutheran University Press, 1965.

Kirby, David. *Northern Europe in the Early Modern Period: The Baltic World, 1492–1772.* London: Longman, 1990.

Klišāns, V. *Livonija 13.-16.gs. pirmajā pusē* (Livonia from the thirteenth to the first half of the sixteenth century). Riga: Latvijas Universitāte, 1992.

Klīve, Adolfs. *Brīvā Latvija* (Independent Latvia). New York: Gramatu Draugs, 1969.

———. *Latvijas neatkarības gadi* (The years of Latvian independence). New York: Gramatu Draugs, 1976.

Kolbergs, Andris. *Dumpis uz laupitāju kuga* (Mutiny on a pirate ship). Riga: Lauku Apgads, 1993.

Kolde, Endel Jakob. "Structural Integration of the Baltic Economies into the Soviet System." *Journal of Baltic Studies* 9 (1978): 164–76.

Komunistiskā totalitārisma un genocīda prakse Latvijā (The practice of totalitarian communism and genocide in Latvia). Riga: Zinātne, 1992.

Kostanda, Odisejs. *Latvijas vēsture* (History of Latvia). Riga: Zvaigzne, 1992.

Krastiņš, J., ed. *Rīga 1860–1917*. Riga: Zinātne, 1978.

Krātiņš, Ojārs. "An Unsung Hero: Krisjanis Barons and His Lifework in Latvian Folk Songs." *Western Folklore* 20 (1961): 239–55.

Krūmiņš, Juris, and Pēteris Zvidriņš. "Recent Mortality Trends in the Three Baltic Republics." *Population Studies* 46 (1992): 259–73.

Krupnikov, P. *Lettland und die Letten im Spiegel deutschen und deutschbaltischer Publizistik, 1895–1950*. Hannover, Germany: H. von Hirschheydt, 1989.

Kundsen, Olav F., and Ovind Jaeger, eds. *The Baltic States Reborn: A Bibliography of Political Affairs in Estonia, Latvia and Lithuania*. Oslo: Norwegian Institute of International Affairs, 1992.

Küng, Andres. *A Dream of Freedom: Four Decades of National Survival versus Russian Imperialism in Estonia, Latvia, and Lithuania, 1940–1980*. Cardiff, Wales: Boreas, 1981.

Labsvīrs, Jānis. *The Sovietization of the Baltic States: Collectivization of Latvian Agriculture, 1944–1956*. N.p: Taurus, 1989.

Lapa, L. "Arodorganizāciju pirmsākumi Latvijā 1905.g." (The beginnings of craft unions in Latvia in 1905). *Latvijas vēstures institūta žurnāls*, no. 2 (1992): 89–106.

Latvia: An Economic Profile. Washington, D.C.: U.S. Department of Commerce, August 1992.

Latvia: The Transition to a Market Economy. World Bank Country Study. Washington, D.C.: World Bank, 1993.

Latvian Research: An International Evaluation. Copenhagen: Danish Research Councils, 1992.

Latviešu nācijas izredzes (The future of the Latvian nation). Proceedings of the Conference "Latviešu nācijas izredzes," held September 28, 1990, in Riga. Riga: Zinātne, 1990.

Latvijas agrārā reforma: agrārās reformas izvešanas darbu noslēgums (The Latvian agrarian reform: Conclusion of the reform implementation). Riga: Ministry of Agriculture, 1938.

Lazda, Paulis. "The Phenomenon of Russophilism in the Development of Latvian Nationalism in the 19th Century." In *National Movements in the Baltic Countries during the 19th Century,* edited by Aleksaner Loit, 129–35. Stockholm: Centre for Baltic Studies, 1985.

Levin, Dov. "Arrests and Deportations of Latvian Jews by the USSR during the Second World War." *Nationalities Papers* 16 (1988): 50–70.

———. "The Jews and the Sovietization of Latvia, 1940–41." *Soviet Jewish Affairs* 5 (1975).

———. "On the Relations between the Baltic Peoples and Their Jewish Neighbors before, during, and after World War II." *Holocaust and Genocide Studies* 5 (1990): 53–56.

Liebel-Weckowicz, Helen. "Nations and Peoples: Baltic-Russian History and the Development of Herder's Theory of Culture." *Canadian Journal of History* 21 (1986): 1–23.

Liepiņa, Dzidra. *Agrārās attiecības Rīgas lauku novadā* (Agrarian relations in the rural districts of Riga). Riga: Latvijas PSR Zinatnu Akademija, 1962.

Lieven, Anatol. *The Baltic Revolution: Latvia, Lithuania, Estonia, and the Path to Independence.* New Haven, Conn.: Yale University Press, 1993.

Littlejohn, David. *Foreign Legions of the Third Reich.* Vol. 4, *Poland, Ukraine, Bulgaria, Romania, Free India, Estonia, Latvia, Lithuania, Finland, and Russia.* San Jose, Calif.: James Bender, 1987.

Liventāls, T., and V. Sadoskis, eds. *Rīga kā Latvijas galvas pilsēta* (Riga as the capital of Latvia). Riga: Rigas pilsetas valde, 1932.

Loeber, Dietrich Andre, ed. *Diktierte Option: Die Umsiedlung der Deutschbalten aus Estland und Lettland 1939–1941: Dokumentation.* Neumunster: Karl Wachholz, 1972.

Loeber, Dietrich André, V. Stanley Vardys, and Laurence P. Kitching, eds. *Regional Identity under Soviet Rule: The Case of the Baltic States.* Hackettstown, N.J.: Association for the Advancement of Baltic Studies, 1990.

Loit, Aleksander, ed. *National Movements in the Baltic Countries during the 19th Century.* Stockholm: University of Stockholm, 1985.

Loit, Aleksander, and John Hiden, eds. *The Baltic in International Relations between the Two World Wars.* Stockholm: University of Stockholm, 1988.

Lūsis, K., and G. Sīmanis, eds. *Krišjānis Valdemārs: Tēvzemei* (Krišjānis Valdemārs: For the fatherland). Riga: Avots, 1991.

Maley, William. *The Politics of Baltic Nationalism.* Canberra: Research School of Pacific Studies, 1990.

Mangulis, Visvaldis. *Latvia in the Wars of the 20th Century.* Princeton Junction, N.J.: Cognition Books, 1983.

Markaus, V., ed. *Agrārās reformas gaita Latvijā 1919–1922* (The process of agrarian reform, 1919–1922). Riga: A. Gulbis, 1922.

Mattiesen, Otto Heinz. *Die Kolonial- und Überseepolitik der Kurländischen Herzoge im 17. und 18. Jahrhundert.* Berlin: Kohlhammer, 1940.

Mednis, Aleksandrs. *Agrārais jautājums un zemes reforma Latvijā* (The agrarian question and land reform in Latvia). Riga: Latvju Kultura, 1924.

Meissner, Boris, ed. *Die Baltische Nationen: Estland, Lettland, und Litauen.* Cologne: Markus Verlag, 1990.

Mendelsohn, Ezra. *The Jews of East Central Europe between the World Wars.* Bloomington: Indiana University Press, 1983.

Mercier, P. R. *Aspects des luttes sociales en URSS: le mouvement democratique des Armeniens, les Baltes, et la question de l'etat de droit.* Paris: P. Bouchereau, 1989.

Mežs, Ilmārs. *Latvieši Latvijā: Etnodemogrāfisks apskats* (Latvian in Latvia: An ethnodemographic description). Kalamazoo, Mich.: Latvian Studies Center, 1992.

Mieriņa, A. *Agrārās attiecības un zemnieku stāvoklis Kurzemē 19.gs. II puse* (Agrarian relation and the condition of the peasantry in the second half of the nineteenth century). Riga: Zinātne, 1963.

Misiunas, Romuald. "The Baltic Republics: Stagnation and Strivings for Sovereignty." In *The Nationalities Factor in Soviet Politics and Society,* edited by Lubomyr Hajda and Mark Beissinger. 204–27. Boulder, Colo.: Westview Press, 1990.

———. "Baltic Nationalism and Soviet Language Policy: From Russification to Constitutional Amendment." In *Soviet Nationality Policies: Ruling Ethnic Groups in the USSR,* edited by Henry Huttenbach. 206–20. London: Mansell, 1990.

Misiunas, Romuald, and Rein Taagepera. *The Baltic States: Years of Dependence, 1940–1990.* Expanded and updated edition. Berkeley: University of California Press, 1993.

Muižnieks, Nīls. "Latvia: Origins, Evolution and Triumph." In *Nations and Politics in the Soviet Successor States,* edited by Ian Bremmer and Ray Taras, 190–91. Cambridge: Cambridge University Press, 1993.

Mylliniemi, Seppo. *Die Neuordnung der Baltischen Länder 1941–1944.* Helsinki: Societas Historica Finlandiae, 1973.

Namsons, Andrīvs. "Die bürgerliche Bewegung in Sowjetrussland und in den baltischen Ländern." *Acta Baltica* 14 (1974): 138–83.

———. "Die Entwicklung der Landwirtschaft in Sowjetlettland." *Acta Baltica* 9 (1969): 135–72.

———. "Die Letten in der Emigration." *Acta Baltica* 6 (1967): 113–28.

———. "Die Umgestaltung der Landwirtschaft in Lettland." *Acta Baltica* 2 (1962): 57–92.

———. "Die Sowjetisierung des Schul- und Bildungswesens in Lettland von 1940 bis 1960." *Acta Baltica* 1 (1960–61): 148–67.

———. "Neue Errungenschaften in der Industrie Lettlands." *Acta Baltica* 9 (1969): 81–134.

————. "Nationale Zusammensetzung und Struktur der Bevölkerung Lettlands nach den Volkszahlungen von 1935, 1959, und 1970." *Acta Baltica* 11 (1971): 61–68.

————. "Stadtentwicklung und Siedlungsformen in Lettland." *Acta Baltica* 7 (1967): 131–69.

Neubert, K. H. *Im Banne Moskaus: Die Evangelisch-luterische Kirche in den Russischen Ostseeprovinzen.* Bermane: H. Klein, 1888.

Neulen, Hans Werner. *An deutscher Seite: Internationale Freiwillige von Wehrmacht und Waffen-SS.* Munich: Universitas, 1985.

Niitemaa, Vilho. *Der Binnenhandel in der Politik der livländischen Städte im Mittelalter.* Helsinki: University of Helsinki, 1952.

————. *Die undeutsche Frage in der Politik der livländischen Städte im Mittelalter.* Helsinki: University of Helsinki, 1949.

Noltein, Erich von. "Die 'Volksfront Lettlands': Entstehung, Programm, und Statuten (Dokumentation)." *Acta Baltica* 27 (1990): 191–224.

Ozoliņa, Dz. *Liepājas pilsētas pašvaldība 1877–1913* (The municipal government of Liepāja, 1877–1913). Riga: Zinātne, 1990.

Ozoliņš, Andris. *Eiropas Kopiena: Latvijas vārti uz Eiropu?* (The European Community: Latvia's gateway to Europe?). Riga: Latvijas ārpolitikas institūts, 1992.

Ozols, Jakob. "Die vor- und frühgeschichtliched Burgen Semgallns." *Commentationes Balticae* 14/15 (1968/70): 105–213.

Paegle, Spricis. *Kā Latvijas valsts tapa* (How the Latvian state was created). Riga: N.p., 1923.

Page, Stanley W. *The Formation of the Baltic States: A Study of the Effects of Great Power Policies on the Emergence of Lithuania, Latvia, Estonia.* Cambridge: Harvard University Press, 1959; New York: Howard Fertig, 1970.

Parming, Tõnu. "Population Processes and the Nationality Issue in the Soviet Baltic." *Soviet Studies* 22 (1980): 398–414.

Pāvulāns, V. *Satiksmes ceļi Latvijā XIII–XVII gs* (Trade routes in Latvia, thirteenth to seventeenth centuries). Riga: Zinātne, 1971.

Peniķis, John J. "Latvian Nationalism: Preface to the Dissenting View." In *Nationalism in the USSR and Eastern Europe in the Era of Brezhnev and Kosygin*, edited by J. Simmond, 157–61. Detroit, Mich.: University of Detroit Press, 1977.

Peniķis, M., ed. *Latvijas atbrīvošanas kara vēsture* (The history of the liberation war in Latvia). Riga: Literatura, 1938.

————. *Pasaules karš 1914., 1915., un 1916. gadā un latviešu strēlnieku bataljonu-pulku cīņas* (The world war in 1914, 1915, and 1916 and the battles of the Latvian rifle battalions). 2 vols. Riga: Militārās literatūras apgādes fonds, 1935.

Plakans, Andrejs. "Agrarian Reform in the Baltic States between the World Wars: The Historical Context." In *An Overview of Rural Development Strategies for the Baltics.* 1–14. Report 93-BR9 of the Center for Agricultural and Rural Development, Iowa State University, Ames, Iowa, March, 1993.

———. "From a Regional Vernacular to the Language of a State: The Case of Latvian." *International Journal of the Sociology of Language*, nos. 100/101 (1993): 203–19.

———. "The Latvians." In *Russification in the Baltic Provinces and Finland 1855–1914*, edited by Edward C. Thaden, 207–84. Princeton, N.J.: Princeton University Press, 1981.

———. "Latvia's Return to Independence." *Journal of Baltic Studies* 22 (1991): 259–65.

———. "Peasants, Intellectuals, and Nationalism in the Russian Baltic Provinces, 1820–1890." *Journal of Modern History* 46 (1974): 445–75.

———. "The Return of the Past: Baltic-Area Nationalism of the Perestroika Period." *Armenian Review* 43 (1990): 109–26.

———. "The Tribulations of Independence: Latvia 1991–1993." *Journal of Baltic Studies* 25 (1994): 63–72.

Plāķis, J. "Baltu tautas un ciltis" (Baltic nations and tribes). In *Latvieši: rakstu krājums*. Vol. 1, edited by F. Balodis and P. Šmits, 45–49. Riga: Valters un Rapa, 1930.

Plotnieks, Andris. "The Evolution of the Soviet Federation and the Independence of Latvia." In *Soviet Federalism, Nationalism, and Economic Decentralisation*, edited by Alistair McAuley. New York: St. Martin's Press, 1991.

Presidential Elections and Independence Referendums in the Baltic States, the Soviet Union, and Successor States: A Compendium of Reports 1991–1992. Washington, D.C.: Commission on Security and Cooperation in Europe, 1992.

Press, Bernard. *Judenmord in Lettland 1941–1945*. 2d ed. Berlin: Metropol-Verlag, 1992.

Putniņš, Aldis. *Latvians in Australia: Alienation and Assimilation*. Canberra: Australian National University Press, 1981.

Radziņš, Pēteris. *Latvijas atbrīvošanas karš* (The war of liberation in Latvia). 1921. Reprint, Riga: Avots, 1991.

Rauch, Georg von. *The Baltic States: The Years of Independence, 1917–1940*. Berkeley: University of California Press, 1974.

Rauch, Georg von, ed. *Geschichte der deutschbaltischen Geschichtsschreibung*. Cologne and Vienna: Bohlau Verlag, 1976.

Raun, Toivo U. "The Latvian and Estonian National Movements, 1860–1914." *Slavonic and East European Review* 64 (1986): 66–80.

———. "Perestroika and Baltic Historiography." *Journal of Soviet Nationalities* 2 (1991): 52–62.

———. "Post-Soviet Estonia, 1991–1993." *Journal of Baltic Studies* 25 (1994): 73–80.

———. "The Revolution of 1905 in the Baltic Provinces and Finland." *Slavic Review* 43 (1984): 453–67.

Rodgers, H. I. *Search for Security: A Study in Baltic Diplomacy, 1920–1934*. Hamden, Conn.: Archon Books, 1975.

Romis, Indulis, ed. *Kārlis Ulmanis un Cietum ā (Karlis Ulmanis in exile and prison)*. Riga: Latvijas Vēstures Institūts, 1994.

Rozītis, Elmārs. "Die evangelisch-luterische Kirche in Sowjetlettland." *Acta Baltica* 1 (1960–61): 93–109.

Rudzītis, J., ed. *Atis Kronvalds: Tagadnei* (Atis Kronvalds: For today). Riga: Liesma, 1987.

Rūķe-Draviņa, Velta. *The Standardization Process in Latvia: 16th Century to the Present*. Stockholm: University of Stockholm, 1977.

Sakwa, Richard. *Gorbachev and His Reforms, 1985–1990*. London: Philip Allen, 1990.

Sapiets, M. " 'Rebirth and Renewal' in the Latvian Lutheran Church." *Religion in Communist Lands* 16 (1988): 237–49.

Schulz-Torge, Ulrich-Joachim. *Who Was Who in the Soviet Union*. München: K.G. Saur, 1992.

Schwabe, A. *Grundriss der Agrargeschichte Lettlands*. Riga: Berhard Lamey, 1928.

Senn, Alfred Erich. "Lithuania's First Two Years of Independence." *Journal of Baltic Studies* 25 (1994): 89–98.

Seraphim, August. *Die Geschichte des Herzogtums Kurland*. Reval: Franz Kluge, 1904.

Serphim, Ernst. *Grundriss der baltischen Geschichte*. Reval: Franz Kluge, 1908.

Seskis, J. *Latvijas valsts izcelšanās* (The founding of the Latvian state). 1937. Reprint, Riga: Balta, n.d.

Smith, G. E. "The Impact of Modernization on the Latvian Soviet Republic." *Coexistence* 6 (1979): 45–64.

———. "Soziale und Geographische Veränderungen in der Bevölkerungstruktur von Estland, Lettland, und Litauen 1918–1940." *Acta Baltica* 19/20 (1979/80): 118–81.

Smith, Graham. "Latvians." In *The Nationalities Question in the Soviet Union*, edited by Graham Smith, 54–71. London: Longmans, 1990.

Smith, Inese, and Marita V. Grunts. *The Baltic States: Estonia, Latvia, Lithuania*. World Bibliographical Series no. 161. Oxford: Clio Press, 1993.

Smith, Jerry C., and Williams L. Urban, eds. *The Livonian Rhymed Chronicle*. Bloomington: Indiana University Press, 1977.

Šmits, P. "Latviešu mitoloğija" (Latvian mythology). In *Latvieši: rakstu krājums*, Balodis and Šmits, 161–77.

Sontag, Raymond, and James Beddie, eds. *Nazi-Soviet Relations, 1939–1941*. Washington, D.C.: U.S. Department of State, 1948.

Spekke, A. *The Ancient Amber Routes and the Geographical Discovery of the Eastern Baltic*. Stockholm: M. Goppers, 1957.

———. *The Baltic Sea in Ancient Maps*. Stockholm: M. Goppers, 1957.

———. *Balts and Slavs: Their Early Relations*. Washington, D.C.: Alpha Printing Co., 1968.

———. "Baltu tautas kristīgās ēras pirmāja gadu tukstotī" (The Baltic nations in the first 1000 years of the Christian era). In *Tautas vēsturei: Veltijums Profesoram Arvēdam Švābem*, edited by B. Ābers, T. Zeids, and T. Zemzaris, 61–76. Riga: A. Gulbis, 1938.

———. *History of Latvia*. Stockholm: M. Goppers, 1957.

———. *Senie dzintara ceļi un austrum-Baltijas ģeogrāfiskā atklāšana* (Ancient amber routes and the geographic discovery of the eastern Baltic). 3d expanded edition. Stockholm: Zelta Abele, 1962.

Stahnke, Astrida B. *Aspazija: Her Life and Her Drama*. London: University Press of America, 1984.

Statistical Yearbook of Latvia. Annual publication. State Committee for Statistics of the Republic of Latvia. Riga, 1992.

Stradiņš, Jānis. "Latvia on the Crossroads of History." *Humanities and Social Sciences. Latvia* 1 (1993): 5–9.

———. *Trešā Atmoda* (The third awakening). Riga: Zinātne, 1992.

Straubergs, Jānis. *Rīgas vēsture* (The history of Riga). Riga: Grāmatu Draugs, n.d.

Streips, Kārlis, comp. *Fifteen Months That Shook the World: Latvian Crisis Chronology January, 1991, to March, 1992*. Rockville, Md.: American Latvian Association, n.d.

Strods, Heinrihs. *Antifeodoālā sabiedriskā doma Latvijā XVIII gs. II pusē - XIX gs I pusē* (Antifeudal social thought in Latvia from the second half of the eighteenth to the first half of the nineteenth century). Riga: Latvijas Universitāte, 1992.

———. "Die herrschende Klasse (Nomenklatur) der Lettischen SSR." *Acta Baltica* 28 (1990): 189–98.

———. *Kurzemes kroņa zemes un zemnieki 1795–1861* (The Courland Crown lands and peasants, 1795–1861). Riga: Zinātne, 1987.

———. *Latvijas lauksaimniecības vēsture* (History of Latvian agriculture). Riga: Zvaigzne, 1991.

———. *Zem melnbrūnā zobena: Vācijas politika Latvijā* (Under the black-brown sword: German policy in Latvia 1939–1945). Riga: Zvaigzne, 1994.

Strods, Heinrihs, ed. *Latviešu etnogrāfija* (Latvian ethnography). Riga: Zinātne, 1969.

———. *Profesors Boļeslavs Brežgo*. Rēzekne: Latvijas Kultūras Centrs, 1990.

Šturms, E. "Der ostbaltische Bernsteinhandel in der vorchristlichen Zeit." *Commentationes Balticae* 1 (1953): 167–205.

Švābe, Arvēds. "Jersikas karaļvalsts" (The kingdoms of Jersika). In Arvēds Švābe, *Straumes un avoti* (Currents and sources). Riga: A. Gulbis, 1938; Lincoln, Neb.: Pilskalns, 1962.

———. "Latviešu Indriķis un viņa chronika" (The Latvian Indriķis and his chronicle). In Arvēds Švābe, *Straumes un avoti*. Vol. 2, 121–220.

———. "Latviešu zemnieks 16. gs. historiogrāfijā" (The Latvian peasants in sixteenth-century historiography). In Arveds Švābe, *Straumes un avoti.* Vol. 3, 53–64.

———. *Latvijas vēsture* (History of Latvia). Vol. 1. Riga: Avots, 1990.

———. *Latvijas vēsture 1800–1914* (History of Latvia, 1800–1914). Stockholm: Daugava, 1958.

———. *Pagasta vēsture* (History of the Pagasts). Vol. 1. Riga: J. Roze, 1926.

———. *Straumes un avoti* (Currents and sources). 3 vols. Riga: A. Gulbis, 1938; Lincoln, Neb.: Pilskalns, 1962.

———. "Tautas dziesmu likteņi" (The history of folk songs). In *Latviešu tautas dziesmas* (Latvian folk songs). Vol. 1, edited by A. Švābe, K. Straubergs, and E. Hauzenberga-Šturma, v–xxv. Copenhagen: Imanta, 1952.

Švābe, Arvēds, ed. *Latvju encikopēdija* (Latvian encyclopedia). 3 vols. Stockholm: Tris Zvaigznes, 1950–51.

Svarāne, M. *Saimnieks un kalps Kurzemē un Vidzemē XIX. gs. vidū* (The farmstead head and farmhands in Courland and Livland in the mid–nineteenth century). Riga: Zinātne, 1971.

Tarulis, A. N. *Soviet Policy toward the Baltic States 1918–1940.* Notre Dame, Ind.: University of Notre Dame Press, 1959.

Tentelis, A. "Latvieši Ordeņa laikmetā" (Latvians in the time of the Livonian Order). In *Latvieši.* Vol. 1, Balodis and Šmits, 121–37.

Tentelis, A., ed. *Dokumenti par "Pēterburgas Avīzēm"* (Documents about "Peterburgas Avizes"). Riga: Latvijas Vesture Institūts, 1937.

Tērauda, Vita. *The Rise of Grass Roots Environmental Groups under Gorbachev: A Case Study of Latvia.* Washington, D.C.: Johns Hopkins University, SAIS, 1989.

Thaden, Edward C. "The Baltic National Movements during the Nineteenth Century." *Journal of Baltic Studies* 16 (1985): 411–21.

———. "Estland, Livland, and the Ukraine: Reflections on Eighteenth-Century Regional Autonomy." *Journal of Baltic Studies* 12 (1981): 312–17.

———. *Russia's Western Borderlands, 1710–1870.* Princeton, N.J.: Princeton University Press, 1984.

These Names Accuse: Nominal List of Latvians Deported to Soviet Russia 1940–1941. Stockholm: Latvian National Foundation, 1982.

Thimme, Heinrich. *Kirche un nationale Frage in Livland während der ersten Hälfte des 19. Jahrunderts.* Königsberg: N.p. 1938.

Thomson, Clare. *The Singing Revolution: A Political Journey through the Baltic States.* London: Michael Joseph, 1992.

Timšāns, Sigizmunds, ed. *Kārlis Ulmanis: Atziņas un runu fragmenti* (Kārlis Ulmanis: Realizations and fragments). Riga: Avize, 1990.

Tolz, Vera, and Melanie Newton, eds. *The USSR in 1990: A Record of Events.* Boulder, Colo.: Westview Press, 1992.

———. *The USSR in 1991: A Record of Events.* Boulder, Colo.: Westview Press, 1993.

Trapāns, Andris. "Die Militarbezirk Baltikum und Aspekte sowjetischer Militarpolitik in den baltischen Staaten." *Acta Baltica* 22 (1982): 164–80.

———. *Soviet Military Power in the Baltic Area.* Stockholm: Latvian National Foundation, 1986.

Trapans, J. A. "Averting Moscow's Baltic Coup." *Orbis* 35 (1991): 427–39.

———. *Impatient for Freedom? The Baltic Struggle for Independence.* European Security Study No. 8. London: Institute for European Defense and Strategic Studies, 1990.

———. "The Sources of Latvia's Popular Movement." In *Toward Independence: The Baltic Popular Movements,* edited by Jan Arved Trapans, 25–41. Boulder, Colo.: Westview Press, 1991.

———. *Toward Independence: The Baltic Popular Movements.* Boulder, Colo.: Westview Press, 1991.

Uibopuu, Henn-Juri. *Die Verfassungs- und Rechtsentwicklung der baltischen Staaten 1988–1990.* Koln: Bundesinstitut fur Ostwissenschaftliche und Internationale Studien, 1990.

Unams, Z. *Krievu laiki Latvijā* (The Russian era in Latvia). Riga: Valters un Rapa, 1936.

Upelnieks, K. *Uzvārdu došana Vidzemes un Kurzemes zemniekiem* (The granting of surnames to the Livland and Courland peasants). Riga: Valters un Rapa, 1938.

Urban, William. *The Baltic Crusade.* De Kalb: Northern Illinois University Press, 1975.

———. *The Livonian Crusade.* Washington, D.C.: University Press of America, 1981.

———. *The Samogitian Crusade.* Chicago: Lithuanian Research Center, 1989.

Vācietis, Jukums. *Latviešu strēlnieku vēsturiskā nozīme* (The historic significance of the Latvian rifle battalions). Riga: Avots, 1989.

Vairogs, Dainis. *Latvian Deportations 1940–Present.* Rockville, Md.: World Federation of Free Latvians, 1986.

Valsts Valoda Latvijā. Riga: Valsts Valodas Centrs, 1992.

Valters, Miķelis. *Mana sarakste ar Kārli Ulmani un Vilhelmu Munteru* (My correspondence with Kārlis Ulmanis and Vilhelms Munters). Västeras, Sweden: Jauna Latvija, 1957.

Vardys, V. Stanley, and Romuald Misiunas, eds. *The Baltic States in Peace and War, 1917–1945.* University Park: Pennsylvania State University Press, 1978.

Vebers, Elmārs. "Demography and Ethnic Politics in Independent Latvia: Some Basic Facts." *Nationalities Papers* 11 (1993): 179–94.

Viese, Saulcerīte. *Krišjānis Barons: The Man and His Work.* Moscow: Raduga, 1985.

Vīķis-Freibergs, Vaira, ed. *Linguistics and Poetics of Latvian Folk Songs.* Montreal: McGill-Queens University Press, 1989.

Vīksniņš, George J. "Current Issues of Soviet Latvia's Economic Growth." *Journal of Baltic Studies* 7 (1976): 343–51.

———. "Evaluating Economic Growth in Latvia." *Journal of Baltic Studies* 12 (1981): 173–88.

Vīksniņš, Nikolajs. *Latvijas vēsture jaunā gaisma* (Latvian history in a new light). Chicago: Draugas, 1968.

Vilks, Andris, ed. *Enciklopēdiskā vārdnica* (Encyclopedic dictionary). 2 vols. Riga: Latvijas Enciklopedijas Redakcija, 1991.

Vizulis, I. J. *The Molotov-Ribbentrop Pact of 1939: The Baltic Case*. New York: Praeger, 1990.

———. *Nations under Duress. The Baltic States*. Port Washington, N.Y.: Associated Faculty Press, 1985.

Widmer, Michael J. "Nationalism and Communism in Latvia: The Latvian Communisty Party under Soviet Rule." Ph.D. diss. Harvard University, 1969.

Žagars, E. *Socialist Transformations in Latvia, 1940–41*. Riga: Zinatne, 1978.

Zeids, Teodors, ed. *Feodālā Rīga* (Feudal Riga). Riga: Zinātne, 1987.

———. *Senākie rakstītie Latvijas vēstures avoti līdz 1800. gadam* (The older sources of Latvian history to the year 1800). Riga: Zvaigzne, 1990.

Ziedonis, Arvids, Rein Taagepera, and Mardi Valgemae, eds. *Problems of Mininations: Baltic Perspectives*. San Jose, Calif.: Association for the Advancement of Baltic Studies, 1973.

Ziedonis, Arvids, William R. Winter, Mardi Valgemae, et al. *Baltic History*. Columbus, Ohio: Association for the Advancement of Baltic Studies, 1974.

Zīle, Roberts. *Changing Ownership in Latvia through Agrarian Reform*. Report 92-BR5 of the Center for Agricultural and Rural Development. Ames, Iowa: Iowa State University, September 1992.

Zīle, Zigurds. "Legal Thought and the Formation of Law and Legal Institutions in the Socialistic Soviet Republic of Latvia, 1917–1920." *Journal of Baltic Studies* 7 (1977): 195–204.

Zutis, J. *Vidzemes un Kurzemes zemnieku brīvlaišana 19.gs.20os gados* (The emancipation of the Livland and Courland peasantry in the nineteenth century). Riga: Zinātne, 1956.

Zvidriņš, P., and I. Vanovska. *Latvieši: statistiski demogrāfisks portrētejums* (Latvians: A statistical and demographic portrait). Riga: Zinātne, 1992.

Index